The Art of War for CEOs

Sun Tzu's Timeless Strategies for Modern Business

Dr. David Leung

BY THE SAME AUTHOR

On a Happy Life: Designing Successful Organisations the Senecan Way

The Finite Advantage: Mastering Time and Leadership the Senecan Way

Bushido Leadership: The Immortal Code of Japan's Warriors

The Golden Mean: Leadership Lessons from Confucius' Doctrine

The Ripple Effect: Leadership Lessons from The Great Learning

Thirty-Six Stratagems: Ancient Chinese Wisdom for Modern Leadership

The Samurai Leader: Management Lessons from The Book of Five Rings

The Resilient Leader: Corporate Wisdom from the Book of Job

The Executive Prince: Adapting Machiavellian Strategies to Modern Leadership

Beyond the Sun: Ecclesiastes' Guide to Modern Leadership

The Hindu Leader: Applying the Bhagavad Gita to Contemporary Management

Wisdom from Proverbs: Biblical Principles for Modern Leadership

The Stoic Leader: Applying Meditations to Modern Management

Enlightened Leadership: Buddhist Principles for Business Success

The Confucian Leader: Transforming Modern Organisations with Classical Philosophy

The Taoist MBA: Leading with Softness, Stillness & Silence

The Taoist CEO: Navigating Business with Ancient Wisdom

Strategy: A Blueprint for Business Warfare

Inside Accounting: The Sociology of Financial Reporting and Auditing

Research Methods for Accounting & Finance: A Guide to Writing Your Dissertation (ed.)

ABOUT THE AUTHOR

Dr. David Leung is a seasoned university lecturer with over 17 years of teaching experience. He holds a PhD and MSc in Science and Technology Studies from the University of Edinburgh, and an MBA from Durham University.

His journey, however, began far beyond the academic world. Before entering academia, he qualified as a Chartered Global Management Accountant with the Chartered Institute of Management Accountants (CIMA), gaining invaluable business experience across diverse industries—ranging from printing and property management to financial services, biotechnology, and tourism.

In 2024, Dr. Leung founded Dragon Business School (www.DragonBusinessSchool.com). This innovative institution aims to become a beacon of excellence, offering cutting-edge online business management courses designed to empower and inspire the next generation of business leaders.

PREFACE

In the fast-paced, ever-evolving world of modern business, the principles of strategy and leadership are more critical than ever. Amidst the whirlwind of technological advancements, market fluctuations, and fierce competition, business leaders are constantly seeking timeless wisdom to guide their decisions and actions. Enter Sun Tzu's *The Art of War*, a 2,500-year-old military treatise whose lessons have transcended the battlefield to become a beacon of strategic thought across various domains, including the corporate arena.

The Art of War for CEOs: Sun Tzu's Timeless Strategies for Modern Business aims to bridge the ancient and the contemporary, providing CEOs and business leaders with actionable insights rooted in the timeless principles of Sun Tzu. This book contains the original translated 13 chapters of *The Art of War*, allowing readers to access the foundational text that has influenced countless leaders throughout history.

The book delves into each of Sun Tzu's chapters, interpreting them through the lens of modern business management. Our goal is to reveal the profound relevance of these ancient strategies in today's corporate world, where the stakes are high, and the challenges are multifaceted. Each chapter contains key aspects of strategy, offering a detailed analysis and practical application for contemporary business scenarios.

Chapters Overview

1. *Laying Plans:* Strategic importance, environmental analysis, leadership, discipline, deception, flexibility, and detailed planning.
2. *Waging War:* Efficient resource management, swift decision-making, motivation, and strategic focus.
3. *Attack by Stratagem:* Strategic planning, competitive positioning, speed and agility, effective leadership, adaptation, and alignment.
4. *Tactical Dispositions:* Preparation, defensive and offensive tactics, strategic positioning, leadership, discipline, and data-driven decision-making.
5. *Energy:* Collective energy, direct and indirect tactics, innovation, momentum, discipline, deception, and talent management.
6. *Weak Points & Strong:* Initiative, preparation, influence, agility, secrecy, concentration, and innovation.
7. *Manoeuvring:* Leadership, resource harmonisation, strategic flexibility, speed and efficiency, intelligence, discipline, and adaptive strategy formulation.
8. *Variation of Tactics:* Flexibility, strategic alliances, risk management, competitive advantage, preparedness, and resilient leadership.
9. *The Army on the March:* Strategic positioning, adaptability, observation, resource management, discipline, anticipation, and strategic patience.
10. *Terrain:* Understanding and navigating different market conditions, strategic decision-making, risk management, leadership, and organisational dynamics.
11. *The Nine Situations:* Understanding different market conditions, adaptive decision-making, leveraging strategic alliances, managing resources, building strong relationships, and strategic patience.
12. *The Attack by Fire:* Resource utilisation, preparation, timing, adaptability, intelligence, innovation, and ethical considerations.
13. *The Use of Spies:* Intelligence gathering, foreknowledge, secrecy, and strategic foresight.

By integrating the timeless strategies of Sun Tzu with contemporary business insights *The Art of War for CEOs* aims to equip leaders with the knowledge and tools needed to thrive in an ever-changing landscape. Whether you are a seasoned executive or an aspiring leader, we invite you to explore these ancient teachings and discover their profound impact on your strategic thinking and decision-making.

Embark on this journey of strategic enlightenment, and may Sun Tzu's ancient wisdom guide your path to modern business success.

CONTENTS

About the Author 3

Preface 4

Sun Tzu 8

Chapter 1 – Laying Plans 10

Chapter 2 – Waging War 20

Chapter 3 – Attack by Stratagem 29

Chapter 4 – Tactical Dispositions 37

Chapter 5 – Energy 45

Chapter 6 – Weak Points & Strong 54

Chapter 7 – Manoeuvring 64

Chapter 8 – Variation of Tactics 75

Chapter 9 – The Army on the March 85

Chapter 10 – Terrain 97

Chapter 11 – The Nine Situations 105

Chapter 12 – The Attack by Fire 117

Chapter 13 – The Use of Spies 134

Conclusion 149

Appendix – SUN TZU ON THE ART OF WAR 152

    I. LAYING PLANS 152

    II. WAGING WAR 153

    III. ATTACK BY STRATAGEM 154

    IV. TACTICAL DISPOSITIONS 155

    V. ENERGY 156

    VI. WEAK POINTS AND STRONG 157

VII. MANOEUVRING 158
VIII. VARIATION OF TACTICS 160
IX. THE ARMY ON THE MARCH 160
X. TERRAIN 162
XI. THE NINE SITUATIONS 164
XII. THE ATTACK BY FIRE 167
XIII. THE USE OF SPIES 167

SUN TZU

Sun Tzu, also known as Sunzi or Sun Wu, was an ancient Chinese military strategist, philosopher, and author whose influence on the art of war and strategy has transcended centuries. Though details of his early life and background are shrouded in mystery, it is believed that he was born around 544 BCE during the late Spring and Autumn period of Chinese history. His birthplace is often cited as the state of Qi, in present-day Shandong Province. Sun Tzu's family background and early education remain largely speculative, but it is presumed that he received a classical education that included teachings on warfare, philosophy, and governance.

The Spring & Autumn Period

The historical context of Sun Tzu's life plays a crucial role in understanding his work. The Spring and Autumn period (771-476 BCE) was marked by political fragmentation and constant warfare among various feudal states in China. This era, named after the *Spring and Autumn Annals* (Chūnqiū 春秋), saw the decline of the Zhou Dynasty's central authority and the rise of powerful regional lords. It was during this tumultuous time that Sun Tzu's insights into military strategy and tactics emerged, reflecting the need for effective leadership and innovative approaches to warfare.

Sun Tzu's Magnum Opus: *The Art of War*

Sun Tzu's most enduring legacy is his seminal work, *The Art of War* (Sūnzǐ Bīngfǎ 孫子兵法). This ancient treatise on military strategy and tactics is composed of 13 chapters, each addressing different aspects of warfare. *The Art of War* has been hailed as a masterpiece of strategic thinking and has influenced military leaders, scholars, and business executives across the globe. While the exact date of its composition remains uncertain, it is widely accepted that Sun Tzu wrote it in the late 6th century BCE.

Key Principles of *The Art of War*

Sun Tzu's *The Art of War* is celebrated for its profound insights into warfare and strategic planning. Some of its key principles include:

- *Know Yourself & Your Enemy:* Sun Tzu emphasises the importance of understanding both your own capabilities and those of your adversary. He famously wrote, "If you know the enemy and know yourself, you need not fear the result of a hundred battles."
- *The Importance of Adaptability:* Sun Tzu advocates for flexibility and the ability to adapt to changing circumstances. He argues that rigid plans can lead to failure, while adaptive strategies can ensure success.
- *Deception & Surprise:* Sun Tzu underscores the value of deception in warfare. He advises leaders to appear weak when they are strong and to strike when the enemy least expects it.
- *Speed & Efficiency:* Sun Tzu emphasises the need for swift and decisive action. He argues that prolonged campaigns can drain resources and morale, making quick and efficient victories preferable.
- *The Role of Leadership:* Sun Tzu places great importance on the qualities of a leader. He believes that wisdom, sincerity, benevolence, courage, and strictness are essential traits for effective leadership.
- *Environmental Awareness:* Sun Tzu stresses the significance of understanding and leveraging the terrain. He advises commanders to use the environment to their advantage and to avoid unfavourable terrain whenever possible.

Sun Tzu's Military Career

While much of Sun Tzu's life remains enigmatic, historical records suggest that he served as a military general and strategist for the state of Wu under King Helü. His strategies and tactics were instrumental in several military campaigns, contributing to the expansion and consolidation of Wu's power. One of the most famous anecdotes about Sun Tzu's military career involves his demonstration of discipline and leadership to King Helü. According to legend, Sun Tzu was tasked with training the king's concubines as soldiers to prove his strategic prowess. Despite initial resistance and mockery, Sun Tzu's strict enforcement of discipline eventually transformed the concubines into a well-coordinated unit, impressing the king and securing Sun Tzu's position as a trusted military advisor.

Influence & Legacy

Sun Tzu's influence extends far beyond ancient China. His teachings have been studied and applied by military leaders, philosophers, and scholars throughout history. Notable figures such as Napoleon Bonaparte, General Douglas MacArthur, and Mao Zedong have drawn inspiration from *The Art of War*. In the modern era, Sun Tzu's principles have found relevance in various fields, including business, sports, and politics. His emphasis on strategic thinking, adaptability, and leadership continues to resonate with individuals and organisations seeking to navigate complex challenges.

The Art of War in Business & Management

One of the most intriguing aspects of Sun Tzu's legacy is the application of his principles to business and management. *The Art of War* has become a popular reference for executives and entrepreneurs looking to develop effective strategies and gain a competitive edge. Key concepts such as "knowing your enemy," "deception and surprise," and "speed and efficiency" have been adapted to the corporate world, guiding decision-making and strategic planning. Business leaders have found value in Sun Tzu's emphasis on understanding market dynamics, anticipating competitors' moves, and leveraging strengths while mitigating weaknesses.

Sun Tzu's Enduring Relevance

Sun Tzu's enduring relevance can be attributed to the timeless nature of his insights. While *The Art of War* was written in a specific historical and cultural context, its principles are universally applicable. The challenges of leadership, competition, and strategic planning are as pertinent today as they were in ancient China. Sun Tzu's ability to distil complex ideas into concise and actionable guidelines has ensured that his work remains a valuable resource for those seeking to excel in various domains.

Controversies & Debates

Despite the widespread acclaim for Sun Tzu's work, there have been controversies and debates surrounding his life and authorship. Some scholars question the historical accuracy of the anecdotes and legends associated with Sun Tzu. Additionally, there are debates about whether *The Art of War* was authored solely by Sun Tzu or if it was a collaborative effort that evolved over time. While these questions remain unresolved, they do not diminish the significance of Sun Tzu's contributions to the fields of strategy and military science.

CHAPTER 1 – LAYING PLANS

Hold out baits to entice the enemy.
Feign disorder, and crush him.

Sun Tzu

Sun Tzu's *Laying Plans* outlines the fundamental principles of strategy and planning. Although conceived in the context of ancient warfare, these timeless insights hold significant relevance for contemporary strategic management.

The Vital Importance of Strategy

Sun Tzu begins by emphasising the paramount importance of strategy, framing it as a matter of life and death for the State. He argues that without a well-thought-out strategy, the State risks falling into chaos, much like a general who ventures into battle unprepared. In the realm of business, effective strategy holds a parallel significance, being the cornerstone of an organisation's survival and growth. Just as in warfare, where a single strategic misstep can lead to utter devastation, in the corporate world, poor strategic decisions can spell financial ruin, loss of competitive edge, and even complete collapse. The consequences of failing to strategise in business are dire; mismanagement and lack of foresight can lead to significant financial losses, erosion of market share, and potentially bankruptcy.

Strategic management, therefore, is not merely a function of business; it is an indispensable element of leadership that requires constant attention and refinement. Business leaders must prioritise strategic planning and execution to navigate the complexities of the modern market landscape effectively. This involves not only devising comprehensive plans but also being able to adapt and respond to unforeseen challenges and opportunities. In a competitive environment, staying ahead often means predicting market trends, understanding the competition, and continuously innovating.

Moreover, Sun Tzu's insights into the need for adaptability and flexibility in strategy are particularly relevant today. The business world is dynamic, with rapid technological advancements, shifting consumer preferences, and volatile economic conditions. Companies that rigidly adhere to outdated strategies without adapting to the changing landscape are likely to falter. Thus, leaders must cultivate a culture of agility, encouraging teams to pivot and innovate when necessary.

The Five Constant Factors

Sun Tzu identifies five constant factors that govern the art of war: The Moral Law, Heaven, Earth, The Commander, and Method and Discipline. These factors serve as a comprehensive framework for strategic planning and decision-making.

<u>The Moral Law:</u>

In Sun Tzu's time, the Moral Law represented the alignment and unity between the ruler and the people, creating a sense of shared purpose and loyalty that was crucial for victory in war. This concept is equally relevant in the modern business world, where it translates to a company's mission, vision, and values. A robust organisational culture, where employees are aligned with the company's goals and values, fosters loyalty, motivation, and a shared sense of purpose. This alignment is not just a superficial agreement but a deep-rooted connection that can drive extraordinary levels of commitment and effort from employees.

When a company has a clear moral compass, guided by ethical leadership, it sets the stage for a thriving workplace environment. Leaders who embody and exemplify the company's values can inspire their teams, creating a ripple effect that enhances engagement and productivity across the organisation. This ethical framework becomes the foundation upon which trust and mutual respect are built, essential elements for any successful business. Employees who see their leaders making decisions based on integrity and ethical considerations are more likely to feel respected and valued, which in turn fosters a stronger emotional connection to the company.

Moreover, a company with strong moral principles can attract like-minded individuals who are drawn to its mission and values. This alignment between personal and organisational values not only improves employee retention but also enhances recruitment efforts, as potential employees are often looking for workplaces that resonate with their own beliefs and ethics. This cultural fit ensures that new hires are not just skilled but are also passionate about contributing to the company's mission, leading to a more cohesive and dedicated workforce.

Additionally, the moral law in business extends to the company's relationship with its customers, partners, and the broader community. Companies that prioritise ethical practices and social responsibility can build stronger, more loyal relationships with their customers, who increasingly value transparency and ethical behaviour. This trust can translate into customer loyalty and advocacy, providing a competitive advantage in the marketplace. Similarly, ethical businesses are better positioned to forge strong partnerships and collaborations, as other organisations are more likely to work with companies that share their values.

Heaven:

In Sun Tzu's framework, the concept of Heaven signifies the external environment, encompassing elements such as time, weather, and seasons. These natural factors were critical in determining the timing and tactics of warfare. In the modern business context, Heaven can be interpreted as the myriad external forces that influence a company's strategic decisions. These include market conditions, economic trends, regulatory landscapes, technological advancements, and even sociopolitical factors. Strategic managers must develop a keen understanding of these external variables to navigate the complex business landscape effectively.

Market conditions are ever-changing, driven by consumer behaviour, competition, and global events. A sudden shift in consumer preferences or the entry of a disruptive competitor can dramatically alter the business environment. Companies that keep a close eye on these shifts can quickly adapt their strategies to capitalise on new opportunities or mitigate emerging threats. For example, a tech company might monitor trends in consumer electronics to anticipate demand for new products, allowing them to innovate and release new gadgets ahead of the competition.

Economic trends, such as inflation rates, interest rates, and economic cycles, also play a significant role in shaping business strategy. During periods of economic growth, companies might focus on expansion and investment, while during downturns, they might prioritise cost-cutting and efficiency improvements. Understanding these economic indicators can help businesses make informed decisions about investments, pricing strategies, and resource allocation.

Technological advancements are another critical component of the external environment. The rapid pace of technological innovation means that companies must stay abreast of the latest developments to remain competitive. This could involve adopting new technologies to improve efficiency, enhance customer experiences, or develop new products. For instance, companies that leverage artificial intelligence and machine learning can gain a competitive edge by automating processes and deriving insights from large datasets.

Regulatory landscapes can also have a profound impact on business operations. Changes in laws and regulations, whether related to environmental standards, data privacy, or labour laws, can necessitate significant adjustments in business practices. Strategic managers must stay informed about regulatory changes and proactively adapt their strategies to ensure compliance and minimise disruptions.

Sociopolitical factors, such as geopolitical tensions, social movements, and cultural shifts, can also influence the business environment. Companies that operate in multiple regions must consider the political and cultural contexts of each market. For example, a global corporation might need to navigate trade restrictions or adapt its marketing strategies to resonate with different cultural norms.

To effectively respond to these external factors, strategic managers must engage in continuous monitoring and analysis. This involves collecting data from various sources, such as market research reports, economic forecasts, and technological trend analyses, and using this information to anticipate changes and refine strategies. By staying attuned to the broader environment, companies can seize opportunities for growth and innovation while mitigating potential risks.

Earth:

In Sun Tzu's military context, Earth represents the physical environment, encompassing distances, terrain, and the probability of encountering danger or securing safety. In the modern business world, Earth can be interpreted as the competitive landscape, industry structure, and the intricate dynamics of the market. These factors create the backdrop against which companies operate, presenting both opportunities and challenges that require keen strategic insights to navigate effectively.

The competitive landscape is akin to the rugged terrain described by Sun Tzu. It includes the relative positions and strengths of various market players, the intensity of competition, and the strategies employed by rivals. To excel in this environment, strategic managers must conduct thorough competitive analyses, identifying the strengths and weaknesses of their competitors. This involves understanding competitors' capabilities, market share, customer loyalty, and strategic initiatives. By analysing this data, companies can anticipate competitors' moves, develop counter-strategies, and position themselves advantageously.

Industry structure refers to the broader framework within which companies operate. This includes the regulatory environment, the level of market concentration, the presence of barriers to entry, and the availability of substitute products or services. Strategic managers must navigate these structural elements to find pathways to success. For instance, in highly regulated industries, companies must ensure compliance while seeking innovative ways to operate efficiently. In markets with high entry barriers, firms might focus on building strong brand loyalty or leveraging economies of scale to maintain a competitive edge.

Market dynamics encompass the ever-changing factors that influence supply and demand, consumer preferences, technological advancements, and economic conditions. These dynamics are constantly in flux, much like the shifting sands of a battlefield. Strategic managers need to stay attuned to these changes, employing market research and data analytics to forecast trends and adapt their strategies accordingly. For instance, a tech company must stay ahead of technological innovations and consumer trends to remain relevant and competitive. By understanding market dynamics, businesses can seize emerging opportunities, such as new customer segments or technological breakthroughs, and mitigate risks like economic downturns or shifts in consumer behaviour.

Assessing the strengths and weaknesses of competitors is just one piece of the puzzle. Strategic managers must also identify and evaluate market opportunities. This involves spotting gaps in the market where unmet customer needs exist or where existing products and services can be improved. For example, a company might identify a niche market that is underserved by current offerings and tailor their products to meet these specific needs. Additionally, recognising global market opportunities can allow companies to expand their reach and diversify their revenue streams.

Understanding the unique challenges of their industry is crucial for strategic managers. Each industry has its own set of hurdles, whether it be regulatory constraints, technological disruptions, or intense competition. By thoroughly understanding these challenges, companies can develop robust strategies to overcome them. For instance, in the pharmaceutical industry, companies must navigate complex regulatory approval processes and invest heavily in research and development to bring new drugs to market. Strategic managers must allocate resources wisely, balancing the need for innovation with the imperative to manage costs and risks.

Equipped with a deep understanding of the competitive landscape, industry structure, and market dynamics, companies can effectively position themselves to capitalise on their strengths and exploit market gaps. This involves leveraging their core competencies, such as unique technological capabilities, strong brand equity, or superior customer service, to differentiate themselves from competitors. For example, a company with a strong reputation for quality might emphasise this attribute in its marketing campaigns to attract discerning customers.

By continuously monitoring the external environment and adapting their strategies, companies can achieve long-term sustainability and growth. This requires a commitment to ongoing learning and agility, as the business landscape is always evolving. Strategic managers must foster a culture of innovation and adaptability within their organisations, encouraging teams to experiment with new ideas and respond swiftly to changes in the market.

The Commander:

This factor represents the quintessential qualities of leadership, encompassing wisdom, sincerity, benevolence, courage, and strictness. These attributes are not just desirable but essential for anyone who seeks to lead with distinction and effectiveness. Wisdom enables leaders to make sound decisions based on a deep understanding of the circumstances and the potential consequences of their actions. This sagacity is crucial for navigating complex challenges and seizing opportunities that align with the organisation's long-term vision.

Sincerity, on the other hand, fosters trust and transparency within the organisation. When leaders are honest and straightforward, they create an environment where open communication and authenticity thrive. This sincerity is the bedrock of ethical leadership, ensuring that decisions are made with integrity and that the organisation's values are upheld.

Benevolence speaks to the compassionate side of leadership. It involves understanding and addressing the needs and concerns of team members, creating a supportive and inclusive workplace. Benevolent leaders prioritise the well-being of their employees, which in turn boosts morale and fosters loyalty. This compassionate approach helps in building strong, cohesive teams that are willing to go the extra mile for the success of the organisation.

Courage is another indispensable quality of effective leadership. It involves the willingness to take calculated risks, make tough decisions, and stand by them even in the face of adversity. Courageous leaders are not afraid to challenge the status quo or make unpopular decisions if they believe it is in the best interest of the organisation. This bravery instils confidence in the team, encouraging them to take initiative and innovate without fear of failure.

Strictness, or the ability to enforce discipline and maintain high standards, ensures that the organisation operates efficiently and effectively. A leader must be able to set clear expectations, hold team members accountable, and ensure that everyone is working towards the same goals. This discipline is necessary for maintaining order and consistency within the organisation, enabling it to achieve its strategic objectives.

Effective leadership is crucial in guiding an organisation through strategic initiatives and ensuring the successful execution of plans. Leaders must possess a balance of strategic vision, ethical integrity, and the ability to inspire and motivate their teams. Strategic vision allows leaders to see the bigger picture, set long-term goals, and chart a course for the future. This foresight is essential for anticipating market trends, identifying growth opportunities, and navigating potential challenges.

Ethical integrity is the cornerstone of responsible leadership. Leaders who uphold strong moral principles earn the respect and trust of their employees, customers, and stakeholders. This integrity ensures that the organisation's actions align with its values, building a positive reputation and fostering a culture of accountability.

The ability to inspire and motivate is what sets great leaders apart. Inspirational leaders communicate a compelling vision and instil a sense of purpose in their teams. They recognise and celebrate achievements, provide constructive feedback, and support professional development. This motivation drives employees to perform at their best, fostering a culture of innovation, resilience, and continuous improvement.

Strong leadership is the driving force behind an organisation's success. It fosters an environment where creativity and innovation are encouraged, allowing the organisation to adapt and thrive in a rapidly changing business landscape. Leaders who embody these qualities create a culture of resilience, where challenges are seen as opportunities for growth and development. This resilience enables the organisation to weather storms and emerge stronger on the other side.

Continuous improvement is another hallmark of effective leadership. Leaders who are committed to ongoing learning and development inspire their teams to do the same. They encourage a mindset of curiosity and experimentation, fostering an environment where new ideas are welcomed, and continuous growth is the norm. This commitment to improvement drives the organisation towards its strategic goals, ensuring long-term sustainability and success.

<u>Method & Discipline:</u>

In Sun Tzu's teachings, method and discipline are fundamental to the successful organisation and management of resources, such as structuring an army, handling supply chain logistics, and maintaining financial control. This concept translates seamlessly into the modern business world, where efficient operational processes, clear organisational structures, and robust financial management are paramount.

Method and discipline in business begin with establishing a solid governance framework. This framework includes the policies, procedures, and structures that guide the company's strategic direction and operational activities. Effective governance ensures that decision-making processes are transparent, accountable, and aligned with the company's goals and values. By setting clear expectations and maintaining consistent oversight, companies can avoid pitfalls and stay on course toward their strategic objectives.

One of the cornerstones of method and discipline is the streamlining of operations. This involves refining and optimising all business processes to eliminate inefficiencies, reduce waste, and improve productivity. Techniques such as Lean management and Six Sigma can be employed to identify and remove bottlenecks, standardise workflows, and enhance overall performance. Streamlined operations not only improve the bottom line but also enable companies to deliver higher quality products and services to their customers.

Clear organisational structures are another critical aspect of method and discipline. A well-defined hierarchy and delineation of roles and responsibilities ensure that everyone in the organisation understands their duties and how they contribute to the company's success. This clarity minimises confusion and overlaps, fostering a cohesive and efficient work environment. It also facilitates better communication and collaboration across different departments and teams.

Robust financial management is equally essential. This includes meticulous budgeting, accurate financial reporting, and effective cash flow management. Companies must regularly monitor their financial performance against set targets and make necessary adjustments to stay on track. Sound financial discipline helps businesses allocate resources wisely, invest in growth opportunities, and weather economic downturns. It also instils confidence in stakeholders, including investors, creditors, and customers, by demonstrating the company's financial health and stability.

Discipline extends to the execution of strategic plans. It's not enough to have a brilliant strategy; companies must also ensure disciplined implementation. This involves setting clear goals, timelines, and performance metrics to track progress and ensure accountability. Regular reviews and audits can help identify deviations from the plan and implement corrective measures promptly. A disciplined approach to strategy execution enables companies to adapt to changing market conditions and seize new opportunities without losing sight of their long-term goals.

Method and discipline also enhance organisational agility. In today's fast-paced business environment, the ability to respond swiftly to changes is a competitive advantage. Companies that maintain disciplined processes and structures are better positioned to pivot quickly when needed. This agility allows them to capitalise on emerging trends, address customer needs more effectively, and stay ahead of competitors.

Furthermore, a disciplined organisation fosters a culture of continuous improvement. Employees are encouraged to identify areas for enhancement and suggest innovative solutions. This proactive mindset drives the organisation forward, ensuring that it remains competitive and relevant in a rapidly evolving market. By continually refining their methods and maintaining strict discipline, companies can achieve sustained growth and success.

Strategic Comparison & Analysis

Sun Tzu strongly advocates for a thorough comparative analysis based on these five fundamental factors. These principles are essential for forecasting victory or defeat in warfare, as they provide a comprehensive understanding of both internal and external conditions. In modern strategic management, this approach translates into the practice of conducting detailed internal and external analyses to develop well-informed strategies that ensure organisational success.

In the realm of business, one of the primary tools for internal analysis is the SWOT framework, which stands for Strengths, Weaknesses, Opportunities, and Threats. This analytical tool enables companies to evaluate their internal capabilities and resources, identifying areas of strength that can be leveraged to gain a competitive advantage. Strengths might include unique technological capabilities, a strong brand reputation, or a highly skilled workforce. By recognising and capitalising on these strengths, companies can develop strategies that enhance their market position and drive growth.

Conversely, the SWOT analysis also highlights weaknesses within the organisation. These could be areas where the company is underperforming or lacks critical resources, such as outdated technology, inadequate financial resources, or poor organisational structure. Identifying weaknesses is crucial for addressing potential vulnerabilities and implementing corrective measures. For example, a company might invest in upgrading its technology infrastructure or providing additional training for employees to bridge skill gaps. Addressing these weaknesses ensures that the company is better equipped to face challenges and maintain its competitive edge.

External analysis, on the other hand, involves evaluating the broader environment in which the company operates. The PESTEL framework is a valuable tool for this purpose, as it considers six key factors: Political, Economic, Social, Technological, Environmental, and Legal. Each of these factors can significantly impact the organisation's strategy and performance. Political factors include government policies, regulations, and political stability, which can influence business operations. Economic factors encompass economic growth, inflation rates, and employment levels, affecting consumer purchasing power and business profitability.

Social factors involve demographic trends, cultural shifts, and changes in consumer behaviour. Understanding these social dynamics allows companies to tailor their products and marketing strategies to meet the needs and preferences of their target audience. Technological factors include advancements and innovations that can disrupt industries and create new opportunities. Companies must stay abreast of technological trends to remain competitive and leverage new technologies to improve efficiency and customer experiences. Environmental factors consider the impact of environmental regulations, climate change, and sustainability concerns on business operations. Companies that prioritise environmental responsibility can build strong reputations and attract environmentally conscious consumers. Legal factors include laws and regulations that govern business practices, such as labour laws, data protection regulations, and intellectual property rights. Ensuring compliance with these legal requirements is essential for avoiding legal disputes and maintaining operational integrity.

By integrating insights from both SWOT and PESTEL analyses, companies can develop informed strategies that leverage their strengths, address weaknesses, capitalise on opportunities, and mitigate threats. This comprehensive approach to strategic comparison and analysis enables organisations to navigate the complexities of the business environment with confidence and foresight. For example, a company that recognises a strength in innovative technology and identifies an opportunity in a growing market for eco-friendly products might develop a new line of sustainable products, positioning itself as a market leader in this niche. Simultaneously, the company can address weaknesses by investing in employee training and upgrading its technology infrastructure, while mitigating threats by staying informed about regulatory changes and adapting its strategies accordingly.

Moreover, strategic comparison and analysis should be an ongoing process, not a one-time exercise. The business landscape is constantly evolving, with new challenges and opportunities emerging regularly. Companies must continuously monitor and reassess their internal capabilities and external environment to remain agile and responsive to change. This proactive approach to strategic management ensures that organisations can quickly adapt to shifts in market dynamics, technological advancements, and regulatory landscapes.

The Role of Deception & Flexibility

Sun Tzu famously posits that all warfare is fundamentally based on deception. This principle, although originating in the context of military strategy, has profound implications in the realm of business. Deception, in this sense, does not imply unethical behaviour, but rather strategic positioning and the clever use of competitive intelligence. Companies must craft perceptions that can subtly influence competitor behaviour and sway market dynamics in their favour. For instance, a company might strategically signal the launch of a new product to deter competitors from entering the market or to mislead them about the company's true strategic intentions. This kind of strategic signalling can create uncertainty and force competitors to make suboptimal decisions, thereby gaining a competitive advantage.

In the business world, creating perceptions involves a deep understanding of market psychology and the behaviour of competitors. It is about knowing when to release information and how to present it to create the desired effect. For example, a tech company might hint at groundbreaking features in their upcoming product to distract competitors and lead them to allocate resources inefficiently. This kind of manoeuvring requires sophisticated market analysis and a keen sense of timing. Deceptive tactics, when used ethically and wisely, can be a powerful tool in a company's strategic arsenal.

Flexibility is another cornerstone of Sun Tzu's strategic philosophy. He advises that plans should be modified according to favourable circumstances, emphasising the necessity of being adaptable in the face of changing conditions. In modern strategic management, this translates to agility and the ability to pivot quickly in response to market changes, technological disruptions, and evolving customer preferences. The business environment today is characterised by rapid change and unpredictability. Companies that are rigid and inflexible in their strategies are likely to fall behind, while those that embrace agility are better positioned to seize new opportunities and respond to threats.

Agility in business requires a culture that encourages innovation and a willingness to change course when necessary. This might involve reconfiguring supply chains in response to geopolitical shifts, adopting new technologies to improve operational efficiency, or even altering business models to better serve changing customer needs. For example, during the COVID-19 pandemic, many businesses demonstrated remarkable agility by pivoting to remote work models, leveraging digital platforms to maintain operations, and exploring new revenue streams to offset losses from traditional channels. This adaptability not only helped them survive the immediate crisis but also positioned them for long-term resilience and growth.

Moreover, being flexible allows organisations to experiment and iterate on their strategies. This iterative approach enables companies to test new ideas, gather feedback, and refine their approaches based on real-world outcomes. For instance, a software company might release a beta version of a new product to a select group of users, gather feedback, and make necessary adjustments before a full-scale launch. This flexibility reduces the risk of failure and increases the likelihood of success by ensuring that strategies are continuously aligned with market realities.

Flexibility also extends to how companies manage their workforce. In a rapidly changing environment, organisations need to be able to redeploy talent quickly to areas of greatest need. This requires cross-training employees, fostering a culture of continuous learning, and encouraging a growth mindset. Employees who are adaptable and willing to learn new skills are invaluable assets in an agile organisation. By investing in their development and creating opportunities for them to grow, companies can build a versatile and resilient workforce capable of navigating any challenge.

The Importance of Calculations & Planning

Sun Tzu places a strong emphasis on the significance of meticulous planning and detailed calculations before engaging in battle. He asserts that the general who achieves victory does so through extensive calculations and preparation, while the one who faces defeat often does so due to a lack of thorough planning. This principle is highly applicable in the business world, where the importance of strategic planning and rigorous analysis cannot be overstated. Companies must invest significant time and resources in developing comprehensive strategic plans, setting clear objectives, and outlining actionable steps to ensure success.

In the realm of business, meticulous strategic planning is akin to laying the groundwork for future success. This involves conducting in-depth research, analysing market trends, and understanding the competitive landscape. Companies must gather and analyse data to make informed decisions about their future direction. This process includes evaluating the strengths and weaknesses of the organisation, identifying opportunities for growth, and recognising potential threats. By thoroughly understanding their internal and external environments, companies can develop strategies that leverage their strengths, mitigate their weaknesses, capitalise on opportunities, and guard against threats.

One crucial aspect of strategic planning is scenario analysis. This involves considering multiple potential scenarios and their possible outcomes. By envisioning different futures, companies can better prepare for uncertainties and develop contingency plans. For example, a company might consider scenarios such as a sudden economic downturn, a new competitor entering the market, or a technological breakthrough that disrupts the industry. By preparing for these possibilities, companies can create flexible strategies that allow them to adapt quickly to changing circumstances.

Risk assessment is another vital component of strategic planning. Companies must identify and evaluate the risks associated with their strategies and operations. This involves understanding the likelihood and potential impact of various risks, such as financial instability, regulatory changes, or supply chain disruptions. By conducting thorough risk assessments, companies can develop strategies to mitigate these risks, ensuring that they are better prepared to handle potential challenges. This proactive approach helps companies avoid costly surprises and maintain stability even in uncertain times.

Resource allocation is also critical in strategic planning. Companies must allocate their resources, including financial, human, and technological assets, in a way that supports their strategic objectives. This requires careful consideration of where to invest and where to cut back, ensuring that resources are used efficiently and effectively. For example, a company might invest in research and development to drive innovation, allocate funds for marketing to increase brand awareness, or allocate human resources to key projects that align with the company's strategic goals. By prioritising resource allocation, companies can ensure that they have the necessary support to execute their strategies successfully.

A well-developed strategic plan also includes clear objectives and actionable steps. Companies must define their goals and outline the specific actions needed to achieve them. This involves setting measurable targets, establishing timelines, and assigning responsibilities to ensure accountability. For example, a company might set a goal to increase market share by 10% within the next year and outline the steps needed to achieve this, such as launching new products, expanding into new markets, or enhancing customer service. By setting clear objectives and actionable steps, companies can track their progress and make necessary adjustments to stay on course.

Moreover, strategic planning is not a one-time exercise but an ongoing process. Companies must continuously monitor their progress, review their strategies, and make adjustments as needed. This involves regularly assessing performance against objectives, analysing new data and market trends, and refining strategies to ensure continued alignment with the company's goals. By maintaining a dynamic approach to strategic planning, companies can stay agile and responsive to changes in the business environment, ensuring long-term success.

Summary

Sun Tzu's *Laying Plans* offers timeless wisdom that is remarkably applicable to modern strategic management. The principles of strategic importance, environmental analysis, leadership, discipline, deception, flexibility, and detailed planning provide a robust framework for navigating the complexities of the business world.

CHAPTER 2 – WAGING WAR

*Bring war material with you from home,
but forage on the enemy.*

Sun Tzu

Sun Tzu's *Waging War* emphasises the importance of efficiency, resource management, and swift decision-making. These principles are directly applicable to modern strategic management, where businesses face fierce competition and complex market dynamics.

The Cost of Engagement

Sun Tzu begins by meticulously detailing the enormous costs associated with waging war, underscoring the immense financial burden that maintaining an army imposes and the strain such endeavours place on resources. In the realm of business, this principle translates seamlessly to the substantial costs involved in entering and competing within a market. Companies must diligently consider the financial implications of their strategic initiatives, which encompass a broad array of expenses including research and development, marketing, production, and distribution. These costs are not merely overheads but critical investments that, if managed poorly, can spell financial disaster. Therefore, effective financial management is paramount. It ensures that resources are not only allocated wisely but are also leveraged to maximise value, thereby maintaining the company's financial viability and competitive edge.

In the modern business landscape, strategic initiatives often require significant upfront investment. Research and development, for example, are crucial for innovation and staying ahead of competitors. However, these activities are expensive and can drain financial resources if not properly managed. Marketing, too, requires substantial investment to build brand awareness and drive customer acquisition. Production and distribution add further layers of cost, particularly in industries that rely on complex supply chains. Each of these areas demands careful budgeting and strategic planning to ensure that expenditures contribute to the overall goals of the organisation.

Moreover, companies must recognise that prolonged engagement in unproductive activities can lead to severe resource depletion, mirroring the effects of extended warfare on a state's resources. Just as prolonged warfare can exhaust a state's financial and material resources, extended periods of unprofitable business endeavours can drain a company's capital and weaken its competitive position. This situation is particularly perilous because it can lead to a vicious cycle of dwindling resources, reduced market share, and declining profitability.

To avoid this pitfall, businesses should prioritise quick wins and the efficient use of resources. Quick wins are smaller, more manageable projects that deliver immediate results and boost morale. These early successes can build momentum and provide the financial support needed to tackle larger, more complex initiatives. By focusing on quick wins, companies can ensure a steady stream of revenue and maintain financial health while pursuing their long-term strategic objectives.

Efficient use of resources is equally critical. This involves optimising processes, reducing waste, and ensuring that every dollar spent contributes to the company's strategic goals. For example, companies can adopt lean manufacturing principles to minimise waste and improve efficiency in production. Similarly, strategic sourcing and procurement practices can reduce costs and enhance the quality of goods and services purchased. Effective resource management also involves investing in technology and systems that improve operational efficiency and enable better decision-making.

Furthermore, strategic financial planning must include rigorous analysis and forecasting. Companies need to develop detailed financial models that project revenues, expenses, and cash flows under various scenarios. This allows them to anticipate potential financial challenges and develop contingency plans. Regular financial reviews and audits are essential to ensure that the company remains on track to meet its financial goals.

In addition to internal financial management, companies must also be aware of external financial risks. These can include fluctuations in currency exchange rates, changes in interest rates, and economic downturns. By hedging against these risks and maintaining a diversified portfolio of investments, companies can protect their financial health and ensure long-term sustainability.

The Importance of Swift Victory

Sun Tzu places immense importance on achieving swift victory, cautioning against the hazards of prolonged campaigns that drain resources and morale. This principle is exceedingly relevant in the business world, where the ability to act with agility and speed can determine an organisation's success or failure. In today's fast-paced market, businesses must not only set strategic objectives but also execute them rapidly to stay ahead of the competition. Prolonged endeavours in the business context can lead to wasted resources, missed opportunities, and diminished competitive advantage, much like a drawn-out war.

In the business landscape, agility translates to the capability to quickly adapt to changing market conditions and customer needs. This requires an organisation to be flexible and responsive, with processes in place that allow for rapid decision-making and implementation. Companies that are slow to react may find themselves overtaken by more nimble competitors who can better meet the dynamic demands of the market. Swift victory in business means being the first to market with innovative solutions, seizing market share before competitors can respond.

Seizing opportunities is another critical aspect of achieving swift victory. Businesses must remain vigilant, constantly scanning the environment for emerging trends, gaps in the market, and new customer demands. When an opportunity arises, swift and decisive action is necessary to capitalise on it before others do. This proactive approach can lead to significant competitive advantages, allowing a company to establish itself as a leader in the market. For instance, recognising a trend towards sustainability, a company might swiftly pivot to eco-friendly products, capturing the growing segment of environmentally conscious consumers and setting itself apart from competitors.

Outmanoeuvring competitors involves not just speed but also strategic foresight. Companies must anticipate the moves of their rivals and position themselves advantageously. This requires a deep understanding of the competitive landscape, including the strengths and weaknesses of competitors. By doing so, businesses can strategically position their products and services to fill gaps that competitors have overlooked or cannot address efficiently. Outmanoeuvring competitors often involves a combination of innovative product development, strategic marketing, and superior customer service, all executed swiftly to gain a decisive edge.

In the technology sector, the importance of rapid innovation cannot be overstated. The fast-paced nature of technological advancement means that companies must continuously innovate and bring new products to market quickly to remain relevant. Industry giants like Apple and Google exemplify this principle through their relentless pursuit of innovation. Apple's ability to consistently introduce groundbreaking products like the iPhone, iPad, and Apple Watch has kept it at the forefront of the technology market. Google's rapid development and release of new services, such as Google Maps, Google Drive, and Google Assistant, have solidified its position as a leader in the tech industry.

Moreover, the concept of swift victory extends beyond product development to include all aspects of business operations. Efficient supply chain management, agile marketing strategies, and rapid customer service response times all contribute to an organisation's ability to achieve swift victory. For example, Amazon's success can be attributed to its highly efficient supply chain and logistics network, which allows it to deliver products to customers faster than many of its competitors. This speed not only enhances customer satisfaction but also deters competitors who cannot match Amazon's delivery times.

Furthermore, achieving swift victory in business requires a culture that embraces change and encourages innovation. Organisations must foster an environment where employees are empowered to take risks, experiment with new ideas, and learn from failures. This culture of agility and continuous improvement ensures that the organisation remains dynamic and can swiftly adapt to new challenges and opportunities. Leadership plays a crucial role in cultivating this culture, setting the tone for the rest of the organisation to follow.

Resource Management & Foraging

Sun Tzu's advice to bring war materials from home while foraging on the enemy is a timeless concept that speaks to the essence of effective resource management. This strategy is as applicable to modern business as it was to ancient warfare, underscoring the importance of leveraging internal strengths and capabilities while also seeking external opportunities to acquire additional resources and capabilities. In the corporate world, this dual approach is essential for maintaining a competitive edge and ensuring long-term sustainability.

In practical terms, this means that companies must first make the most of their internal resources. These can include anything from proprietary technology and skilled personnel to established processes and brand equity. By optimising these internal assets, companies can create a strong foundation upon which to build their strategic initiatives. For example, a company with a robust research and development team might focus on leveraging this internal capability to drive innovation and develop new products. Similarly, a firm with a well-established brand can use its market reputation to introduce new product lines or enter new markets with greater ease.

However, relying solely on internal resources is often not enough to stay ahead in a highly competitive market. This is where the concept of foraging on the enemy comes into play. In the business context, this translates to looking beyond the company's own resources and capabilities to acquire what is needed from external sources. Strategic alliances, mergers, and acquisitions are modern equivalents of this ancient tactic. By partnering with or acquiring other companies, businesses can gain access to new technologies, markets, and expertise, thereby enhancing their competitive position and accelerating growth.

Strategic alliances are partnerships between companies that allow them to share resources and collaborate on projects that benefit both parties. These alliances can take many forms, such as joint ventures, research collaborations, or marketing partnerships. For example, two technology companies might form an alliance to co-develop a new product, leveraging each other's strengths and sharing the costs and risks involved. This collaboration can result in a product that neither company could have developed on its own, thereby creating a competitive advantage.

Mergers and acquisitions (M&A) are more formal and permanent forms of foraging on the enemy. Through M&A, companies can acquire new capabilities, enter new markets, and achieve economies of scale. For instance, a company looking to expand its presence in a particular region might acquire a local competitor to gain immediate market access and customer base. Similarly, acquiring a company with cutting-edge technology can provide the acquirer with a significant competitive edge. The tech industry provides numerous examples of successful M&A strategies. Facebook's acquisition of Instagram and WhatsApp, for instance, allowed it to expand its social media dominance and diversify its product offerings. These acquisitions provided Facebook with new platforms and user bases, strengthening its overall market position and increasing its revenue streams.

Effective resource management also involves the integration of acquired assets and capabilities into the existing organisational structure. This can be a complex process that requires careful planning and execution. Companies must ensure that the newly acquired resources are aligned with their strategic objectives and that any potential cultural or operational differences are addressed. Successful integration maximises the value of the acquisition and enhances the company's overall capabilities.

Furthermore, companies must continuously evaluate their resource management strategies to ensure they remain aligned with changing market conditions and strategic goals. This involves regularly reviewing internal capabilities, assessing the effectiveness of strategic alliances, and identifying potential acquisition targets. By staying proactive and agile, companies can adapt to evolving circumstances and maintain their competitive advantage.

In addition to strategic alliances and M&A, businesses can also explore other forms of external resource acquisition, such as licensing agreements, franchising, and outsourcing. Licensing allows companies to use patented technology or proprietary processes owned by another company, providing access to valuable resources without the need for ownership. Franchising enables companies to expand their market presence by allowing third parties to operate under their brand and business model. Outsourcing involves contracting external service providers to handle specific business functions, such as manufacturing or customer support, allowing companies to focus on their core competencies.

Managing Proximity & Costs

Sun Tzu astutely notes the economic impact of an army's proximity to the people, observing that high prices and heavy exactions can severely drain the populace's resources. This principle translates seamlessly into the corporate world, where managing operational costs and maintaining efficiency are paramount. Companies must strike a delicate balance in their operational footprint to avoid incurring excessive costs that could significantly erode profitability. Effective cost management is not just a financial imperative but a strategic one that ensures long-term sustainability and competitive advantage.

In the corporate context, managing proximity involves strategically positioning operations to optimise costs and enhance efficiency. This might include selecting manufacturing sites, distribution centres, and offices based on factors like labour costs, transportation expenses, and proximity to key markets. By carefully considering these variables, companies can minimise overheads and improve operational efficiency. For instance, a company might choose to establish a production facility in a region with lower labour costs and favourable tax incentives, thereby reducing production expenses and boosting profit margins.

Outsourcing and offshoring are common strategies that companies employ to manage costs effectively. Outsourcing involves contracting external vendors to handle specific business functions, such as customer service, IT support, or manufacturing. This allows companies to focus on their core competencies while benefiting from the specialised expertise and cost advantages of external providers. Offshoring, on the other hand, involves relocating certain operations to regions with lower labour and production costs. By moving operations to countries with more favourable economic conditions, businesses can achieve significant cost savings and enhance their bottom line.

However, while outsourcing and offshoring offer substantial benefits, they also come with potential risks and challenges. Quality control is a critical concern, as outsourcing production to external vendors or offshoring to distant locations can result in inconsistencies in product quality. To mitigate this risk, companies must establish rigorous quality assurance processes and maintain close oversight of their external partners. Regular audits, comprehensive training programmes, and clear communication channels can help ensure that quality standards are upheld.

Supply chain disruptions are another significant risk associated with outsourcing and offshoring. Natural disasters, political instability, and logistical challenges can disrupt the supply chain and lead to delays or shortages. To address this, companies must develop robust supply chain management strategies that include contingency planning and diversification of suppliers. By maintaining a diverse network of suppliers and establishing backup plans, businesses can enhance their resilience and minimise the impact of disruptions.

Additionally, companies must consider the broader economic and regulatory environment when making decisions about outsourcing and offshoring. Changes in trade policies, tariffs, and labour laws can affect the feasibility and cost-effectiveness of these strategies. Staying informed about regulatory developments and proactively adapting to changes can help companies navigate these challenges and maintain operational stability.

Beyond outsourcing and offshoring, companies can explore other cost management strategies such as automation and process optimisation. Automation involves leveraging technology to streamline operations and reduce reliance on manual labour. This can lead to significant cost savings and efficiency gains. For example, implementing automated manufacturing systems can increase production speed and reduce labour costs. Process optimisation, on the other hand, focuses on identifying and eliminating inefficiencies within existing workflows. Techniques such as Lean management and Six Sigma can help companies improve processes, reduce waste, and enhance overall productivity.

Effective financial management also plays a crucial role in managing costs and maintaining profitability. Companies must develop comprehensive budgeting and forecasting processes to ensure that resources are allocated efficiently. Regular financial reviews and performance assessments can help identify areas of overspending and implement corrective measures. By maintaining strict financial discipline, companies can avoid unnecessary expenditures and focus their resources on strategic initiatives that drive growth and profitability.

Motivating & Rewarding Employees

Sun Tzu emphasises the critical importance of motivating soldiers through rewards and recognition, underscoring that a well-motivated force is more likely to achieve victory. This principle holds immense relevance in the modern business world, where employee motivation and engagement are pivotal to organisational success. Creating a culture that recognises and rewards employees' contributions is essential for fostering a sense of ownership, commitment, and loyalty among the workforce.

Employee motivation starts with the establishment of a recognition culture. This involves acknowledging and appreciating employees' efforts and achievements regularly. Simple acts of recognition, such as verbal praise, thank-you notes, or public acknowledgments, can significantly boost morale and reinforce positive behaviours. Employees who feel valued and appreciated are more likely to be engaged and committed to their work, leading to higher productivity and job satisfaction. For example, a company might implement a "Employee of the Month" programme to highlight outstanding performance and inspire others.

Performance-based incentives are another powerful tool for motivating employees. These incentives can take various forms, including bonuses, commissions, profit-sharing, or stock options. By tying rewards to specific performance metrics, companies can align employees' efforts with organisational goals. For instance, a sales team might receive bonuses based on meeting or exceeding sales targets, encouraging them to work harder to achieve these objectives. Performance-based incentives not only drive results but also foster a competitive spirit that can lead to continuous improvement and innovation.

Recognition programmes are designed to celebrate employees' accomplishments and milestones. These programmes can include awards ceremonies, employee appreciation events, or even simple gestures like gift cards or extra time off. Recognition programmes create a positive work environment where employees feel valued and motivated to excel. For example, a company might host an annual awards banquet to honour top performers in various categories, such as innovation, leadership, and teamwork. Such events not only recognise individual achievements but also strengthen the sense of community and camaraderie among employees.

Opportunities for career advancement are also crucial for employee motivation and engagement. Providing clear pathways for growth and development within the organisation helps employees see a future with the company and motivates them to invest in their careers. This can include offering training programmes, mentorship opportunities, and career development plans. For instance, a company might establish a leadership development programme that identifies high-potential employees and provides them with the skills and experiences needed to advance to higher-level positions. By investing in employees' professional growth, companies can retain top talent and build a strong leadership pipeline.

Aligning individual goals with organisational objectives is essential for maximising employee motivation and overall performance. When employees understand how their work contributes to the company's success, they are more likely to be engaged and committed. This alignment can be achieved through regular goal-setting and performance reviews, where managers work with employees to set clear, measurable objectives that support the company's strategic goals. For example, a marketing team might set goals related to increasing brand awareness or driving lead generation, directly contributing to the company's revenue growth. By aligning individual and organisational goals, companies can create a sense of purpose and direction that motivates employees to perform at their best.

Moreover, fostering a culture of innovation is critical for keeping employees motivated and engaged. Companies that encourage creativity and experimentation create an environment where employees feel empowered to take risks and develop new ideas. This culture of innovation can be supported through initiatives such as hackathons, innovation labs, or suggestion programmes. For example, a technology company might host regular hackathons where employees can collaborate on innovative projects, with the best ideas receiving funding and support for further development. By promoting innovation, companies can drive continuous improvement and stay ahead of the competition.

Google serves as an exemplary model of a company that has successfully implemented these principles. Known for its innovative work environment and employee-centric policies, Google has created a culture where employees are motivated to excel and contribute to the company's success. Google's recognition programmes, performance-based incentives, and opportunities for career advancement have made it one of the most desirable places to work. The company's commitment to fostering a culture of innovation and continuous improvement has not only attracted top talent but also driven significant advancements in technology and business practices.

Utilising Conquered Resources

Sun Tzu advises making use of the enemy's provisions and integrating captured soldiers to strengthen one's own forces. This principle is directly applicable to the modern business context, where it translates to leveraging acquired assets and integrating new capabilities from mergers and acquisitions (M&A). When companies undertake M&A activities, it is crucial to effectively incorporate the new resources, talents, and capabilities they acquire to maximise value and achieve strategic goals.

The process of successfully integrating acquired resources requires meticulous planning and execution. Companies must approach integration with a comprehensive strategy that aligns the acquired entity's operations, culture, and systems with their own. This ensures a seamless transition and the full realisation of the benefits of the merger or acquisition. For instance, when a company acquires another firm, it must integrate various aspects such as human resources, technology platforms, supply chains, and customer service protocols. This alignment helps in creating a cohesive and unified organisation that operates efficiently and effectively.

Cultural integration is a critical component of successful M&A. Each company has its own unique culture, shaped by its history, values, and practices. When two companies merge, these cultures must be harmonised to foster a collaborative and productive work environment. This involves identifying and addressing cultural differences, promoting shared values, and fostering open communication. For example, Disney's acquisition of Pixar and Marvel not only brought new creative assets and capabilities but also required careful cultural integration. Disney successfully embraced the innovative and distinct cultures of Pixar and Marvel, allowing them to maintain their creative autonomy while aligning with Disney's broader strategic objectives. This cultural integration contributed to the substantial value creation and success of these acquisitions.

Operational integration is another crucial aspect that requires attention. Companies must ensure that their operational processes, systems, and workflows are aligned and optimised for efficiency. This may involve integrating IT systems, standardising processes, and streamlining supply chains. Effective operational integration helps in eliminating redundancies, reducing costs, and improving overall performance. For instance, a company acquiring a competitor in the same industry may find opportunities to consolidate production facilities, harmonise procurement practices, and integrate logistics operations. This can lead to cost savings and improved efficiency, enhancing the company's competitive position.

Moreover, financial integration is essential to ensure that the combined entity operates smoothly from a financial perspective. This includes consolidating financial statements, aligning budgeting and forecasting processes, and integrating financial reporting systems. Companies must also address any financial risks associated with the acquisition and ensure compliance with regulatory requirements. Effective financial integration helps in maintaining financial stability and achieving the anticipated financial synergies of the merger or acquisition.

Human resources integration is equally important in leveraging the talent and capabilities acquired through M&A. Companies must develop strategies to retain key employees, integrate HR policies, and align performance management systems. Providing clear communication, offering development opportunities, and fostering a positive work environment can help in retaining top talent and ensuring their engagement and productivity. For example, during the integration process, a company might conduct workshops and training sessions to help employees from both organisations understand the new structure, culture, and strategic objectives. This facilitates a smoother transition and promotes a sense of unity and collaboration among employees.

The successful integration of acquired resources also involves leveraging new technologies and capabilities to drive innovation and growth. Companies must identify opportunities to incorporate the technological strengths and expertise of the acquired entity into their operations. This may involve adopting new technologies, enhancing product offerings, or entering new markets. For instance, a technology company acquiring a startup with cutting-edge innovations can integrate these technologies into its existing product portfolio, enhancing its competitive edge and accelerating growth.

Strategic Focus & Leadership

Sun Tzu concludes his teachings by emphasising that the ultimate objective of war is victory, not prolonged campaigns. This principle is profoundly relevant in the business world, highlighting the importance of strategic focus and decisive leadership. Companies must prioritise their strategic objectives and avoid getting bogged down in unproductive activities that can drain resources and hinder progress. Strategic focus means concentrating efforts on the most critical initiatives that drive the organisation towards its long-term goals. It involves setting clear priorities, allocating resources effectively, and maintaining a laser-sharp focus on achieving key milestones.

Effective leadership is crucial in guiding organisations toward their strategic goals. Leaders play a pivotal role in setting the direction, making informed decisions, and fostering a culture of excellence. They must have a deep understanding of the market dynamics, competitive landscape, and internal capabilities to make strategic choices that propel the organisation forward. This involves continuous learning and staying abreast of industry trends to anticipate changes and adapt strategies accordingly.

A critical aspect of effective leadership is the ability to communicate a clear vision. A compelling vision provides a sense of purpose and direction for the entire organisation. It inspires and motivates employees, creating a shared sense of mission. Leaders must articulate this vision in a way that resonates with their teams, ensuring that everyone understands how their individual contributions align with the broader organisational goals. This alignment fosters unity and collaboration, driving collective efforts toward achieving the vision.

In addition to communicating the vision, leaders must inspire their teams to achieve excellence. This involves creating an environment where employees feel valued, empowered, and motivated to perform at their best. Leaders should recognise and celebrate achievements, provide constructive feedback, and support professional development. By fostering a culture of recognition and growth, leaders can enhance employee engagement and commitment, leading to higher productivity and better outcomes.

Maintaining strategic focus requires leaders to be disciplined in their approach. They must resist the temptation to chase every new opportunity or trend and instead concentrate on initiatives that align with the strategic objectives. This involves setting clear goals, establishing measurable targets, and regularly reviewing progress. Leaders must be vigilant in identifying activities that do not contribute to the strategic goals and reallocate resources to more impactful initiatives. This disciplined approach ensures that efforts are concentrated on areas that drive the most significant value.

Decisive leadership is also about making tough decisions when necessary. Leaders must have the courage to make bold choices, even when faced with uncertainty or resistance. This could involve pivoting the business model, entering new markets, or discontinuing unprofitable products. Decisive leaders weigh the risks and benefits, gather insights from various sources, and take swift action to capitalise on opportunities or mitigate threats. Their ability to make timely decisions can be the difference between seizing a market advantage and falling behind competitors.

Furthermore, effective leaders cultivate resilience within their organisations. They understand that setbacks and challenges are inevitable, but they use these experiences as learning opportunities. Resilient leaders encourage their teams to adapt, innovate, and persist in the face of adversity. They create a supportive environment where employees feel safe to take calculated risks and learn from failures. This resilience not only helps the organisation navigate challenges but also builds a strong foundation for long-term success.

Leaders must also foster a culture of continuous improvement. They should encourage their teams to constantly seek ways to enhance processes, products, and services. This involves promoting a mindset of innovation and encouraging creative problem-solving. Leaders can support this culture by providing resources for research and development, facilitating cross-functional collaboration, and rewarding innovative ideas. Continuous improvement ensures that the organisation remains competitive and responsive to evolving market demands.

Summary

Sun Tzu's *Waging War* offers timeless insights that are highly relevant to modern strategic management. The principles of efficient resource management, swift decision-making, motivation, and strategic focus provide a robust framework for navigating the challenges of the business world.

CHAPTER 3 – ATTACK BY STRATAGEM

*...the skilful leader subdues the enemy's troops
without any fighting...*

Sun Tzu

Sun Tzu's *Attack by Stratagem* emphasises the importance of strategic planning, deception, and the effective use of resources. These principles are highly relevant to modern strategic management, where businesses must navigate competitive landscapes, manage resources efficiently, and outmanoeuvre rivals to achieve success.

Strategic Planning & Intelligence

Sun Tzu begins this chapter by asserting that the most effective strategy is to take the enemy's country whole and intact rather than destroy it. This principle applies directly to the business world, where the goal is to gain market share and competitive advantage without engaging in destructive competition. Companies should strive to capture value and expand their market presence through well-crafted strategic planning and intelligence, avoiding price wars and tactics that erode profitability and harm the industry.

Strategic planning in the business context involves a thorough analysis of market trends to anticipate future shifts and opportunities. This includes studying economic indicators, consumer behaviour patterns, technological advancements, and regulatory changes. Companies that stay ahead of these trends can better position themselves to take advantage of new opportunities and navigate potential threats. For instance, a company might analyse the growing demand for sustainable products and decide to invest in eco-friendly innovations to capture a new segment of environmentally conscious consumers.

Understanding competitor strengths and weaknesses is another critical component of strategic planning. This involves conducting competitive analysis to identify what competitors do well and where they fall short. Companies can then develop strategies to leverage their own strengths against competitors' weaknesses. For example, a company might find that a competitor has a strong product lineup but weak customer service. In response, the company could focus on enhancing its customer service to differentiate itself and attract dissatisfied customers from the competitor.

Identifying growth opportunities requires a keen understanding of the market landscape and consumer needs. This involves not only recognising existing gaps in the market but also anticipating future demand. Companies can use market research, surveys, and data analytics to gather insights into customer preferences and emerging trends. By addressing these needs, companies can develop new products or services that capture additional market share and create value for customers. For instance, a company might discover a rising interest in health and wellness products and decide to launch a new line of organic and natural goods.

Gathering and analysing intelligence is essential for informed decision-making. This process involves collecting data from various sources, such as industry reports, customer feedback, social media, and competitive analysis. By synthesising this information, companies can develop a comprehensive understanding of the market and make strategic decisions that align with their objectives. For example, a company might use social media analytics to monitor consumer sentiment and identify potential issues with its products. By addressing these issues proactively, the company can improve customer satisfaction and maintain a positive brand image.

Apple is a prime example of a company that has consistently leveraged its strategic planning and intelligence capabilities to gain market share and maintain a competitive edge. Apple's success can be attributed to its strong brand, innovative capabilities, and loyal customer base. The company's ability to anticipate market trends and consumer needs has allowed it to introduce groundbreaking products, such as the iPhone, iPad, and Apple Watch. These innovations have not only captured significant market share but also set new standards for the industry.

Furthermore, Apple's strategic focus on maintaining premium pricing and avoiding price wars has helped preserve its profitability and brand value. Rather than competing on price, Apple differentiates itself through product quality, design, and customer experience. This approach has enabled Apple to build a loyal customer base willing to pay a premium for its products, resulting in strong financial performance and sustained growth.

In addition to product innovation, Apple's strategic planning extends to its supply chain management and global operations. The company has developed a highly efficient supply chain that allows it to produce and deliver products quickly and cost-effectively. This operational efficiency is a key component of Apple's competitive advantage, enabling it to respond swiftly to market demand and maintain high levels of customer satisfaction.

Apple's success also highlights the importance of aligning strategic planning with organisational capabilities. The company's focus on fostering a culture of innovation and continuous improvement has been instrumental in driving its success. By investing in research and development, Apple ensures that it remains at the forefront of technological advancements. The company's emphasis on design and user experience further enhances its competitive position, as customers consistently seek out Apple products for their superior quality and functionality.

Deception & Competitive Positioning

Sun Tzu teaches that supreme excellence in warfare lies in breaking the enemy's resistance without engaging in actual combat. This timeless principle is equally pertinent in the business world, where achieving competitive advantage without destructive competition can lead to sustainable success. In business, this principle translates into the importance of competitive positioning and the strategic use of deception to outmanoeuvre rivals. Companies can craft perceptions that influence competitor behaviour and market dynamics, thereby securing a strategic edge.

Competitive positioning is all about creating a unique value proposition that sets a company apart from its competitors. This begins with a deep understanding of customer needs, preferences, and pain points. By conducting thorough market research and engaging with customers, companies can gain valuable insights into what drives purchasing decisions. Armed with this knowledge, businesses can develop products and services that offer superior value, thereby attracting and retaining a loyal customer base. For instance, a company that identifies a growing demand for eco-friendly products can position itself as a leader in sustainability, thereby differentiating itself from competitors and appealing to environmentally conscious consumers.

Developing a compelling value proposition requires innovation and a keen sense of market trends. Companies must continuously innovate to meet evolving customer expectations and stay ahead of the competition. This might involve investing in research and development, exploring new technologies, or enhancing existing products and services. By offering unique and high-quality solutions, companies can create a strong competitive position that is difficult for rivals to replicate. For example, a tech company that consistently introduces cutting-edge gadgets with advanced features can establish itself as an industry leader, attracting tech-savvy customers and building brand loyalty.

Strategic deception, another crucial aspect highlighted by Sun Tzu, involves creating perceptions that mislead competitors about a company's true intentions. This can be a powerful tool for gaining a competitive advantage without direct confrontation. For instance, a company might signal a future product launch or expansion plans to deter competitors from entering a particular market or investing in similar initiatives. This type of strategic signalling can create uncertainty and force competitors to allocate resources inefficiently, thereby weakening their position.

The art of strategic deception extends to various aspects of business operations. Companies can use marketing and public relations to shape perceptions and influence competitor behaviour. For instance, a company might generate buzz about a new product through strategic leaks or teaser campaigns, creating anticipation and diverting attention from competitors. At the same time, the company can secretly focus on improving other aspects of its business, such as customer service or supply chain efficiency, gaining an edge that competitors did not anticipate.

Another example of strategic deception is the use of alliances and partnerships to mislead competitors. By forming strategic alliances with other companies, businesses can create the illusion of strengthening certain capabilities while actually focusing on different areas of growth. For instance, a company might partner with a leading technology firm to signal an emphasis on technological innovation, while its real focus remains on expanding market reach through improved distribution channels. This tactic can divert competitors' attention and resources, allowing the company to achieve its strategic objectives unchallenged.

Furthermore, strategic deception can involve misleading competitors about financial health and market positioning. Companies can use financial reports, press releases, and other communications to present a controlled narrative that influences competitor perceptions. For example, a company might downplay its financial strength and market ambitions to avoid attracting competitive threats, while internally executing an aggressive growth strategy. This approach can buy valuable time and resources to solidify market presence and build competitive advantage.

To effectively implement competitive positioning and strategic deception, companies must foster a culture of strategic thinking and innovation. This involves encouraging employees to think creatively, take calculated risks, and explore unconventional approaches to problem-solving. By promoting a mindset of continuous improvement and adaptability, companies can stay agile and responsive to market changes.

The Importance of Speed & Agility

Sun Tzu advises against besieging walled cities, emphasising the high costs and risks associated with prolonged engagements. This principle is profoundly relevant in modern strategic management, highlighting the importance of speed and agility in achieving strategic objectives. In today's fast-paced business environment, companies must be able to rapidly adapt to changing market conditions, seize opportunities, and outmanoeuvre competitors. The ability to move quickly and efficiently is essential for maintaining a competitive edge and achieving sustainable growth.

Speed in business refers to the ability to act swiftly in response to market changes, emerging opportunities, and competitive threats. Companies that can rapidly pivot their strategies and operations are better positioned to capitalise on new opportunities and mitigate potential risks. This requires a proactive approach to monitoring the market and staying attuned to industry trends. For instance, a company that quickly identifies a shift in consumer preferences can adjust its product offerings and marketing strategies to meet the new demand, thereby gaining a first-mover advantage.

Agility, on the other hand, involves being flexible and responsive to both internal and external changes. This encompasses the ability to quickly reconfigure processes, redeploy resources, and adapt to new challenges. Companies can enhance their agility by adopting flexible organisational structures that support rapid decision-making and execution. For example, a company might implement cross-functional teams that can collaborate seamlessly and respond quickly to new initiatives. This approach fosters a culture of agility and innovation, enabling the organisation to stay ahead of the curve.

Streamlining decision-making processes is another critical aspect of enhancing agility. Traditional hierarchical structures can slow down decision-making and impede responsiveness. To overcome this, companies can adopt flatter organisational structures that empower employees to make decisions at various levels. This decentralisation of authority allows for faster decision-making and implementation. For instance, a retail company might empower store managers to make inventory decisions based on local market conditions, rather than waiting for approval from the central office. This autonomy enables the company to respond more effectively to changing customer demands.

Investing in technology is also essential for enhancing speed and agility. Advanced technologies, such as artificial intelligence, machine learning, and big data analytics, enable companies to gather and analyse real-time data, providing valuable insights that inform strategic decisions. For example, a company that leverages real-time data analytics can quickly identify trends and patterns, allowing it to adjust its strategies and operations accordingly. This technological capability enhances the company's ability to respond to market changes and maintain a competitive edge.

Amazon serves as an exemplary model of a company that has mastered the principles of speed and agility. Amazon's ability to quickly adapt to market trends and customer preferences has been a key factor in its sustained growth and success. The company's agile approach to business is evident in its continuous innovation and rapid expansion into new markets. For example, Amazon's swift response to the growing demand for e-commerce led to the development of its highly efficient logistics and delivery network, which has become a cornerstone of its competitive advantage.

Furthermore, Amazon's investment in technology has enabled it to maintain its competitive edge. The company leverages advanced data analytics to monitor customer behaviour and preferences, allowing it to personalise the shopping experience and anticipate future demand. This real-time data analysis informs Amazon's strategic decisions, from product recommendations to inventory management. The company's focus on technological innovation is also evident in its development of cloud computing services through Amazon Web Services (AWS), which has become a significant revenue stream and a key driver of growth.

In addition to technological investments, Amazon's organisational structure supports agility and rapid decision-making. The company operates with a decentralised structure that empowers teams to act autonomously and make decisions quickly. This approach fosters a culture of innovation and continuous improvement, enabling Amazon to stay ahead of the competition. For example, the company encourages experimentation and rapid prototyping, allowing teams to test new ideas and bring successful innovations to market quickly.

The importance of speed and agility is not limited to large corporations like Amazon. Businesses of all sizes can benefit from adopting these principles. Small and medium-sized enterprises (SMEs) can leverage their inherent flexibility and agility to compete with larger competitors. By focusing on niche markets, quickly adapting to customer needs, and embracing innovation, SMEs can carve out a competitive advantage and achieve sustainable growth.

The Role of Leadership

Sun Tzu asserts that the general is the bulwark of the state, and the strength of the state fundamentally depends on the strength of its leadership. This principle translates directly to the business world, where effective leadership is the cornerstone of an organisation's ability to navigate strategic challenges and achieve success. Leaders must possess not only a strategic vision but also robust decision-making capabilities and the ability to inspire and motivate their teams. This multifaceted role requires a combination of skills, character traits, and strategic acumen to guide the organisation towards its goals.

Effective leadership begins with the setting of clear strategic objectives. Leaders must articulate these objectives in a manner that is both specific and actionable. These goals should align with the long-term vision of the company, ensuring that every member of the organisation understands their role in achieving them. For instance, a technology company may set a strategic objective to become a leader in artificial intelligence within five years. This overarching goal would then be broken down into specific, measurable targets, such as investing in R&D, forming strategic partnerships, and expanding the talent pool with AI expertise. By establishing clear objectives, leaders provide a roadmap that guides the organisation's efforts and resources.

Communicating a compelling vision is another critical aspect of leadership. A vision provides a sense of purpose and direction, inspiring employees to work towards a common goal. Leaders must be able to communicate this vision effectively, using language and storytelling that resonate with their audience. This involves not only articulating the vision but also demonstrating a commitment to it through actions and decisions. For example, a leader who envisions creating a customer-centric company must embody this vision by prioritising customer needs in every decision and encouraging a culture of customer service excellence.

Fostering a culture of collaboration and innovation is essential for driving organisational success. Leaders must create an environment where collaboration is encouraged and valued. This involves promoting open communication, breaking down silos, and facilitating cross-functional teamwork. By fostering collaboration, leaders can harness the diverse perspectives and skills within the organisation, leading to more innovative solutions and improved problem-solving. Additionally, leaders must cultivate a culture of innovation by encouraging experimentation, risk-taking, and continuous learning. This can be achieved by providing employees with the resources and autonomy to explore new ideas, recognising and rewarding innovation, and learning from failures as well as successes.

Informed decision-making is a hallmark of effective leadership. Leaders must gather and analyse information from both internal and external sources to make well-informed decisions. This involves understanding the internal dynamics of the organisation, such as employee morale, resource allocation, and operational efficiency, as well as external factors like market trends, competitive landscape, and regulatory changes. By conducting thorough analyses, leaders can identify opportunities and threats, assess the impact of potential decisions, and choose the best course of action. For example, a company considering entering a new market must evaluate factors such as market demand, competition, legal requirements, and cultural differences before making a decision.

Providing direction and support is crucial for empowering teams to execute strategic initiatives. Leaders must offer clear guidance on expectations, priorities, and desired outcomes. This includes setting performance standards, providing feedback, and addressing any obstacles that may hinder progress. Support also involves equipping teams with the necessary resources, training, and tools to perform their tasks effectively. By removing barriers and facilitating access to resources, leaders enable their teams to focus on delivering results.

In addition to strategic vision, effective communication, collaboration, and informed decision-making, leaders must also possess emotional intelligence. This involves being aware of and managing one's own emotions, as well as understanding and influencing the emotions of others. Emotional intelligence enables leaders to build strong relationships, foster a positive work environment, and effectively navigate interpersonal dynamics. For example, a leader who demonstrates empathy and active listening can better understand and address the concerns of their employees, leading to higher levels of trust and engagement.

Moreover, effective leadership requires adaptability and resilience. The business landscape is constantly evolving, and leaders must be able to adapt to changing circumstances and recover from setbacks. This involves being open to new ideas, embracing change, and maintaining a positive attitude in the face of challenges. By demonstrating adaptability and resilience, leaders can inspire their teams to persevere and remain focused on achieving their goals.

Adaptation & Flexibility

Sun Tzu highlights the critical importance of adapting to changing circumstances and modifying plans based on favourable conditions. This principle is paramount in modern strategic management, underscoring the necessity for flexibility and adaptability. In today's fast-paced business environment, companies must possess the ability to pivot their strategies in response to market changes, technological disruptions, and evolving customer preferences. The capacity to adapt swiftly and effectively can mean the difference between thriving and failing in a highly competitive market.

Adaptation involves a multifaceted approach, starting with the continuous monitoring of the external environment. This includes staying attuned to market trends, competitor actions, regulatory changes, and technological advancements. By keeping a finger on the pulse of the external environment, companies can anticipate changes and proactively adjust their strategies. For instance, a business that closely monitors consumer behaviour trends may notice a growing preference for online shopping and shift its focus from brick-and-mortar stores to e-commerce platforms, thus staying ahead of the curve.

Gathering intelligence is another crucial aspect of adaptation. Companies must collect and analyse data from various sources to inform their strategic decisions. This data-driven approach enables organisations to make informed choices, minimise risks, and capitalise on opportunities. For example, by leveraging big data analytics, a retail company can gain insights into customer preferences and buying patterns, allowing it to tailor its product offerings and marketing strategies to better meet customer needs. This intelligence-driven decision-making process enhances the company's ability to respond to market dynamics swiftly and effectively.

Flexibility is also about fostering a culture of continuous learning and improvement within the organisation. Companies that encourage a growth mindset and promote ongoing education and skills development are better equipped to adapt to change. This involves providing employees with access to training programmes, workshops, and resources that enhance their knowledge and capabilities. By investing in employee development, companies create a workforce that is agile, innovative, and prepared to tackle new challenges. For instance, a tech company might offer coding boot camps and certifications to keep its developers up-to-date with the latest programming languages and technologies, ensuring they remain competitive and innovative.

Encouraging innovation is another key element of fostering adaptability. Companies should create an environment where creativity and experimentation are valued and rewarded. This can be achieved by establishing innovation labs, hosting hackathons, and promoting cross-functional collaboration. By encouraging employees to think outside the box and explore new ideas, companies can drive continuous improvement and stay ahead of the competition. For instance, Google's "20% time" policy, which allows employees to spend 20% of their time working on passion projects, has led to the development of innovative products like Gmail and Google Maps.

Investing in research and development (R&D) is also crucial for maintaining flexibility and adaptability. Companies that allocate resources to R&D are better positioned to innovate and respond to technological disruptions. This involves exploring new technologies, developing new products, and improving existing offerings. For example, pharmaceutical companies invest heavily in R&D to discover new drugs and therapies, enabling them to address emerging health challenges and maintain a competitive edge in the market. Similarly, a software company might invest in developing artificial intelligence capabilities to enhance its products and services, staying ahead of technological advancements.

Netflix serves as a prime example of a company that has successfully embraced adaptation and flexibility. Originally a DVD rental service, Netflix recognised the shifting landscape of media consumption and the growing demand for online streaming. By leveraging its understanding of market trends and investing in streaming technology, Netflix transformed itself into a leading streaming platform. This strategic pivot allowed Netflix to capture a significant share of the market and establish itself as a dominant player in the entertainment industry. Furthermore, Netflix continues to adapt by producing original content, leveraging data analytics to personalise user experiences, and expanding its global reach.

Unity & Alignment

Sun Tzu emphasises the crucial importance of unity and alignment within the ranks of an army, asserting that coordinated and cohesive efforts are essential for achieving victory. This principle is profoundly relevant in the business context, where organisational success hinges on the alignment and cohesion of all employees. Companies must ensure that every team member is fully aligned with the strategic objectives and is working harmoniously towards common goals. The power of a unified organisation cannot be overstated, as it drives efficiency, fosters innovation, and enhances overall performance.

Achieving alignment begins with creating a shared sense of purpose that resonates with every employee. This involves articulating the company's mission, vision, and values in a way that inspires and motivates the workforce. When employees understand the broader purpose behind their work, they are more likely to be engaged and committed. For instance, a company might emphasise its commitment to sustainability and environmental responsibility, creating a sense of pride and purpose among employees who share these values. This shared sense of purpose unites the workforce and aligns their efforts towards common objectives.

Fostering a culture of collaboration and teamwork is another critical aspect of achieving alignment. Companies must create an environment where teamwork is encouraged and valued, and where employees feel empowered to contribute their ideas and skills. This involves promoting open communication, breaking down silos, and facilitating cross-functional collaboration. By encouraging employees to work together towards shared goals, companies can harness the collective intelligence and creativity of their workforce. For example, a company might implement team-building activities, collaborative projects, and regular cross-departmental meetings to strengthen bonds and promote a spirit of teamwork.

Setting clear goals is essential for ensuring alignment within the organisation. Leaders must establish specific, measurable, achievable, relevant, and time-bound (SMART) objectives that provide a clear roadmap for employees. These goals should be communicated transparently and consistently, ensuring that every team member understands what is expected of them and how their efforts contribute to the broader organisational objectives. For instance, a sales team might have clear quarterly targets for revenue growth, customer acquisition, and market expansion, providing a focused direction for their efforts.

Communicating a compelling vision is another vital component of achieving alignment. A vision provides a long-term perspective and a sense of direction for the organisation. Leaders must articulate this vision in a way that resonates with employees and inspires them to strive for excellence. This involves using storytelling, visual aids, and regular updates to keep the vision alive and relevant. For example, a technology company might communicate its vision of becoming a leader in innovation and digital transformation, inspiring employees to contribute to groundbreaking projects and initiatives.

Providing incentives that align individual performance with organisational objectives is crucial for maintaining alignment. Incentives can take various forms, including financial rewards, recognition programmes, career development opportunities, and non-monetary benefits. By aligning incentives with performance metrics, companies can motivate employees to achieve their goals and contribute to the overall success of the organisation. For instance, a company might offer performance-based bonuses, employee of the month awards, and opportunities for career advancement to recognise and reward exceptional performance. These incentives reinforce desired behaviours and drive employees to exceed expectations.

Google serves as an exemplary model of a company that has successfully achieved alignment through a collaborative and innovative culture. Google's emphasis on open communication, teamwork, and continuous learning has created an environment where employees feel valued and empowered. The company's clear goals, compelling vision, and performance-based incentives have enabled it to attract and retain top talent, driving organisational success. For example, Google's OKR (Objectives and Key Results) framework provides a structured approach to goal-setting, ensuring that every employee's efforts are aligned with the company's strategic priorities.

Moreover, Google's investment in employee well-being and development further reinforces alignment and cohesion within the organisation. The company offers a range of benefits, including wellness programmes, professional development opportunities, and flexible work arrangements, to support employees' physical, mental, and professional growth. By prioritising employee well-being and development, Google creates a positive work environment that fosters loyalty, engagement, and high performance.

Summary

Sun Tzu's *Attack by Stratagem* offers timeless insights that are highly relevant to modern strategic management. The principles of strategic planning, competitive positioning, speed and agility, effective leadership, adaptation, and alignment provide a robust framework for navigating the complexities of the business world.

CHAPTER 4 – TACTICAL DISPOSITIONS

The general who is skilled in defence hides in the most secret recesses of the earth; he who is skilled in attack flashes forth from the topmost heights of heaven.

Sun Tzu

Sun Tzu's *Tactical Dispositions* offers particularly valuable lessons for modern strategic management. This chapter emphasises the importance of preparation, adaptability, and strategic positioning—principles that are essential for navigating the complexities of today's business environment.

The Foundation of Defence & Preparation

Sun Tzu asserts that exceptional fighters first secure themselves against the possibility of defeat and then wait for an opportunity to overcome their adversaries. This timeless wisdom translates seamlessly into the business world, where it underscores the crucial importance of building a strong, resilient foundation before pursuing aggressive growth strategies. Companies must meticulously invest in their core capabilities, ensure financial stability, and establish robust operational processes to create a solid base capable of withstanding market fluctuations and competitive pressures.

Building a strong foundation begins with investing in core capabilities. These include the fundamental skills, technologies, and resources that give a company its competitive edge. For instance, a technology firm might focus on developing advanced software engineering capabilities and investing in cutting-edge research and development. By honing these core capabilities, companies can ensure they have a distinct advantage that sets them apart from competitors. This involves continuous learning, upgrading skills, and staying abreast of industry advancements to maintain a leading position.

Financial stability is another critical aspect of building a resilient foundation. Companies must ensure they have a solid financial footing, with adequate reserves to weather economic downturns and unforeseen challenges. This involves prudent financial management, including maintaining healthy cash flow, reducing debt, and diversifying revenue streams. For example, a retail company might focus on optimising its inventory management to reduce costs and improve cash flow. By maintaining financial stability, companies can navigate market volatility and invest in growth opportunities without compromising their long-term viability.

Establishing robust operational processes is equally important. Companies must streamline their operations to enhance efficiency, reduce waste, and improve overall performance. This involves implementing best practices, standardising procedures, and leveraging technology to automate repetitive tasks. For example, a manufacturing company might adopt Lean manufacturing principles to minimise waste and improve productivity. By creating efficient operational processes, companies can ensure they deliver high-quality products and services consistently, meeting customer expectations and building a strong reputation in the market.

Strengthening the supply chain is a key component of building a resilient foundation. Companies must ensure their supply chain is robust and capable of withstanding disruptions. This involves diversifying suppliers, optimising logistics, and implementing contingency plans to address potential risks. For instance, a company might establish relationships with multiple suppliers to mitigate the risk of supply chain disruptions caused by geopolitical tensions or natural disasters. By strengthening the supply chain, companies can maintain continuity in their operations and deliver products to customers without delays.

Improving product quality is another essential aspect of building a strong foundation. Companies must focus on delivering products that meet or exceed customer expectations. This involves implementing rigorous quality control measures, conducting regular inspections, and continuously seeking ways to enhance product performance. For example, a consumer electronics company might invest in advanced testing equipment and employ skilled technicians to ensure its products meet high-quality standards. By consistently delivering high-quality products, companies can build a loyal customer base and enhance their brand reputation.

Building a loyal customer base is crucial for long-term success. Companies must prioritise customer satisfaction and create meaningful relationships with their customers. This involves understanding customer needs, providing exceptional service, and fostering engagement through personalised experiences. For instance, a hospitality company might implement a loyalty programme that rewards repeat customers with exclusive benefits and personalised offers. By building a loyal customer base, companies can generate repeat business, reduce customer acquisition costs, and create brand advocates who promote their products and services.

Once a strong foundation is established, companies are better positioned to pursue aggressive growth strategies and seize opportunities when they arise. A company that has strengthened its supply chain, improved product quality, and built a loyal customer base is well-prepared to expand into new markets, introduce new products, and take on competitors. For example, an e-commerce company that has optimised its logistics and built a strong online presence can leverage its foundation to expand into international markets, reaching new customers and driving growth.

Defensive Tactics & Offensive Opportunities

Sun Tzu draws a critical distinction between defensive and offensive tactics, emphasising that while security against defeat is achieved through defensive measures, the ability to overcome the enemy requires proactive offensive action. In the business realm, this principle underscores the necessity for a balanced strategy that harmoniously incorporates both defensive and offensive elements. Businesses must adeptly blend these two strategic approaches to safeguard their market position and simultaneously drive growth and innovation.

Defensive tactics in business are those measures that protect the company's current position and assets. These may include robust risk management practices, ensuring compliance with all relevant regulations, and safeguarding intellectual property. Risk management involves identifying potential threats to the company, such as financial risks, operational risks, or market risks, and developing strategies to mitigate these threats. This proactive approach helps the company to prepare for and respond to unforeseen challenges, thereby maintaining stability and continuity. Compliance with regulations is equally important, as it ensures that the company operates within the legal framework and avoids penalties that could damage its reputation and financial standing. Safeguarding intellectual property is another critical defensive measure, protecting the company's innovations, patents, trademarks, and copyrights from infringement by competitors.

On the other hand, offensive opportunities involve actions that aim to advance the company's position in the market. This includes innovative product development, which is the lifeblood of any successful business. By continuously developing new and improved products, companies can meet the evolving needs of their customers and stay ahead of competitors. Market expansion is another offensive strategy, where companies seek to enter new geographic regions or demographic segments to grow their customer base. Competitive differentiation involves creating a unique value proposition that sets the company apart from its rivals. This could be achieved through superior product quality, exceptional customer service, or innovative marketing strategies.

Companies must be adept at both defending their market position and identifying opportunities for growth. For instance, a technology company might invest heavily in cybersecurity measures to protect its data and systems from cyber threats, thereby ensuring the integrity and confidentiality of its operations (defensive tactic). Simultaneously, the same company might allocate resources to research and development to create cutting-edge software solutions that address emerging market needs and capture new market segments (offensive opportunity). This dual approach ensures that the company is not only secure from potential threats but is also actively pursuing growth and innovation.

The ability to seamlessly integrate defensive and offensive strategies is a hallmark of effective strategic management. This requires a comprehensive understanding of the internal and external environment, as well as the agility to respond to changing circumstances. Leaders must be vigilant in monitoring the market landscape, identifying potential risks and opportunities, and making informed decisions that balance both defensive and offensive elements. For example, a pharmaceutical company might engage in rigorous regulatory compliance to ensure the safety and efficacy of its products (defensive tactic) while also investing in the development of new therapies that address unmet medical needs (offensive opportunity). This balanced approach enables the company to maintain its market position and drive future growth.

Moreover, the integration of defensive and offensive strategies involves aligning them with the overall strategic goals of the company. This requires clear communication and coordination across all levels of the organisation. Employees must understand the importance of both defensive and offensive tactics and how their roles contribute to achieving the company's objectives. For instance, the marketing team must work closely with the product development team to ensure that new products are effectively promoted and meet customer needs, while the legal team ensures that all intellectual property is protected. This collaborative approach ensures that the company operates as a cohesive unit, with all functions aligned towards common goals.

The Significance of Strategic Positioning

Sun Tzu asserts that a skilled fighter places himself in a position that makes defeat impossible and seizes the moment to defeat the enemy. This principle underscores the paramount importance of strategic positioning and timing in achieving a competitive advantage. For businesses, strategic positioning involves carefully assessing their market position, understanding the competitive landscape, and identifying the most opportune moments for strategic initiatives. Companies must leverage their unique strengths to create a formidable position that can withstand market pressures and ensure long-term success.

Strategic positioning is the art of differentiating a company's products or services in a way that stands out from the competition. This differentiation can be achieved through various means, such as superior product quality, exceptional customer service, innovative features, or unique branding. By understanding customer needs and preferences, companies can develop offerings that provide unmatched value and resonate with their target audience. For example, a company might focus on sustainability by creating eco-friendly products that appeal to environmentally conscious consumers. This unique value proposition not only attracts customers but also fosters loyalty and long-term relationships.

Targeting the right customer segments is another critical component of strategic positioning. Companies must conduct thorough market research to identify the most promising segments that align with their offerings. By tailoring products and marketing strategies to meet the specific needs of these segments, businesses can maximise their impact and build a loyal customer base. For instance, a luxury car manufacturer might target affluent consumers who value premium quality and cutting-edge technology. By aligning their offerings with the preferences of this segment, the manufacturer can establish a strong market presence and command higher prices.

Leveraging unique capabilities is essential for creating a competitive edge. Companies must identify and capitalise on their core competencies, such as proprietary technology, skilled workforce, or robust supply chain. These unique capabilities provide a foundation for differentiation and enable companies to deliver superior value to customers. For example, a technology company with advanced research and development capabilities can continuously innovate and introduce groundbreaking products that set it apart from competitors. By leveraging these capabilities, the company can maintain its competitive edge and drive growth.

Timing is equally crucial in strategic positioning. Companies must launch new products, enter new markets, or execute strategic initiatives at the most opportune moments to maximise their impact. This requires a keen understanding of market dynamics, competitive actions, and emerging trends. By carefully timing their initiatives, companies can capture market opportunities and gain a first-mover advantage. For example, a company that recognises a growing demand for wearable technology might expedite the development and launch of smartwatches to capitalise on this trend. By being the first to market, the company can establish a strong position and build brand recognition before competitors catch up.

A prime example of effective strategic positioning and timing is Apple's approach to product launches. Apple has consistently positioned its products as premium, high-quality offerings that deliver exceptional value. This strategic positioning is reinforced by meticulous attention to design, innovation, and user experience. Apple's brand is synonymous with quality and cutting-edge technology, attracting a loyal customer base willing to pay a premium for its products. By leveraging its unique capabilities in design and innovation, Apple has created a formidable market position that competitors find challenging to replicate.

Timing has been a critical factor in Apple's success. The company has a history of carefully timing its product releases to coincide with market demand and technological advancements. For instance, the launch of the iPhone revolutionised the smartphone industry and set new standards for mobile technology. Apple's ability to anticipate market trends and deliver products that exceed customer expectations has allowed it to capture significant market share and sustain its competitive advantage. Additionally, Apple's strategic timing extends to its marketing and promotional activities, creating anticipation and excitement around new product launches. This approach ensures maximum impact and drives strong sales performance.

Moreover, Apple's strategic positioning and timing are complemented by its focus on customer experience. The company invests heavily in creating seamless and intuitive user experiences, from the design of its products to the layout of its retail stores. This emphasis on customer experience strengthens Apple's brand loyalty and differentiates it from competitors. By consistently delivering superior value and memorable experiences, Apple maintains its position as a market leader and sets itself apart in a crowded marketplace.

The Role of Leadership & Discipline

Sun Tzu underscores the critical importance of leadership and discipline in achieving success. He highlights the essential need for leaders to cultivate the moral law, adhere to method and discipline, and ensure that they make no mistakes. These principles are as relevant today as they were in ancient times. In the modern context of strategic management, effective leadership is paramount for navigating organisations through strategic challenges and ensuring the disciplined execution of strategic plans. The role of a leader is multifaceted, encompassing strategic vision, ethical integrity, and the ability to inspire and motivate teams.

Leaders must first and foremost possess a clear strategic vision. This vision serves as a guiding star for the organisation, providing direction and purpose. It is the leader's responsibility to articulate this vision in a compelling manner that resonates with employees, stakeholders, and customers. A well-defined vision helps align the efforts of all members of the organisation, fostering unity and focus. For example, a leader who envisions transforming their company into a pioneer of sustainable practices must communicate this vision effectively and outline the strategic steps necessary to achieve it. This ensures that everyone within the organisation understands their role in contributing to this overarching goal.

Ethical integrity is another cornerstone of effective leadership. Leaders must set the tone for the organisation by demonstrating unwavering commitment to ethical principles and values. This includes making decisions that are not only legally compliant but also morally sound. Leaders who act with integrity earn the trust and respect of their teams, customers, and the broader community. For instance, a leader who prioritises transparency and accountability in their business practices fosters a culture of honesty and trust, which can lead to stronger relationships and a positive reputation.

The ability to inspire and motivate teams is a vital aspect of leadership. Inspirational leaders have the capacity to ignite passion and enthusiasm within their teams, encouraging them to strive for excellence. This involves recognising and celebrating achievements, providing constructive feedback, and supporting professional development. By creating an environment where employees feel valued and motivated, leaders can enhance productivity and drive overall performance. For example, a leader who regularly acknowledges the contributions of their team members and provides opportunities for growth and advancement can boost morale and foster a sense of loyalty and commitment.

Ensuring that the organisation operates with discipline is equally crucial. Leaders must establish and maintain processes and standards that promote efficiency and consistency. This involves setting clear expectations, implementing robust performance management systems, and ensuring compliance with policies and regulations. Discipline in operations minimises errors, reduces waste, and enhances the quality of products and services. For example, a manufacturing company that adheres to stringent quality control standards can ensure that its products meet customer expectations and regulatory requirements, thereby reducing the risk of recalls and enhancing customer satisfaction.

Fostering a culture of discipline and continuous improvement is essential for organisational resilience. Leaders must create an environment where discipline is valued and continuous improvement is a core principle. This involves encouraging employees to identify areas for improvement, experiment with new ideas, and learn from failures. By promoting a culture of innovation and adaptability, leaders can ensure that their organisations remain competitive and responsive to changing market dynamics. For example, a technology company that prioritises continuous improvement and innovation can stay ahead of industry trends and deliver cutting-edge solutions to its customers.

Amazon's leadership under Jeff Bezos serves as a prime example of the importance of leadership and discipline. Bezos emphasised customer obsession, innovation, and operational excellence, creating a culture of relentless pursuit of improvement. This disciplined approach enabled Amazon to consistently deliver value to customers and maintain its market leadership. Bezos's strategic vision of transforming Amazon into the world's most customer-centric company guided the organisation's efforts and priorities. His commitment to ethical integrity and transparency built trust and loyalty among customers and stakeholders.

Bezos's ability to inspire and motivate his teams was evident in Amazon's culture of innovation and experimentation. He encouraged employees to take risks, think big, and embrace failure as a learning opportunity. This culture of continuous improvement and disciplined execution drove Amazon's success in various ventures, from e-commerce and cloud computing to artificial intelligence and logistics.

Measurement, Calculation, & Strategic Decision-Making

Sun Tzu's timeless wisdom emphasises the importance of a methodical approach to strategy, which includes measurement, estimation of quantity, calculation, balancing of chances, and ultimately achieving victory. This analytical framework is extraordinarily relevant to modern strategic decision-making. Companies must adopt data-driven approaches to thoroughly assess market opportunities, evaluate risks, and make well-informed strategic decisions that drive success.

Measurement is the foundational step in this methodical approach, involving the meticulous gathering of data on various factors such as market conditions, customer preferences, and competitor actions. Companies can utilise an array of tools and technologies to collect this data, including market research surveys, social media analytics, and customer feedback mechanisms. By obtaining accurate and comprehensive data, businesses can gain valuable insights into the current state of the market and the external factors influencing their operations. For example, a retail company might gather data on seasonal shopping trends, consumer spending habits, and competitor pricing strategies to better understand the market landscape.

Estimation of quantity and calculation are the next crucial steps, where the gathered data is analysed to identify trends, forecast demand, and assess the potential impact of strategic initiatives. This involves using advanced analytical techniques such as statistical modelling, predictive analytics, and machine learning algorithms. By analysing the data, companies can uncover patterns and correlations that inform their strategic decisions. For instance, a manufacturer might analyse production data to forecast future demand for their products, allowing them to optimise inventory levels and production schedules. This data-driven approach ensures that decisions are based on empirical evidence rather than intuition or guesswork.

Balancing of chances involves weighing the risks and rewards of different strategic options to identify the most promising course of action. This step requires a careful evaluation of potential outcomes, considering both the likelihood of success and the potential impact on the organisation. Companies must conduct thorough risk assessments, considering factors such as market volatility, competitive actions, and economic conditions. By balancing the risks and rewards, businesses can prioritise initiatives that offer the greatest potential for success while mitigating potential downsides. For example, a tech company considering entering a new market might evaluate the potential revenue gains against the risks of regulatory challenges and market competition. This comprehensive analysis helps ensure that strategic decisions are well-informed and aligned with the company's long-term goals.

Adopting a methodical, data-driven approach to strategic decision-making enhances a company's ability to navigate uncertainties and achieve strategic objectives. This approach allows organisations to be more agile and responsive to changing market conditions, as they can quickly adjust their strategies based on new data and insights. It also fosters a culture of continuous improvement, as businesses can regularly review and refine their strategies based on performance metrics and feedback. By integrating data-driven decision-making into their strategic planning processes, companies can build a solid foundation for sustained success.

Netflix serves as a prime example of the power of a data-driven approach to strategic decision-making. The company uses advanced data analytics to gain a deep understanding of viewer preferences and behaviours. By analysing vast amounts of data on what viewers watch, how long they watch, and what they search for, Netflix can identify trends and preferences that inform its content creation and acquisition decisions. This data-driven strategy enables Netflix to deliver compelling content that resonates with its audience, driving subscriber growth and engagement. For instance, Netflix's decision to invest in original content like "Stranger Things" and "The Crown" was based on insights from viewer data, allowing the company to cater to audience preferences and differentiate itself from competitors.

Furthermore, Netflix's data-driven approach extends to its marketing and user experience strategies. The company uses data to personalise recommendations, enhance user interfaces, and optimise marketing campaigns. This tailored approach enhances the overall viewer experience, increasing customer satisfaction and loyalty. By continuously analysing data and refining its strategies, Netflix can stay ahead of market trends and maintain its competitive edge.

Achieving Victory with Strategic Focus

Sun Tzu concludes his teachings by emphasising that true victory is achieved by those who make no mistakes and excel in winning with ease. This principle underscores the vital importance of strategic focus and the relentless pursuit of excellence in the business world. For companies to achieve sustained success, they must prioritise their strategic objectives, diligently avoid unnecessary risks, and strive for operational excellence across all facets of their operations. The pursuit of strategic focus is not merely about setting goals but about executing them with precision and unwavering dedication.

Strategic focus begins with the clear articulation of a company's vision and goals. This involves defining a long-term vision that serves as the North Star, guiding all strategic decisions and initiatives. The vision should be bold and inspiring, motivating employees to rally behind a common cause. Once the vision is established, leaders must identify the critical initiatives that align with this vision and allocate resources accordingly. This process requires rigorous analysis and prioritisation to ensure that resources are concentrated on the most impactful projects. For example, a healthcare company with a vision to revolutionise patient care might prioritise initiatives related to telemedicine, AI-driven diagnostics, and personalised treatment plans. By focusing resources on these key areas, the company can drive meaningful progress towards its vision.

Avoiding distractions is another crucial aspect of maintaining strategic focus. In the fast-paced and ever-changing business environment, it is easy to get sidetracked by emerging trends, new opportunities, or competitive pressures. However, companies must remain disciplined and stay true to their strategic priorities. This involves saying no to initiatives that do not align with the company's core objectives, even if they seem attractive in the short term. For instance, a technology company focused on developing cutting-edge software might choose to forgo opportunities in hardware manufacturing to maintain its strategic focus and expertise in software innovation. By avoiding distractions, companies can ensure that their efforts are directed towards achieving their long-term goals.

Operational excellence is integral to the successful execution of strategic initiatives. This involves optimising processes, enhancing efficiency, and ensuring high-quality outcomes. Companies must adopt best practices and continuous improvement methodologies to streamline operations and eliminate inefficiencies. For example, implementing Lean and Six Sigma principles can help companies reduce waste, improve productivity, and deliver consistent quality. Operational excellence also requires a commitment to innovation and agility. Companies must be willing to adapt and evolve their processes in response to changing market conditions and technological advancements. For instance, a manufacturing company might invest in automation and smart factory technologies to enhance production efficiency and maintain a competitive edge.

Tesla exemplifies the power of strategic focus and the pursuit of excellence. The company's unwavering commitment to electric vehicles (EVs) and renewable energy solutions has positioned it as a market leader in innovation and sustainability. From its inception, Tesla's vision has been to accelerate the world's transition to sustainable energy. This clear and compelling vision has guided the company's strategic decisions and resource allocation. Tesla has prioritised critical initiatives such as the development of high-performance EVs, the expansion of its Gigafactory network, and the integration of solar energy solutions. By concentrating resources on these key areas, Tesla has driven significant advancements in EV technology, battery storage, and renewable energy integration.

Moreover, Tesla's ability to avoid distractions and maintain a clear strategic direction has been instrumental in its success. Despite facing numerous challenges and competitive pressures, Tesla has remained focused on its core mission. This discipline has enabled the company to make bold and strategic decisions, such as investing heavily in battery technology and expanding its charging infrastructure. By staying true to its strategic priorities, Tesla has built a strong brand, a loyal customer base, and a competitive moat that is difficult for rivals to replicate.

Tesla's pursuit of operational excellence is evident in its commitment to innovation, quality, and continuous improvement. The company has implemented advanced manufacturing techniques, such as automation and robotics, to enhance production efficiency and ensure high-quality outcomes. Tesla's focus on innovation is reflected in its continuous development of cutting-edge technologies, from autonomous driving capabilities to energy storage solutions. This relentless pursuit of excellence has enabled Tesla to deliver superior products, drive customer satisfaction, and achieve sustained growth.

Summary

Sun Tzu's *Tactical Dispositions* offers timeless insights that are highly relevant to modern strategic management. The principles of preparation, defensive and offensive tactics, strategic positioning, leadership, discipline, and data-driven decision-making provide a robust framework for navigating the complexities of the business world.

CHAPTER 5 – ENERGY

The quality of decision is like the well-timed swoop of a falcon which enables it to strike and destroy its victim.

Sun Tzu

Sun Tzu's *Energy* provides invaluable insights into the principles of force and momentum in warfare, which can be seamlessly translated into the realm of modern strategic management. This chapter emphasises the importance of harnessing collective energy, employing direct and indirect strategies, and making timely decisions. These concepts are vital for contemporary businesses aiming to navigate competitive landscapes and achieve sustainable growth.

Collective Energy & Division of Labour

Sun Tzu begins by stating that the control of a large force is the same as the control of a few men; it is merely a question of dividing up their numbers. In a business context, this principle highlights the paramount importance of an effective organisational structure and a well-considered division of labour. Companies must efficiently divide tasks and responsibilities to maximise productivity and ensure that all parts of the organisation work cohesively towards common goals. By doing so, they can harness the collective energy of their workforce to achieve strategic objectives and drive success.

A well-organised structure is the backbone of any successful organisation. It begins with a clear understanding of the company's vision, mission, and strategic goals. Leaders must translate these overarching goals into specific, actionable objectives for each department and team. This requires a deep understanding of the strengths and capabilities of different functions within the organisation. For example, a tech company might have departments focused on research and development, marketing, sales, customer service, and operations. Each of these departments plays a critical role in achieving the company's overall objectives, and their efforts must be synchronised to ensure seamless execution.

Specialised teams are essential for addressing the diverse aspects of business operations. By establishing teams focused on different areas such as marketing, product development, and customer service, companies can leverage specialised skills and expertise. Marketing teams, for instance, can concentrate on understanding market trends, developing compelling campaigns, and driving brand awareness. Product development teams can focus on innovation, designing new products, and improving existing offerings. Customer service teams can dedicate their efforts to enhancing customer satisfaction and addressing inquiries and concerns. Each team, with its specialised knowledge and skills, contributes to the collective success of the organisation.

Clearly defining roles and responsibilities is crucial for effective division of labour. Employees need to understand their specific roles, what is expected of them, and how their work contributes to the larger organisational goals. This clarity helps prevent overlaps, reduces confusion, and ensures that all tasks are covered without gaps. For instance, a sales team should know whether their primary focus is on acquiring new customers or maintaining relationships with existing ones. Clear role definitions enable employees to work with confidence and accountability, knowing that their contributions are valued and aligned with the company's objectives.

Effective communication and collaboration are vital to harnessing the collective energy of the workforce. Companies must establish channels for regular communication, both within and between teams. This includes meetings, reports, and digital collaboration tools that facilitate the sharing of information and ideas. Open communication fosters a culture of transparency and trust, where employees feel comfortable sharing their insights and feedback. For example, a weekly cross-departmental meeting can ensure that marketing, sales, and product development teams are aligned on upcoming product launches and marketing campaigns. This collaborative approach helps identify potential issues early and allows for joint problem-solving.

Moreover, fostering a collaborative culture encourages innovation and continuous improvement. When employees from different departments work together, they bring diverse perspectives and ideas that can lead to creative solutions. Encouraging cross-functional projects and initiatives can drive innovation and enhance the company's ability to adapt to changing market conditions. For instance, a collaborative project between the R&D and marketing teams can result in the development of a product that not only meets technical specifications but also resonates with customer needs and preferences.

Investing in technology and tools that support collaboration and productivity is also essential. Companies should leverage digital platforms that enable real-time communication, project management, and data sharing. Tools such as Slack, Trello, and Microsoft Teams can facilitate efficient collaboration and ensure that team members stay connected and informed. These technologies enhance the ability of teams to work together, regardless of geographic location, and contribute to a more agile and responsive organisation.

Leadership plays a critical role in fostering effective organisational structure and division of labour. Leaders must set the tone for collaboration and ensure that teams have the resources and support they need to succeed. This involves providing clear direction, removing obstacles, and empowering employees to take ownership of their tasks. Leaders should also recognise and celebrate team achievements, reinforcing the importance of collective effort and motivating employees to continue striving for excellence.

For example, Amazon's organisational structure and division of labour under Jeff Bezos's leadership have been instrumental in its success. Amazon established specialised teams focused on various aspects of the business, such as e-commerce, cloud computing, logistics, and customer service. Each team operates with clear roles and responsibilities, contributing to the company's overall strategic goals. Effective communication and collaboration are encouraged through regular meetings, performance reviews, and a culture of innovation. By harnessing the collective energy of its workforce, Amazon has been able to achieve remarkable growth and maintain its market leadership.

Direct & Indirect Tactics

Sun Tzu emphasises that while the direct method can be used to engage in battle, achieving true victory often requires the use of indirect methods. This principle is highly relevant in the business world, where a combination of direct and indirect strategies can provide a significant competitive advantage. Companies that can master both types of tactics are better positioned to navigate complex market dynamics and outmanoeuvre their competitors.

Direct strategies in business involve straightforward actions that are clear and immediate. These might include launching a new product, entering a new market, or executing a marketing campaign. For example, a company might introduce a groundbreaking new product to the market, drawing immediate attention and capturing significant market share. Such direct actions are essential for making bold moves and establishing a strong market presence. However, while direct strategies can create immediate impact, they are often visible to competitors and can be easily countered.

Indirect strategies, on the other hand, are more subtle and creative. These involve building strategic alliances, leveraging brand reputation, employing competitive intelligence, and other nuanced approaches that are not immediately apparent to competitors. For instance, a company might form strategic partnerships with suppliers, distributors, or even competitors to strengthen its market position. These alliances can provide access to new markets, enhance supply chain efficiency, and create synergies that drive competitive advantage. Leveraging brand reputation is another powerful indirect strategy. By cultivating a strong brand image and maintaining customer loyalty, a company can create a competitive moat that is difficult for rivals to breach. Competitive intelligence, which involves gathering and analysing information about competitors, allows companies to anticipate and counter rivals' moves without direct confrontation.

The combination of direct and indirect strategies enables companies to achieve a balanced approach to strategic management. For example, a technology company might use direct strategies to launch an innovative new product, capturing immediate market attention and generating sales. Simultaneously, it might employ indirect strategies such as building a robust ecosystem of partners and developers, enhancing its brand reputation through thought leadership, and using data analytics to understand customer behaviour and preferences. This dual approach ensures that the company not only gains market share but also builds long-term resilience and sustainability.

Effective strategic management requires the seamless integration of direct and indirect tactics. Leaders must be adept at identifying when to use each type of strategy and how to combine them for maximum impact. This involves a deep understanding of the market landscape, competitive dynamics, and the company's own strengths and weaknesses. For instance, a retail company facing intense competition might use direct tactics such as aggressive pricing and promotions to attract customers. At the same time, it could use indirect tactics such as enhancing customer experience, building a loyalty programme, and investing in community engagement to create a strong, differentiated brand that resonates with customers.

The ability to pivot between direct and indirect tactics is also crucial in responding to market changes and disruptions. Companies that are flexible and adaptable can quickly shift their strategies to address new opportunities or threats. For example, during an economic downturn, a company might reduce direct marketing expenses and focus on indirect tactics such as improving operational efficiency and strengthening customer relationships. This balanced approach allows the company to maintain stability while positioning itself for future growth when the market recovers.

A prime example of the effective use of direct and indirect tactics is Apple's strategic approach. Apple employs direct strategies through the launch of innovative products like the iPhone, iPad, and Apple Watch, which generate significant market buzz and sales. Concurrently, Apple uses indirect strategies to build a loyal customer base and strong brand equity. This includes creating an ecosystem of products and services that work seamlessly together, investing in high-quality customer service, and maintaining a strong presence in media and public discourse. By combining direct and indirect tactics, Apple has built a powerful competitive advantage that is difficult for rivals to replicate.

The Endless Possibilities of Combination

Sun Tzu draws vivid parallels between the infinite combinations of musical notes, colours, and tastes to illustrate the limitless possibilities of combining direct and indirect tactics in warfare. This principle extends seamlessly to the business world, where the fusion of creativity and strategy is paramount for achieving competitive advantage and differentiation. The notion of endless possibilities underscores the importance of innovation and creativity in strategy formulation, as companies continuously explore new combinations of tactics and approaches to carve out unique value propositions and capture market opportunities.

In business, innovation involves thinking beyond conventional boundaries and experimenting with novel ideas and solutions. It is the lifeblood of progress and a key driver of competitive advantage. Companies that foster a culture of innovation encourage their employees to think creatively, challenge the status quo, and explore uncharted territories. By promoting an environment where experimentation is valued and failures are seen as learning opportunities, organisations can unleash the full potential of their workforce and drive continuous improvement.

One of the primary ways companies can explore new combinations of tactics is through cross-functional collaboration. Bringing together diverse teams with different expertise and perspectives can lead to the generation of innovative ideas that transcend traditional boundaries. For example, a marketing team might collaborate with product developers to create a new offering that not only meets customer needs but also leverages cutting-edge technology. This collaborative approach ensures that the final product is both innovative and aligned with market demands, creating a unique value proposition that sets the company apart from competitors.

Additionally, companies must continuously analyse market trends, customer preferences, and competitor actions to identify opportunities for innovation. This involves staying attuned to industry developments, conducting market research, and gathering feedback from customers. By understanding the evolving landscape, companies can anticipate changes and proactively develop strategies that address emerging needs. For instance, a company that identifies a growing trend towards sustainable products might invest in developing eco-friendly solutions, thereby capturing a new segment of environmentally conscious consumers.

Strategic alliances and partnerships are another avenue for exploring new combinations of tactics. By collaborating with other organisations, companies can pool resources, share expertise, and co-create innovative solutions. These partnerships can open up new markets, enhance product offerings, and drive mutual growth. For example, a technology company might partner with a healthcare provider to develop advanced medical devices that leverage cutting-edge technology. This alliance not only expands the reach of both companies but also creates a unique value proposition that addresses a critical need in the healthcare industry.

Furthermore, the integration of technology plays a crucial role in enabling innovation and creativity. Advanced technologies such as artificial intelligence, machine learning, and data analytics provide companies with the tools to analyse vast amounts of data, gain actionable insights, and make informed decisions. By leveraging these technologies, companies can identify patterns, predict trends, and optimise their strategies. For example, a retail company might use data analytics to personalise the shopping experience, recommending products based on individual customer preferences and behaviours. This level of personalisation creates a unique and engaging customer experience, driving loyalty and retention.

The role of leadership is also pivotal in fostering a culture of innovation and creativity. Leaders must set the tone by championing innovation, providing resources and support, and recognising and rewarding creative efforts. This involves creating an environment where employees feel empowered to take risks, experiment with new ideas, and learn from failures. For instance, a company might implement an innovation programme that encourages employees to submit their ideas for new products or process improvements. By providing funding and resources for the most promising ideas, leaders can nurture a culture of innovation that drives continuous improvement and growth.

Companies like Google and Tesla exemplify the power of embracing innovation and continuously exploring new ways to create value. Google's commitment to innovation is evident in its wide array of products and services, from search engines and cloud computing to artificial intelligence and autonomous vehicles. The company's focus on fostering a culture of creativity and experimentation has led to groundbreaking innovations that have transformed industries and set new standards. Similarly, Tesla's relentless pursuit of innovation in electric vehicles and renewable energy solutions has positioned it as a leader in sustainability and technological advancement. By continuously pushing the boundaries of what is possible, Tesla has created a unique value proposition that resonates with environmentally conscious consumers and investors.

Momentum & Timing

Sun Tzu likens the onset of troops to the rush of a torrent and the quality of decision to the well-timed swoop of a falcon. These vivid metaphors emphasise the crucial importance of momentum and timing in achieving success. In the business world, momentum involves building and maintaining a positive trajectory, while timing refers to making strategic decisions at the most opportune moments. The combination of these elements can create a powerful force that propels an organisation towards its goals.

Generating and sustaining momentum requires companies to set clear goals that provide direction and purpose. These goals must be specific, measurable, achievable, relevant, and time-bound (SMART) to ensure that everyone in the organisation understands what they are working towards. By establishing clear objectives, companies can maintain focus and ensure that their efforts are aligned with their strategic vision. For example, a technology company might set a goal to become a leader in artificial intelligence within five years. This overarching goal would then be broken down into specific targets, such as developing new AI products, forming strategic partnerships, and expanding the talent pool with AI expertise.

Maintaining focus is essential for sustaining momentum. Companies must prioritise their initiatives and allocate resources to the most critical projects. This involves regularly reviewing progress, identifying potential obstacles, and making necessary adjustments to stay on track. For instance, a company might conduct quarterly performance reviews to assess the progress of its strategic initiatives and make data-driven decisions to optimise its efforts. By staying focused and adaptable, companies can keep the momentum going and avoid distractions that could derail their progress.

Executing strategies effectively is another key component of generating and sustaining momentum. This involves implementing well-defined processes and ensuring that all team members are equipped with the necessary tools and resources to perform their tasks efficiently. Companies must also foster a culture of accountability, where employees take ownership of their responsibilities and are committed to delivering results. For example, a manufacturing company might implement lean management principles to streamline operations, reduce waste, and improve productivity. By executing strategies effectively, companies can drive continuous improvement and maintain a positive trajectory.

Timing is equally crucial in achieving success. Companies must launch new products, enter new markets, or execute strategic initiatives at the right moment to maximise impact. This requires a keen understanding of market dynamics, customer preferences, and competitive actions. By carefully timing their initiatives, companies can capitalise on market opportunities and gain a first-mover advantage. For instance, a company that identifies a growing demand for wearable technology might expedite the development and launch of smartwatches to capture this trend. By being the first to market, the company can establish a strong position and build brand recognition before competitors catch up.

The ability to make strategic decisions at the most opportune moments involves gathering and analysing data from various sources. Companies must monitor market trends, conduct competitive analysis, and gather customer feedback to inform their decision-making. Advanced data analytics and business intelligence tools can provide valuable insights that help companies identify the best timing for their initiatives. For example, a retail company might use data analytics to track seasonal trends and determine the optimal timing for product launches and marketing campaigns. By leveraging data-driven insights, companies can make informed decisions that enhance their chances of success.

A prime example of effective momentum and timing is Apple's approach to product launches. Apple has mastered the art of creating and sustaining momentum through its strategic timing of product releases. The company positions its products as premium, high-quality offerings and meticulously times their launches to coincide with market demand and technological advancements. This approach has enabled Apple to consistently capture market attention and drive sales growth. The anticipation and excitement surrounding Apple's product launches create a positive trajectory that fuels the company's success.

Apple's ability to generate and sustain momentum is also evident in its focus on innovation and customer experience. The company continuously develops new products that meet evolving customer needs and preferences, ensuring that it stays ahead of the competition. For example, the launch of the iPhone revolutionised the smartphone industry and set new standards for mobile technology. Apple's strategic timing and commitment to innovation have enabled it to maintain its competitive edge and achieve significant market impact.

Furthermore, Apple's disciplined approach to executing strategies and maintaining focus has been instrumental in sustaining its momentum. The company's emphasis on design, quality, and user experience ensures that its products consistently deliver value to customers. By adhering to its strategic vision and maintaining a clear direction, Apple has built a loyal customer base and a strong brand reputation that continues to drive its success.

Discipline & Deception

Sun Tzu astutely emphasises the importance of discipline and the strategic use of deception. He notes that simulated disorder postulates perfect discipline, and hiding order beneath the cloak of disorder is a tactical disposition. This principle is profoundly relevant in the modern business context. Discipline involves adhering to established processes, maintaining operational excellence, and ensuring consistent performance, while deception entails creating perceptions that mislead competitors about a company's true intentions. The harmonious integration of these two elements can significantly enhance an organisation's strategic positioning and competitive edge.

Effective discipline is the cornerstone of organisational success. It ensures that the company operates smoothly and can respond to challenges with agility and precision. Discipline involves the rigorous implementation of best practices, adherence to regulatory standards, and the meticulous execution of operational procedures. For example, a manufacturing company that maintains strict quality control measures ensures that its products meet high standards consistently, thereby building a reputation for reliability and excellence. This disciplined approach minimises errors, reduces waste, and enhances productivity, contributing to the overall efficiency and effectiveness of the organisation.

Furthermore, discipline in business extends to financial management, where careful budgeting, forecasting, and cost control are essential. Companies must establish financial discipline to ensure sustainable growth and profitability. This involves monitoring expenses, optimising resource allocation, and implementing robust financial controls to prevent fraud and mismanagement. For instance, a company that maintains financial discipline can weather economic downturns, invest in strategic initiatives, and capitalise on market opportunities without compromising its financial stability.

In addition to operational and financial discipline, companies must also foster a culture of discipline within their workforce. This involves setting clear expectations, providing regular feedback, and holding employees accountable for their performance. By promoting a disciplined work environment, companies can enhance employee productivity, job satisfaction, and overall organisational morale. For example, a sales team that operates with discipline, adhering to a structured sales process and consistently meeting targets, can drive significant revenue growth and strengthen the company's market position.

Deception, on the other hand, is a strategic tool that can be employed to create competitive advantages. It involves crafting perceptions that mislead competitors about a company's true intentions, thereby gaining a strategic edge. Strategic deception can take various forms, such as signalling a future product launch to deter competitors or misguiding them about strategic priorities. For instance, a company might announce plans to enter a new market, causing competitors to divert resources and focus on defending their positions, while the company's actual strategy is to strengthen its core operations and enhance its existing market share.

The art of strategic deception requires a deep understanding of the competitive landscape and the ability to anticipate competitors' reactions. Companies must be adept at gathering intelligence, analysing competitor behaviour, and crafting messages that influence perceptions. For example, a tech company might use strategic leaks to create buzz about a new product, generating excitement and anticipation among customers and investors, while simultaneously diverting competitors' attention from its true strategic initiatives. This approach can create a competitive advantage by shaping market dynamics in the company's favour.

Moreover, deception can be used to protect proprietary information and maintain a competitive edge. Companies can employ tactics to disguise their true capabilities, innovations, or market strategies. For instance, a pharmaceutical company might file multiple patents with varying levels of detail to obscure its actual research focus, thereby preventing competitors from gaining insights into its drug development pipeline. This protective measure allows the company to advance its research and development efforts without the threat of competitive imitation.

The seamless integration of discipline and deception is a hallmark of effective strategic management. Companies that master this balance can navigate competitive landscapes more effectively, responding to challenges with agility and precision while outmanoeuvring competitors. This requires a cohesive approach, where disciplined operations provide a stable foundation, and strategic deception enhances competitive positioning.

A prime example of an organisation that has effectively employed both discipline and deception is Amazon. Under Jeff Bezos's leadership, Amazon has demonstrated a relentless commitment to customer obsession, innovation, and operational excellence. The company's disciplined approach to logistics, supply chain management, and customer service has enabled it to consistently deliver value to customers and maintain its market leadership. Amazon's rigorous adherence to best practices and continuous improvement has built a reputation for reliability and efficiency.

Simultaneously, Amazon has employed strategic deception to navigate competitive landscapes. For example, the company has strategically misled competitors about its expansion plans, product launches, and technological capabilities. This has allowed Amazon to execute its strategies without significant competitive interference and maintain a first-mover advantage in various markets. By signalling intentions in one direction while pursuing actual initiatives in another, Amazon has effectively diverted competitors' attention and resources, creating opportunities for growth and innovation.

Leveraging Combined Energy

Sun Tzu emphasises the crucial importance of leveraging combined energy and choosing the right individuals to achieve success. This principle is deeply relevant in the business context, where teamwork and effective utilisation of talent are paramount. Companies must harness the collective energy of their workforce by fostering collaboration, aligning individual goals with organisational objectives, and creating an empowering environment that allows employees to perform at their best.

Harnessing the collective energy of the workforce starts with fostering a culture of collaboration. Companies need to create an environment where teamwork is encouraged and valued. This involves promoting open communication, breaking down silos, and encouraging cross-functional collaboration. By facilitating collaboration, companies can ensure that diverse perspectives and skills are brought together to solve complex problems and drive innovation. For instance, a company might implement team-building activities, collaborative projects, and cross-departmental meetings to strengthen bonds and promote a spirit of teamwork. When employees feel connected and supported, they are more likely to contribute their best efforts and achieve remarkable results.

Aligning individual goals with organisational objectives is another critical aspect of leveraging combined energy. Employees need to understand how their work contributes to the broader goals of the organisation. This alignment helps create a sense of purpose and direction, motivating employees to work towards common objectives. For example, during goal-setting sessions, managers can work with their team members to set specific, measurable, achievable, relevant, and time-bound (SMART) goals that align with the company's strategic priorities. By ensuring that individual goals are linked to organisational objectives, companies can drive a unified effort towards achieving success.

Creating an empowering environment is essential for maximising the potential of the workforce. This involves providing employees with the resources, tools, and support they need to excel. Leaders should foster a culture of trust and empowerment, where employees are encouraged to take ownership of their work, experiment with new ideas, and learn from failures. For instance, a technology company might provide its developers with state-of-the-art tools and technologies, along with the autonomy to explore innovative solutions. By creating a supportive and empowering environment, companies can unleash the full potential of their workforce and drive continuous improvement.

Effective talent management is a cornerstone of leveraging combined energy. This begins with recruiting the right people who align with the company's values and possess the necessary skills and expertise. A rigorous recruitment process ensures that the organisation attracts top talent who can contribute to its success. For example, a company might implement structured interview processes, skill assessments, and cultural fit evaluations to identify the best candidates. By hiring individuals who are not only skilled but also aligned with the company's mission, companies can build a strong and cohesive team.

Providing opportunities for professional development is also crucial for talent management. Companies must invest in training and development programmes that enhance employees' skills and knowledge. This includes offering workshops, online courses, mentorship programmes, and certifications that support career growth. For instance, a company might establish a leadership development programme that identifies high-potential employees and provides them with the training and experiences needed to advance to higher-level positions. By investing in professional development, companies can retain top talent, foster loyalty, and ensure that employees are equipped to meet evolving business challenges.

Recognising and rewarding performance is another key aspect of effective talent management. Companies should implement recognition programmes that celebrate employees' achievements and contributions. This can include monetary rewards, promotions, public recognition, and non-monetary incentives such as extra time off or special projects. For example, a company might establish an "Employee of the Month" programme to highlight outstanding performance and inspire others. Recognising and rewarding employees not only boosts morale but also reinforces desired behaviours and motivates employees to continue striving for excellence.

By leveraging combined energy and maximising the potential of their workforce, companies can achieve higher levels of productivity and innovation. This holistic approach to talent management ensures that employees are engaged, motivated, and aligned with the organisation's goals. For instance, companies like Microsoft and Amazon invest heavily in talent management and employee engagement to drive organisational success. Microsoft's commitment to a growth mindset and continuous learning has fostered a culture of innovation and excellence. The company provides extensive training and development programmes, encourages cross-functional collaboration, and recognises and rewards employee contributions. Similarly, Amazon's focus on customer obsession, operational excellence, and innovation has been driven by its investment in talent management. The company empowers its employees to take ownership, experiment with new ideas, and drive continuous improvement.

Summary

Sun Tzu's *Energy* offers timeless insights that are highly relevant to modern strategic management. The principles of collective energy, direct and indirect tactics, innovation, momentum, discipline, deception, and talent management provide a robust framework for navigating the complexities of the business world.

CHAPTER 6 – WEAK POINTS & STRONG

O divine art of subtlety and secrecy!
Through you we learn to be invisible,
through you inaudible; and hence we can hold
the enemy's fate in our hands.

Sun Tzu

Sun Tzu's *Weak Points & Strong* delves into the principles of identifying and exploiting weaknesses while safeguarding one's own strengths. These timeless insights are remarkably relevant to modern strategic management, where businesses must navigate competitive landscapes, anticipate market dynamics, and leverage their unique capabilities to achieve sustainable success.

The Importance of Initiative & Preparation

Sun Tzu begins by emphasising the critical importance of being first in the field and awaiting the enemy. This principle, deeply rooted in strategic military thinking, translates seamlessly into the business world, underscoring the significance of initiative and preparation. Companies that proactively identify opportunities and strategically position themselves are far better equipped to capitalise on market dynamics and outmanoeuvre competitors. By being the first to market or the first to adopt innovative practices, businesses can establish a formidable competitive position and secure a significant advantage over their rivals.

Initiative in business is about seizing opportunities before competitors do. It involves a proactive mindset, where companies constantly scan the horizon for emerging trends, unmet customer needs, and technological advancements. By taking the lead, businesses can capture market share and set industry standards. For instance, a tech company that quickly adopts a breakthrough technology can redefine customer expectations and position itself as a market leader. This proactive approach not only drives growth but also creates a lasting competitive edge.

Preparation, on the other hand, involves laying the groundwork to ensure readiness and resilience. This includes thorough market research, strategic planning, and the development of robust capabilities. Market research is the foundation of effective preparation, as it provides critical insights into market trends, customer preferences, and competitor behaviour. By gathering and analysing data, companies can make informed decisions and anticipate changes in the market. For example, a retail company might conduct surveys, focus groups, and data analysis to understand shifting consumer preferences, enabling it to adapt its product offerings and marketing strategies accordingly.

Strategic planning is another essential component of preparation. Companies must develop comprehensive strategic plans that outline their vision, goals, and the steps needed to achieve them. This involves setting clear objectives, identifying key performance indicators, and establishing timelines. Strategic planning helps organisations stay focused, allocate resources effectively, and navigate uncertainties. For example, a pharmaceutical company might develop a strategic plan to bring a new drug to market, outlining the stages of research, clinical trials, regulatory approvals, and commercialisation. By having a clear roadmap, the company can coordinate efforts, manage risks, and achieve its strategic objectives.

The development of robust capabilities is crucial for sustaining a competitive advantage. This includes building a strong talent pool, investing in technology and innovation, and enhancing operational efficiency. Companies must ensure that they have the necessary resources and competencies to execute their strategies effectively. For instance, a manufacturing company might invest in advanced automation technologies to improve production efficiency and reduce costs. By continuously developing and refining their capabilities, businesses can maintain their competitive edge and respond effectively to market changes.

A prime example of a company that has excelled in initiative and preparation is Amazon. From its inception, Amazon has demonstrated a proactive approach to identifying opportunities and positioning itself advantageously. The company's early entry into e-commerce allowed it to establish a strong foothold in the online retail market. By being the first to market with a comprehensive online shopping platform, Amazon set the standard for e-commerce and captured a significant market share.

Amazon's success can also be attributed to its meticulous preparation. The company invests heavily in logistics and technology to create a seamless and efficient supply chain. This includes developing state-of-the-art fulfilment centres, implementing advanced inventory management systems, and leveraging data analytics to optimise operations. Amazon's investment in technology extends to its customer service, with innovations like the Alexa voice assistant and the Amazon Prime subscription service enhancing the customer experience and driving loyalty.

Moreover, Amazon's strategic planning and market research have enabled it to continuously expand its product offerings and enter new markets. The company's foray into cloud computing with Amazon Web Services (AWS) is a testament to its ability to identify emerging trends and capitalise on them. AWS has become a market leader in cloud services, contributing significantly to Amazon's overall revenue and growth. This diversification strategy showcases Amazon's proactive mindset and its ability to anticipate and respond to market opportunities.

Imposing Will & Influencing Behaviour

Sun Tzu asserts that the clever combatant imposes his will on the enemy and does not allow the enemy's will to be imposed on him. This timeless principle is profoundly relevant in the corporate world, where shaping market dynamics and influencing competitor behaviour are essential for achieving strategic dominance. Companies can achieve this by creating compelling value propositions, setting industry standards, and strategically positioning their products and services. By offering unique advantages and benefits, businesses can attract customers, deter competitors, and shape the competitive landscape to their advantage.

In the modern business environment, imposing one's will on the market involves a multifaceted approach. It starts with the development of a compelling value proposition that clearly communicates the unique benefits and advantages of a company's products or services. This value proposition should resonate with target customers and differentiate the company from its competitors. For instance, a company might emphasise the superior quality, innovative features, or exceptional customer service of its offerings. By highlighting these unique aspects, the company can attract and retain a loyal customer base, creating a strong market presence.

Setting industry standards is another powerful way to impose one's will on the market. Companies that lead in innovation and quality often set benchmarks that competitors must follow. This can be achieved through continuous improvement, research and development, and a commitment to excellence. By consistently raising the bar, companies can establish themselves as industry leaders and influence the direction of the market. For example, a tech company that pioneers new technologies and sets high standards for product performance can compel competitors to innovate and improve their offerings, thereby shaping the competitive landscape.

Strategically positioning products and services is crucial for influencing market dynamics. This involves identifying the most advantageous market segments, understanding customer needs, and aligning offerings to meet those needs effectively. Companies must analyse market trends, customer preferences, and competitor actions to determine the optimal positioning strategy. For instance, a luxury brand might position its products as premium offerings, targeting affluent consumers who value exclusivity and quality. By doing so, the company can create a distinct market niche and build a strong brand identity that competitors find difficult to replicate.

One of the most compelling examples of imposing will and influencing behaviour in the business world is Apple's approach to design, innovation, and user experience. Apple's emphasis on these elements has set it apart from competitors and established it as a leader in the technology industry. By prioritising sleek, intuitive design and cutting-edge technology, Apple has created a loyal customer base that eagerly anticipates each new product release. This focus on innovation and user experience has allowed Apple to shape consumer preferences and set industry standards that competitors strive to match.

Apple's strategy goes beyond just product design; it extends to the entire customer experience. From the moment a customer walks into an Apple Store to the seamless integration of Apple devices, the company has meticulously crafted every aspect of the user journey. This holistic approach reinforces Apple's brand identity and creates a strong emotional connection with customers. By delivering a consistently exceptional experience, Apple has imposed its will on the market, influencing not only consumer behaviour but also competitor strategies.

Furthermore, Apple strategically positions its products in the market to maximise impact. The company's product launches are carefully timed to generate excitement and anticipation. By creating a sense of exclusivity and urgency, Apple drives strong initial sales and maintains momentum. This strategic timing, combined with innovative marketing campaigns, ensures that Apple captures significant market attention and drives sales growth. Competitors are often left scrambling to respond, trying to match Apple's innovation and market positioning.

In addition to its focus on design and user experience, Apple has also leveraged strategic alliances and partnerships to strengthen its market position. Collaborations with other leading companies, such as partnerships with content providers for Apple TV+ or collaborations with healthcare organisations for Apple Watch health features, have expanded Apple's ecosystem and enhanced its value proposition. These strategic alliances have allowed Apple to offer unique benefits that attract customers and set it apart from competitors.

Exploiting Weaknesses & Creating Opportunities

Sun Tzu emphasises the critical importance of identifying and exploiting the enemy's weak points while safeguarding one's own strengths. This principle is profoundly relevant in the business world, where companies must conduct thorough analyses of their competitors to identify vulnerabilities and opportunities. By doing so, they can develop strategic initiatives that exploit these weaknesses, creating competitive advantages and positioning themselves for success.

In the modern business landscape, conducting a comprehensive analysis of competitors involves utilising a range of analytical tools and techniques. One of the most valuable tools for this purpose is the SWOT analysis, which stands for Strengths, Weaknesses, Opportunities, and Threats. A SWOT analysis enables companies to evaluate their internal strengths and weaknesses, as well as external opportunities and threats, providing a holistic view of their competitive landscape.

Internal strengths may include factors such as proprietary technology, skilled workforce, strong brand reputation, and efficient supply chain management. By identifying these strengths, companies can leverage them to their advantage, enhancing their competitive position. For example, a company with a robust research and development (R&D) department can capitalise on its technological capabilities to innovate and introduce new products that meet market demand.

Conversely, internal weaknesses may involve outdated technology, limited financial resources, poor organisational structure, or gaps in employee skills. Recognising these weaknesses is crucial for addressing them proactively and minimising their impact on the company's performance. For instance, a company with outdated technology might invest in upgrading its infrastructure to improve efficiency and remain competitive.

External opportunities refer to favourable conditions in the market that companies can capitalise on to achieve growth and success. These may include emerging market trends, technological advancements, changes in consumer behaviour, or regulatory shifts. By staying attuned to these opportunities, companies can develop strategies to seize them and expand their market presence. For example, a company might identify a growing demand for sustainable products and launch a new line of eco-friendly offerings to capture this market segment.

External threats, on the other hand, encompass factors that could negatively impact the company's performance, such as economic downturns, increased competition, or changing regulations. Identifying these threats enables companies to develop contingency plans and risk mitigation strategies. For example, a company facing increased competition might enhance its marketing efforts and invest in customer loyalty programmes to retain its customer base.

By leveraging their strengths and addressing their weaknesses, companies can enhance their competitive position and create new opportunities for growth. A prime example of this is Netflix, which identified traditional cable TV's weakness in flexibility and on-demand content. Recognising this gap, Netflix capitalised on it by offering a convenient streaming service that allows users to access content anytime, anywhere. This innovative approach disrupted the entertainment industry, transforming Netflix into a dominant player in the market.

Netflix's success can be attributed to its strategic focus on exploiting weaknesses and creating opportunities. The company continuously analyses market trends, customer preferences, and competitive actions to stay ahead of the curve. By leveraging its strengths in technology and content delivery, Netflix has consistently introduced features and services that enhance the user experience and differentiate it from competitors.

Moreover, Netflix's ability to create opportunities extends to its investment in original content. Recognising the growing demand for exclusive and high-quality programming, the company has invested heavily in producing its own shows and movies. This strategic initiative has not only attracted a global audience but also strengthened Netflix's brand and competitive position. By offering unique and compelling content, Netflix has built a loyal subscriber base and increased its market share.

Another example of exploiting weaknesses and creating opportunities can be seen in the technology sector. Companies like Apple and Samsung continuously analyse their competitors' weaknesses and develop strategies to gain a competitive edge. For instance, Apple identified a gap in the smartphone market for premium, user-friendly devices and capitalised on it by introducing the iPhone. This innovation set new standards in the industry and positioned Apple as a market leader.

Samsung, on the other hand, recognised the need for a diverse product portfolio and invested in developing a wide range of devices to cater to different consumer segments. By offering products at various price points and features, Samsung has captured a broad customer base and maintained its competitive position.

The Role of Agility & Adaptability

Sun Tzu emphasises the paramount importance of agility and adaptability in warfare, noting that one should appear at points which the enemy must defend and march swiftly to places where one is not expected. This principle is profoundly applicable in modern strategic management, where the ability to quickly and effectively respond to changing market conditions and stay ahead of competitors is crucial for business success. In today's fast-paced and ever-evolving business environment, companies that embrace agility and adaptability are better positioned to navigate uncertainties, capitalise on opportunities, and maintain a competitive edge.

Agility in the business context involves the ability to quickly adjust strategies, processes, and operations in response to market dynamics. This requires a proactive approach to monitoring the external environment, anticipating changes, and making data-driven decisions. Companies can enhance their agility by fostering a culture of innovation that encourages experimentation, risk-taking, and continuous improvement. By promoting an innovative mindset, businesses can develop new solutions, products, and services that meet evolving customer needs and market demands. For instance, a technology company might encourage its employees to explore and prototype new ideas, leading to the development of groundbreaking products that differentiate the company from competitors.

Implementing flexible organisational structures is another key aspect of enhancing agility. Traditional hierarchical structures can impede swift decision-making and slow down the organisation's response to changes. In contrast, flexible structures, such as cross-functional teams and decentralised decision-making, empower employees to act quickly and effectively. For example, a company might establish agile teams that bring together members from different departments to collaborate on specific projects. These teams operate with a high degree of autonomy, allowing them to make rapid decisions, iterate on solutions, and adapt to changing circumstances without waiting for approval from higher management.

Investing in technology that enables real-time data analysis and decision-making is also essential for maintaining agility. Advanced technologies, such as artificial intelligence, machine learning, and big data analytics, provide companies with the tools to gather and analyse vast amounts of data, gain actionable insights, and make informed decisions swiftly. For example, a retail company might use data analytics to monitor sales trends, inventory levels, and customer behaviour in real-time, allowing it to adjust pricing strategies, stock levels, and marketing campaigns on the fly. This real-time responsiveness enhances the company's ability to meet customer demands, optimise operations, and stay ahead of competitors.

Zara, a renowned fashion retailer, exemplifies the power of agility and adaptability in business. Zara has built its business model around rapid production cycles and the ability to quickly respond to fashion trends. The company's agile supply chain enables it to design, produce, and deliver new fashion items to stores in a matter of weeks, rather than the traditional months-long cycle. This speed allows Zara to capitalise on emerging fashion trends, meet customer preferences, and maintain a fresh and up-to-date product offering. By embracing agility, Zara has established itself as a leader in the fast fashion industry and gained a significant competitive advantage.

In addition to rapid production cycles, Zara's flexible organisational structure and innovative approach to inventory management contribute to its agility. The company operates with a flat organisational structure that empowers store managers to make decisions based on local market conditions. Store managers have the autonomy to reorder popular items and provide feedback to designers on customer preferences. This decentralised decision-making process ensures that Zara can quickly adapt to changing market demands and maintain a customer-centric approach.

Zara also leverages technology to enhance its agility. The company uses data analytics to monitor sales, track inventory levels, and forecast demand. This data-driven approach enables Zara to optimise its supply chain, reduce excess inventory, and minimise markdowns. By integrating technology into its operations, Zara can make informed decisions, respond to market trends in real-time, and maintain operational efficiency.

Moreover, Zara's commitment to continuous improvement and innovation drives its agility. The company invests in research and development to explore new materials, production techniques, and sustainable practices. For example, Zara has introduced eco-friendly collections made from organic and recycled materials, appealing to environmentally conscious consumers. By continuously innovating and adapting to market trends, Zara ensures its long-term relevance and success.

Secrecy & Subtlety

Sun Tzu extols the virtues of subtlety and secrecy, noting that being invisible and inaudible allows one to hold the enemy's fate in one's hands. In the business world, this principle translates into the critical importance of maintaining confidentiality and strategically managing information. Companies must vigilantly safeguard proprietary information, trade secrets, and strategic plans to prevent competitors from gaining an advantage. This involves creating robust information security protocols, ensuring that sensitive data is accessible only to those who need it, and fostering a culture of discretion and trust within the organisation.

Maintaining confidentiality begins with understanding the value of the information at hand. Companies must identify what constitutes proprietary information and establish clear guidelines for handling and protecting it. This includes everything from intellectual property, such as patents and trademarks, to strategic plans and financial data. By implementing stringent access controls, encryption technologies, and regular security audits, companies can ensure that sensitive information remains protected. For example, a technology firm developing a breakthrough product must keep its research and development details under wraps to prevent competitors from gaining an early advantage.

Secrecy also involves training employees to recognise the importance of confidentiality and the potential risks of information breaches. Regular training sessions can educate staff on best practices for information security, such as using strong passwords, avoiding phishing scams, and securely disposing of sensitive documents. By fostering a culture of vigilance, companies can reduce the likelihood of accidental information leaks and ensure that employees understand their role in protecting the organisation's assets.

Beyond protecting information, secrecy in business also entails the strategic use of deception to mislead competitors about one's intentions. This can be a powerful tool for creating uncertainty and ambiguity, forcing competitors to spread their resources thin and make suboptimal decisions. Strategic deception can take various forms, such as signalling a future product launch to distract competitors while secretly working on a different strategic initiative. For example, a consumer electronics company might announce plans to release a new smartphone model, generating buzz and drawing competitors' attention, while its actual focus is on developing an innovative wearable device.

The art of strategic deception requires a deep understanding of the competitive landscape and the ability to anticipate competitors' reactions. Companies must carefully craft their messages and actions to influence competitors' perceptions without revealing their true intentions. This might involve controlled leaks, strategic partnerships, or deliberate misinformation campaigns. For instance, a retail company might collaborate with a well-known designer to create a limited-edition product line, generating significant media coverage and distracting competitors from its broader strategy of expanding its online presence.

In addition to misleading competitors, secrecy and subtlety can also be used to protect ongoing projects and initiatives. By keeping strategic plans under wraps, companies can avoid tipping off competitors and maintain a first-mover advantage. This is particularly important in highly competitive industries, where the race to market can be a key determinant of success. For example, a pharmaceutical company developing a new drug must keep its research and clinical trial results confidential to prevent competitors from duplicating its efforts and launching similar products.

Moreover, secrecy can be employed to manage public relations and shape market perceptions. Companies can strategically release information to create buzz, manage expectations, and control the narrative around their brand. This involves carefully timing announcements, coordinating media coverage, and using social media to engage with customers and stakeholders. By managing the flow of information, companies can build anticipation and excitement around their products and services, enhancing their market position.

A prime example of effective secrecy and subtlety in business is Apple's approach to product development and launches. Apple is renowned for its ability to maintain strict confidentiality around its new products, creating an aura of mystery and anticipation. The company implements rigorous security measures to ensure that information about upcoming products does not leak. This includes requiring employees and partners to sign non-disclosure agreements, conducting regular security audits, and compartmentalising information so that only a select few have access to the full picture.

Apple's strategic use of secrecy extends to its marketing and public relations efforts. The company carefully orchestrates product launches, building suspense through teaser campaigns and media speculation. By keeping details under wraps until the official unveiling, Apple generates significant buzz and excitement, driving strong initial sales and reinforcing its brand image as a leader in innovation. This approach not only deters competitors but also captivates consumers, creating a loyal customer base that eagerly anticipates each new release.

Concentration of Forces & Unity

Sun Tzu wisely advises concentrating forces and maintaining unity, emphasising that a single united body is more powerful than divided factions. This principle is profoundly relevant in the business world, where the alignment of organisational efforts and resources towards common strategic goals is paramount. Companies must ensure that all departments and teams are working cohesively to achieve organisational objectives, fostering a sense of unity and purpose that drives success.

Achieving this alignment begins with setting clear, well-defined goals. These goals should be specific, measurable, attainable, relevant, and time-bound (SMART) to provide a clear roadmap for the organisation. By establishing clear objectives, companies can ensure that every team member understands their role in contributing to the broader mission. For instance, a technology company might set a goal to develop a groundbreaking product within a certain timeframe, breaking down this goal into specific tasks for research, development, marketing, and sales teams. This clarity helps to ensure that all efforts are directed towards the same end.

Communicating a compelling vision is another crucial aspect of fostering unity. A well-articulated vision provides direction and inspiration, helping employees understand the bigger picture and their part in it. Leaders must convey this vision consistently and passionately, using various channels such as meetings, emails, and company events. For example, a company committed to sustainability might articulate a vision of becoming a leader in green technology, inspiring employees to innovate and align their work with this goal. When employees are connected to a compelling vision, they are more likely to be engaged and motivated, driving collective efforts towards success.

Fostering collaboration across the organisation is essential for harnessing the collective energy of the workforce. This involves promoting open communication, breaking down silos, and encouraging cross-functional teamwork. Companies can create environments that support collaboration by implementing collaborative technologies, designing open workspaces, and encouraging regular interdepartmental meetings. For instance, a company might use collaboration tools like Slack or Microsoft Teams to facilitate real-time communication and project management. By enabling employees to share ideas and work together seamlessly, companies can enhance innovation and problem-solving capabilities.

Effective leadership is key to maintaining unity and concentration of forces. Leaders must set the tone for collaboration and ensure that resources are allocated efficiently. This includes providing teams with the necessary tools, training, and support to achieve their objectives. Leaders should also recognise and celebrate collaborative efforts, reinforcing the importance of teamwork. For example, a leader might highlight successful cross-functional projects in company newsletters or during all-hands meetings, fostering a culture of appreciation and collaboration. By demonstrating a commitment to unity and collaboration, leaders can inspire their teams to work together towards common goals.

Aligning efforts and resources also involves ensuring that all parts of the organisation are working in harmony. This requires clear role definitions, accountability, and effective performance management. Companies must establish processes for tracking progress, measuring performance, and addressing issues promptly. For example, a sales team might use performance metrics to track individual and team achievements, with regular reviews to ensure alignment with company goals. This structured approach helps to maintain focus and ensures that all efforts are contributing to the overall success of the organisation.

Furthermore, fostering a culture of continuous improvement is essential for maintaining unity and concentration of forces. Companies should encourage employees to seek ways to enhance processes, innovate, and adapt to changing market conditions. This involves providing opportunities for professional development, supporting creative initiatives, and fostering a growth mindset. For instance, a company might offer training programmes, workshops, and mentorship opportunities to help employees develop new skills and contribute to the company's success. By promoting a culture of continuous improvement, companies can ensure that they remain agile, resilient, and aligned with their strategic goals.

A prime example of a company that has successfully leveraged concentration of forces and unity is Google. Google's emphasis on a collaborative and innovative culture has enabled it to align its resources and efforts towards achieving technological advancements and market leadership. The company's clear goals, compelling vision, and commitment to fostering collaboration have created a unified workforce that drives continuous innovation. Google's investment in cutting-edge technologies, such as artificial intelligence and cloud computing, has been supported by a cohesive strategy that aligns all departments towards common objectives. This alignment has enabled Google to maintain its competitive edge and achieve sustained growth.

Strategic Flexibility & Innovation

Sun Tzu emphasises the crucial need for strategic flexibility and the ability to adapt tactics based on the opponent's actions. This principle, deeply ingrained in ancient military strategy, is incredibly relevant in the realm of modern strategic management. It underscores the importance of innovation and the continuous evolution of strategies to respond to dynamic market conditions, technological advancements, and competitive pressures. Companies that are adept at adapting their tactics and innovating consistently are more likely to sustain a competitive advantage and thrive in ever-changing environments.

Strategic flexibility involves a company's capacity to pivot and adjust its strategies in real-time. This requires an agile mindset and the ability to respond swiftly to external changes, such as shifts in consumer behaviour, economic fluctuations, and technological breakthroughs. For example, a retail company that monitors customer preferences and swiftly adjusts its inventory and marketing strategies can better meet consumer demands and maintain a competitive edge. By being flexible, companies can avoid the pitfalls of rigid planning and remain resilient in the face of uncertainty.

Innovation, on the other hand, is about exploring new ideas, experimenting with novel approaches, and continuously improving products and services. It is the engine that drives strategic flexibility. A culture of innovation encourages employees to think creatively, challenge the status quo, and pursue bold initiatives. Companies can foster innovation by providing the necessary resources, creating an environment that values experimentation, and supporting risk-taking. For instance, a technology company might set up an innovation lab where employees can work on cutting-edge projects and collaborate on new solutions. This proactive approach to innovation ensures that the company stays ahead of industry trends and can swiftly respond to emerging opportunities.

Exploring new ideas is fundamental to innovation. Companies must encourage their teams to brainstorm and propose creative solutions to existing problems. This involves creating channels for idea generation and collaboration, such as hackathons, innovation workshops, and cross-functional teams. By leveraging diverse perspectives and expertise, companies can uncover innovative approaches that drive competitive advantage. For example, a software company might hold regular brainstorming sessions where developers, designers, and marketers collaborate to create new features that enhance the user experience. This collaborative effort fosters a sense of ownership and encourages employees to think outside the box.

Experimenting with new approaches is also vital for fostering innovation. Companies should be willing to pilot new initiatives and learn from the outcomes. This might involve launching small-scale projects to test new concepts before rolling them out on a larger scale. By embracing a test-and-learn mindset, companies can iterate on their ideas and refine their strategies based on real-world feedback. For instance, a consumer goods company might launch a limited-edition product to gauge market interest and gather customer feedback before deciding to scale up production. This iterative process allows the company to make data-driven decisions and mitigate risks.

Continuous improvement is another cornerstone of innovation. Companies must commit to constantly enhancing their products, services, and processes. This involves regularly assessing performance, gathering feedback, and identifying areas for improvement. By fostering a culture of continuous improvement, companies can ensure that they remain competitive and responsive to changing market conditions. For example, a manufacturing company might implement Lean principles to streamline operations, reduce waste, and improve efficiency. By continuously seeking ways to enhance its processes, the company can maintain high-quality standards and deliver superior value to customers.

Tesla is a prime example of a company that has thrived by embracing innovation and continuously exploring new ways to create value in the electric vehicle (EV) market. Tesla's strategic flexibility and commitment to innovation have been key drivers of its success. The company has consistently pushed the boundaries of what is possible in the automotive industry, from developing high-performance electric vehicles to pioneering advancements in autonomous driving and battery technology. Tesla's focus on innovation has enabled it to capture significant market share and establish itself as a leader in the EV market.

Tesla's ability to adapt its tactics in response to market changes and technological advancements has been instrumental in its growth. The company has leveraged its innovative capabilities to address emerging trends, such as the growing demand for sustainable transportation solutions. By continuously investing in research and development, Tesla has introduced groundbreaking products that set new standards for performance, safety, and energy efficiency. For example, the launch of the Tesla Model S redefined consumer expectations for electric vehicles, combining long-range capabilities with luxury and performance.

Furthermore, Tesla's strategic flexibility extends to its business model and market approach. The company has adopted a direct-to-consumer sales model, bypassing traditional dealership networks and creating a seamless purchasing experience for customers. This approach has allowed Tesla to maintain greater control over its brand and customer interactions, resulting in higher customer satisfaction and loyalty. Additionally, Tesla has diversified its product offerings to include energy solutions, such as solar panels and energy storage systems, positioning itself as a comprehensive provider of sustainable energy solutions.

Tesla's commitment to continuous improvement is evident in its iterative approach to product development. The company regularly releases over-the-air software updates to enhance the performance and features of its vehicles, ensuring that customers benefit from the latest advancements. This focus on continuous improvement has not only strengthened Tesla's competitive position but also fostered a loyal customer base that values innovation and quality.

Summary

Sun Tzu's *Weak Points & Strong* offers timeless insights that are highly relevant to modern strategic management. The principles of initiative, preparation, influence, agility, secrecy, concentration, and innovation provide a robust framework for navigating the complexities of the business world.

CHAPTER 7 – MANOEUVRING

*Let your plans be dark and impenetrable as night,
and when you move, fall like a thunderbolt.*

Sun Tzu

Sun Tzu's *Manoeuvring* offers valuable insights into the complexities of tactical manoeuvres and strategic decision-making. These principles are highly relevant to modern strategic management, where businesses must navigate competitive landscapes, manage resources efficiently, and adapt to changing market conditions.

The Importance of Leadership & Command

Sun Tzu begins the chapter on manoeuvring by emphasising that in war, the general receives his commands from the sovereign. This principle underscores the crucial importance of leadership and the alignment of strategic objectives with organisational goals. In the business world, effective leadership is paramount for guiding an organisation through strategic initiatives and ensuring that all efforts are cohesively aligned with the company's mission and vision. Leaders serve as the linchpin that connects the overarching strategic vision with the daily operations of the organisation, driving both direction and execution.

Effective leadership begins with the communication of clear directives. Leaders must articulate the strategic objectives and expectations in a manner that is understandable and actionable for all team members. This involves not only setting clear goals but also explaining the rationale behind them, helping employees see how their individual contributions fit into the larger picture. For instance, a company aiming to expand its market share might set a directive to increase sales by 20% over the next fiscal year. The leader's role is to break down this goal into specific targets and tasks for each department, ensuring that everyone understands their part in achieving the collective objective.

In addition to clear communication, leaders must inspire and motivate their teams to achieve common goals. This involves creating a compelling vision that resonates with employees and ignites their passion and commitment. A compelling vision provides a sense of purpose and direction, guiding employees' efforts and encouraging them to go above and beyond in their roles. For example, a leader who envisions creating a world-class customer service experience must inspire their team to prioritise customer satisfaction and continually seek ways to improve service delivery. By connecting the vision to everyday actions, leaders can cultivate a motivated and engaged workforce.

Fostering a culture of collaboration is essential for aligning organisational efforts. Leaders must create an environment where teamwork is encouraged and valued, and where employees feel empowered to share ideas and work together towards common objectives. This involves promoting open communication, facilitating cross-functional collaboration, and providing opportunities for team-building activities. For instance, a leader might organise regular interdepartmental meetings to discuss progress on strategic initiatives, share insights, and address any challenges. By fostering a collaborative culture, leaders can harness the collective intelligence and creativity of their teams, driving innovation and problem-solving.

Accountability is another critical aspect of effective leadership. Leaders must establish clear roles and responsibilities, ensuring that each team member is accountable for their contributions. This involves setting performance standards, providing regular feedback, and recognising and rewarding achievements. By holding employees accountable, leaders can maintain high levels of performance and ensure that everyone is working towards the same strategic objectives. For example, a leader might implement a performance management system that tracks individual and team achievements, with regular reviews to assess progress and provide constructive feedback. This structured approach helps to maintain focus and drive continuous improvement.

Leaders must also be adaptable and resilient, ready to pivot and adjust strategies in response to changing circumstances. This involves staying attuned to market dynamics, technological advancements, and competitive pressures, and being willing to make bold decisions when necessary. For example, during a market downturn, a leader might decide to shift resources towards more profitable product lines or explore new revenue streams. By demonstrating adaptability and resilience, leaders can navigate uncertainties and guide their organisations towards sustained success.

An exemplary illustration of effective leadership and command in action is Satya Nadella's tenure as CEO of Microsoft. Under his leadership, Microsoft has successfully aligned its strategic initiatives with its overarching vision of empowering every person and organisation on the planet to achieve more. Nadella's leadership has been characterised by clear communication, inspiring vision, and a commitment to fostering a collaborative and accountable culture. He has championed a growth mindset, encouraging continuous learning and innovation across the organisation. This cultural transformation has driven significant advancements in cloud computing, artificial intelligence, and productivity solutions, positioning Microsoft as a leader in the technology industry.

Nadella's emphasis on collaboration and teamwork has been instrumental in breaking down silos and promoting cross-functional initiatives. For example, the integration of LinkedIn and GitHub into Microsoft's ecosystem has facilitated collaboration between different teams, enhancing product development and customer engagement. By fostering a collaborative culture, Nadella has harnessed the collective energy of Microsoft's workforce, driving innovation and growth.

Furthermore, Nadella's leadership has instilled a strong sense of accountability within Microsoft. He has implemented performance management systems that track individual and team progress, with regular reviews to ensure alignment with strategic objectives. By holding employees accountable and recognising their contributions, Nadella has created a high-performing and motivated workforce. This focus on accountability has been key to Microsoft's success in executing its strategic initiatives and achieving its vision.

Harmonising & Blending Resources

Sun Tzu asserts that after collecting an army and concentrating forces, the general must blend and harmonise the different elements before pitching camp. This timeless principle is highly applicable in the business context, where resource integration and optimisation are critical for creating a cohesive and efficient organisation. Companies must ensure that their resources, capabilities, and processes are seamlessly harmonised to work towards common objectives, ultimately enhancing overall performance and achieving strategic goals.

Resource harmonisation begins with aligning different departments, functions, and teams to work seamlessly together. This involves breaking down organisational silos that often impede communication and collaboration. Siloed departments can lead to inefficiencies, duplicated efforts, and missed opportunities. Therefore, companies must foster a culture of cross-functional collaboration where information flows freely, and teams can leverage each other's strengths. For instance, a company might establish interdepartmental committees or task forces to address specific challenges or projects, ensuring that diverse perspectives are considered and integrated into the decision-making process.

Effective communication is a cornerstone of resource harmonisation. Leaders must establish clear channels for communication and ensure that all team members are informed about the organisation's goals, priorities, and progress. This includes regular updates, meetings, and transparent reporting mechanisms. For example, a technology company might implement a weekly all-hands meeting where leaders share updates on strategic initiatives, celebrate successes, and address any challenges. By maintaining open lines of communication, companies can ensure that everyone is on the same page and working towards the same objectives.

Fostering a collaborative culture is essential for optimising resource utilisation. This involves encouraging teamwork, promoting mutual respect, and creating an environment where employees feel valued and empowered to contribute their ideas. Companies can facilitate collaboration by designing open and flexible workspaces, implementing collaborative technologies, and recognising and rewarding collaborative efforts. For instance, a marketing team and a product development team might collaborate on the launch of a new product, working together to create a cohesive marketing strategy that highlights the product's unique features and benefits. By leveraging the strengths of each team, the company can create a more compelling value proposition for customers.

Implementing robust processes and systems is another key aspect of resource harmonisation. Companies must ensure that their processes are efficient, scalable, and adaptable to changing needs. This involves continuously evaluating and improving workflows, automating repetitive tasks, and adopting best practices. For example, a manufacturing company might implement a lean manufacturing system that focuses on eliminating waste, improving quality, and increasing efficiency. By streamlining processes, the company can reduce costs, enhance productivity, and deliver higher value to customers.

Technology plays a crucial role in harmonising resources and optimising operations. Companies must invest in technologies that enable seamless collaboration, data sharing, and real-time decision-making. Advanced analytics, cloud computing, and project management tools can provide valuable insights, enhance transparency, and improve coordination across departments. For instance, a company might use an integrated enterprise resource planning (ERP) system to manage inventory, track sales, and monitor production processes. This integrated approach ensures that all relevant information is accessible to decision-makers, enabling them to make informed choices that align with the organisation's goals.

Continuous improvement is a fundamental principle of resource harmonisation. Companies must foster a culture of continuous learning and development, encouraging employees to seek ways to enhance processes, innovate, and adapt to new challenges. This involves providing opportunities for professional development, supporting creative initiatives, and fostering a growth mindset. For example, a company might offer training programmes, workshops, and mentorship opportunities to help employees develop new skills and contribute to the company's success. By promoting a culture of continuous improvement, companies can ensure that they remain agile, resilient, and aligned with their strategic goals.

A prime example of a company that has successfully harmonised and blended its resources is Toyota. Toyota's adoption of the lean manufacturing system, known as the Toyota Production System (TPS), has been instrumental in achieving high levels of efficiency and productivity. The TPS emphasises teamwork, continuous improvement, and the elimination of waste. By fostering a collaborative culture and empowering employees to identify and address inefficiencies, Toyota has created a cohesive and efficient organisation that consistently delivers high-quality products.

Toyota's success in resource harmonisation extends beyond manufacturing. The company has implemented robust processes and systems across all functions, from supply chain management to customer service. This integrated approach ensures that all departments work together seamlessly, leveraging their unique capabilities to achieve common goals. For example, Toyota's supply chain management system integrates suppliers, production facilities, and distribution centres, enabling the company to respond quickly to changes in demand and maintain optimal inventory levels. This holistic approach to resource harmonisation has enabled Toyota to maintain its competitive edge and achieve sustained growth.

Tactical Manoeuvring & Strategic Flexibility

Sun Tzu eloquently highlights the inherent challenges of tactical manoeuvring, underscoring the critical importance of transforming devious actions into direct paths and converting misfortune into gain. In the realm of modern strategic management, this principle emphasises the necessity for strategic flexibility and the adeptness to adapt to ever-changing circumstances. Companies must cultivate the ability to pivot their strategies dynamically in response to evolving market dynamics, intensifying competitive pressures, and emerging opportunities. This agility is paramount for sustaining a competitive edge and driving long-term success.

Strategic flexibility begins with the continuous monitoring of the external environment. This involves staying attuned to market trends, economic shifts, technological advancements, and regulatory changes. By gathering intelligence from various sources, such as market research reports, industry analysis, and customer feedback, companies can gain a comprehensive understanding of the external factors influencing their business. For example, a retail company might analyse consumer purchasing patterns and competitor activities to identify emerging trends and adjust its product offerings accordingly. This proactive approach ensures that the company remains responsive and well-prepared to capitalise on new opportunities.

Gathering intelligence is a crucial component of strategic flexibility. Companies must collect and analyse data to make informed, data-driven decisions. This process involves utilising advanced data analytics tools and technologies to derive actionable insights from vast amounts of information. For instance, a financial services firm might use predictive analytics to forecast market trends and identify potential investment opportunities. By leveraging data-driven insights, companies can make strategic decisions with greater precision and confidence, minimising risks and maximising returns.

Adopting agile methodologies is another vital aspect of enhancing strategic flexibility. Agile practices, such as iterative planning, continuous feedback loops, and adaptive project management, enable companies to respond swiftly to changing circumstances. By breaking down large projects into smaller, manageable tasks, companies can iterate and refine their strategies based on real-time feedback. For example, a software development company might implement agile methodologies to deliver incremental updates and enhancements, allowing it to respond quickly to user needs and market demands. This iterative approach fosters a culture of adaptability and continuous improvement, ensuring that the company remains agile and resilient.

Implementing adaptive planning processes is also essential for maintaining strategic flexibility. Companies must develop flexible planning frameworks that allow for adjustments and revisions based on evolving conditions. This involves setting clear objectives, identifying key performance indicators, and regularly reviewing progress to ensure alignment with strategic goals. For instance, a manufacturing company might adopt a rolling planning process, where strategic plans are revisited and updated quarterly based on market conditions and operational performance. By maintaining flexible planning processes, companies can stay agile and responsive, making timely adjustments to their strategies as needed.

Fostering a culture of innovation is critical for driving strategic flexibility. Companies should create an environment that encourages creativity, experimentation, and risk-taking. This involves providing employees with the resources and autonomy to explore new ideas and develop innovative solutions. For example, a technology company might establish an innovation lab where employees can collaborate on cutting-edge projects and prototype new products. By promoting a culture of innovation, companies can drive continuous improvement and stay ahead of industry trends.

Netflix serves as a prime example of a company that has excelled in strategic flexibility and innovation. Originally a DVD rental service, Netflix demonstrated remarkable adaptability by transforming its business model to embrace streaming services. This strategic pivot allowed Netflix to capitalise on the growing demand for digital content consumption, positioning itself as a market leader. Furthermore, Netflix continued to innovate by investing in original content production, creating a vast library of exclusive shows and movies. This move not only differentiated Netflix from competitors but also established it as a powerhouse in the entertainment industry.

Netflix's ability to adapt its business model exemplifies the power of strategic flexibility. By continuously monitoring market trends and gathering intelligence, Netflix identified the shift in consumer preferences towards on-demand streaming. The company leveraged data analytics to understand viewer behaviour and inform content creation decisions, ensuring that its offerings resonated with audiences. This data-driven approach allowed Netflix to make informed strategic decisions, reducing the risk of missteps and maximising its competitive advantage.

Moreover, Netflix's adoption of agile methodologies and adaptive planning processes enabled it to stay responsive to changing market conditions. The company implemented iterative development practices, allowing it to release new features and updates based on user feedback. This agile approach ensured that Netflix remained at the forefront of technological advancements and continuously improved its platform. Additionally, Netflix fostered a culture of innovation, encouraging employees to experiment with new ideas and take calculated risks. This culture of creativity and adaptability has been instrumental in driving Netflix's sustained growth and market leadership.

Speed & Efficiency

Sun Tzu advises that in order to succeed, one must move swiftly and efficiently, akin to a falcon striking with precision. This principle underscores the importance of speed and agility in the business world, where the ability to swiftly respond to market changes, seize opportunities, and outmanoeuvre competitors is paramount for achieving strategic objectives. Companies that can rapidly adapt to evolving conditions, make timely decisions, and expedite their processes are more likely to gain a competitive edge and achieve long-term success.

Speed in business encompasses several dimensions, starting with the ability to make timely decisions. Rapid decision-making involves assessing situations quickly, analysing relevant data, and executing plans without undue delay. This requires a combination of analytical skills, intuition, and confidence. Leaders must cultivate a culture where decisions are made promptly, leveraging real-time data and insights. For instance, a retail company that swiftly adjusts its pricing strategy based on real-time sales data can capitalise on consumer demand and maximise revenue. By fostering a sense of urgency and empowerment, companies can ensure that they remain agile and responsive to market dynamics.

Accelerating product development cycles is another crucial aspect of speed. Companies must streamline their product development processes to bring innovations to market quickly. This involves adopting agile methodologies, such as iterative development, rapid prototyping, and continuous feedback loops. By breaking down projects into smaller, manageable tasks, companies can iterate and refine their products based on user feedback, ensuring that they meet customer needs and expectations. For example, a technology company might use agile development to release incremental updates and enhancements, allowing it to stay ahead of competitors and deliver cutting-edge solutions. This approach not only speeds up product development but also enhances product quality and customer satisfaction.

Quickly bringing innovations to market is essential for capturing early adopters and gaining a first-mover advantage. Companies that can launch new products and services ahead of competitors can establish a strong market presence and build brand recognition. This involves efficient supply chain management, effective marketing strategies, and seamless execution. For instance, a consumer electronics company that rapidly brings a new gadget to market can generate buzz and excitement, attracting tech-savvy customers and setting industry trends. By prioritising speed to market, companies can drive growth and secure a competitive edge.

Agility, on the other hand, involves the ability to adapt and pivot strategies in response to changing conditions. This requires a flexible mindset and the willingness to embrace change. Companies must develop adaptive planning processes that allow for adjustments and revisions based on real-time feedback and evolving circumstances. For example, a manufacturing company that monitors global supply chain disruptions and quickly adjusts its sourcing strategy can mitigate risks and maintain operational continuity. By fostering a culture of agility, companies can stay resilient and responsive, navigating uncertainties and capturing new opportunities.

The combination of speed and agility is exemplified by Amazon's approach to business. Amazon's emphasis on rapid innovation and customer-centricity has enabled it to quickly adapt to market trends and maintain its market leadership. The company's commitment to speed is evident in its streamlined logistics and fulfilment operations. Amazon's vast network of fulfilment centres, advanced inventory management systems, and efficient delivery processes ensure that products are delivered to customers swiftly. This focus on speed not only enhances the customer experience but also drives customer loyalty and repeat business.

Furthermore, Amazon's agile approach to innovation has been instrumental in its success. The company continuously explores new ideas and experiments with novel approaches, from launching new product categories to expanding into cloud computing and artificial intelligence. For example, Amazon Web Services (AWS) was born out of the company's agility and willingness to venture into new territories. AWS has since become a market leader in cloud services, contributing significantly to Amazon's overall growth and profitability. This ability to pivot and innovate has allowed Amazon to stay ahead of competitors and capture new market opportunities.

Amazon's customer-centric culture is another cornerstone of its speed and agility. The company prioritises understanding and meeting customer needs, from personalised recommendations to responsive customer service. By leveraging data analytics and machine learning, Amazon continuously improves its offerings and enhances the customer experience. This customer-centric approach ensures that Amazon remains relevant and competitive in a rapidly changing market.

The Role of Intelligence & Local Knowledge

Sun Tzu asserts that a general must be intimately familiar with the terrain—the mountains, forests, pitfalls, and precipices—before leading an army on a march. This ancient wisdom translates seamlessly into the business world, where the role of market intelligence and local knowledge is paramount. Companies must diligently gather and analyse market data, comprehend local conditions, and leverage these insights to inform strategic decisions. In doing so, businesses can navigate complex market landscapes with precision and confidence, ultimately enhancing their competitive edge.

Market intelligence is the backbone of strategic decision-making. It involves conducting thorough research to collect data on market conditions, consumer behaviours, competitor activities, and industry trends. This data provides valuable insights that help companies anticipate changes and make informed decisions. For example, a retail company might use market intelligence to identify emerging consumer preferences for sustainable products, enabling it to adjust its inventory and marketing strategies accordingly. By staying ahead of market trends, companies can better meet customer needs and maintain a competitive advantage.

Understanding customer needs and preferences is a critical component of market intelligence. Companies must gather feedback from customers through surveys, focus groups, and social media interactions to gain insights into their preferences and pain points. This information allows businesses to tailor their products and services to better meet customer expectations, thereby enhancing customer satisfaction and loyalty. For instance, a technology company might use customer feedback to improve the usability and features of its software, resulting in higher user satisfaction and retention rates.

Local knowledge is equally important in strategic decision-making. It involves understanding the unique cultural, economic, and regulatory conditions of different markets. This knowledge helps companies adapt their strategies to local contexts, ensuring that their offerings resonate with local customers. For example, a food and beverage company entering a new market might study local dietary preferences, cultural traditions, and regulatory requirements to develop products that appeal to local tastes and comply with regulations. By leveraging local knowledge, companies can create a more relevant and appealing brand presence in new markets.

The importance of local knowledge extends to economic and regulatory conditions. Companies must be aware of the economic factors that influence consumer spending, such as income levels, inflation rates, and employment trends. This understanding helps businesses adjust their pricing strategies and product offerings to align with local economic conditions. Additionally, companies must navigate the regulatory environment, ensuring compliance with local laws and standards. For instance, a pharmaceutical company expanding into a new country must understand the local regulatory framework for drug approvals and adhere to all requirements to avoid legal issues and delays.

By combining market intelligence and local knowledge, companies can develop strategies that are tailored to specific market conditions and enhance their competitiveness. This integrated approach ensures that businesses are well-informed and agile, capable of responding swiftly to changes and capitalising on opportunities. For example, an e-commerce company might use market intelligence to identify a growing demand for online shopping in a particular region and leverage local knowledge to optimise its logistics and delivery network to meet this demand efficiently. This strategic alignment of market intelligence and local knowledge enables the company to provide a seamless and convenient shopping experience, driving customer satisfaction and loyalty.

Starbucks serves as a prime example of a company that has successfully leveraged market intelligence and local knowledge to achieve international success. The coffee giant's ability to adapt its offerings and marketing strategies to local preferences and cultural nuances has been a key driver of its global expansion. In each new market, Starbucks conducts extensive market research to understand local consumer preferences, behaviours, and cultural traditions. This information informs the development of products and store designs that resonate with local customers. For instance, in Japan, Starbucks offers seasonal beverages that incorporate traditional Japanese flavours, such as matcha and sakura, appealing to local tastes and enhancing the brand's cultural relevance.

Moreover, Starbucks's deep understanding of local economic and regulatory conditions has enabled it to navigate complex market environments successfully. The company ensures compliance with local laws and standards, builds strong relationships with local suppliers, and invests in community engagement initiatives. By integrating market intelligence and local knowledge into its strategic planning, Starbucks has created a strong and adaptable business model that drives sustained growth and market leadership.

Discipline & Coordination

Sun Tzu emphasises the critical importance of discipline and coordination in achieving success. He advises making use of signal-fires, drums, flags, and banners to influence the ears and eyes of the army and maintain coordination. This principle, rooted in ancient military strategy, translates seamlessly into the business world, where maintaining discipline and ensuring effective communication and coordination are paramount for organisational success.

Discipline in business involves adhering to established processes, maintaining operational excellence, and ensuring consistent performance. It is the backbone of an efficient organisation, providing structure and reliability. Companies must implement clear policies and procedures that guide daily operations and decision-making. This includes standardised workflows, quality control measures, and performance benchmarks. For instance, a manufacturing company might have strict protocols for production processes, ensuring that each step is executed with precision and consistency. By maintaining high standards of discipline, businesses can minimise errors, reduce waste, and enhance productivity.

Operational excellence is a key component of discipline. It involves continuously improving processes and systems to achieve superior performance. Companies must adopt best practices and strive for efficiency in all areas of their operations. This might include implementing Lean management principles, utilising automation technologies, and conducting regular audits to identify areas for improvement. For example, a logistics company might streamline its supply chain by optimising routes, reducing lead times, and enhancing inventory management. By prioritising operational excellence, companies can deliver consistent quality and meet customer expectations.

Consistency in performance is also crucial for maintaining discipline. Companies must set clear performance standards and monitor progress regularly. This involves establishing key performance indicators (KPIs) and conducting regular reviews to assess performance against targets. For instance, a sales team might have monthly targets for revenue generation, customer acquisition, and market expansion. By tracking these metrics and providing feedback, companies can ensure that employees remain focused and aligned with organisational goals. Consistent performance builds trust and credibility with customers, stakeholders, and employees.

Coordination, on the other hand, involves effective communication and collaboration among different teams and departments. It ensures that all parts of the organisation are working cohesively towards common objectives. Effective communication is the foundation of coordination, enabling the smooth flow of information and fostering a culture of transparency. Companies must establish clear communication channels and encourage open dialogue among employees. This might include regular team meetings, project updates, and digital collaboration tools. For example, a tech company might use platforms like Slack or Microsoft Teams to facilitate real-time communication and information sharing. By promoting open communication, companies can enhance collaboration and ensure that everyone is on the same page.

Collaboration among teams is essential for achieving synergy and driving innovation. Companies must encourage cross-functional collaboration, bringing together diverse perspectives and expertise. This involves breaking down silos and fostering a culture of teamwork. For instance, a product development team might collaborate with marketing, sales, and customer service teams to create a new product that meets customer needs and market demands. By leveraging the collective knowledge and skills of different teams, companies can develop more comprehensive and innovative solutions.

Southwest Airlines serves as a prime example of a company that has excelled in discipline and coordination. The airline's emphasis on disciplined operations and effective communication has enabled it to achieve high levels of customer satisfaction and operational efficiency. Southwest Airlines implements rigorous processes and standards to ensure consistent performance across its operations. This includes meticulous aircraft maintenance procedures, efficient boarding processes, and standardised customer service protocols. By maintaining discipline in its operations, Southwest Airlines ensures safety, reliability, and quality.

Effective communication and coordination are also central to Southwest Airlines' success. The airline fosters a culture of collaboration and transparency, encouraging open dialogue among employees at all levels. This involves regular team meetings, cross-departmental collaborations, and digital communication platforms. For example, Southwest Airlines conducts daily operations meetings to review performance, address issues, and align strategies. By promoting open communication and teamwork, the airline ensures that all employees are working towards common goals and delivering a seamless customer experience.

Moreover, Southwest Airlines' focus on discipline and coordination extends to its customer interactions. The airline emphasises consistent and high-quality customer service, ensuring that passengers have a positive experience from booking to arrival. This involves training employees to adhere to service standards, providing them with the tools and resources to assist customers effectively, and recognising exceptional performance. By maintaining discipline in customer service and fostering coordination among frontline staff, Southwest Airlines builds strong customer loyalty and satisfaction.

Studying Circumstances & Adapting Strategies

Sun Tzu astutely underscores the importance of meticulously studying circumstances and adapting strategies based on the prevailing situation. He advises avoiding an enemy when its spirit is keen and attacking when it is sluggish and inclined to retreat. This principle is profoundly relevant in modern strategic management, emphasising the critical necessity of situational analysis and adaptive strategy formulation. Companies that master these elements are better equipped to navigate the complexities of the market, respond to competitive pressures, and achieve their strategic objectives.

Situational analysis is the cornerstone of informed strategic decision-making. It involves a comprehensive assessment of the external environment to identify factors that could impact the organisation. This includes evaluating economic conditions, industry trends, regulatory changes, and technological advancements. For instance, a company might analyse macroeconomic indicators such as GDP growth, inflation rates, and consumer spending patterns to gauge the overall health of the economy. By understanding these factors, companies can anticipate potential challenges and opportunities, allowing them to develop more effective strategies.

Evaluating competitive dynamics is another critical aspect of situational analysis. Companies must thoroughly analyse their competitors' strengths, weaknesses, strategies, and market positions. This involves studying competitors' product offerings, pricing strategies, marketing tactics, and customer base. For example, a company in the tech industry might analyse its competitors' latest innovations, market share, and customer reviews to identify gaps in the market and areas for differentiation. By understanding the competitive landscape, companies can develop strategies that capitalise on their own strengths while exploiting competitors' weaknesses.

Understanding market conditions is also essential for situational analysis. This involves gathering data on customer preferences, buying behaviours, and emerging trends. Companies can use surveys, focus groups, social media analytics, and market research reports to gain insights into what drives customer decisions. For instance, a fashion retailer might analyse trends in consumer spending, popular styles, and seasonal demand to tailor its product offerings and marketing campaigns. By staying attuned to market conditions, companies can remain relevant and responsive to customer needs.

Adaptive strategy formulation is the process of developing flexible strategies that can be adjusted based on changing circumstances. This involves creating a strategic framework that allows for continuous evaluation and adjustment. Companies must be willing to pivot their strategies when necessary, responding to new information and shifting market dynamics. For example, a company might implement a rolling strategic plan, where goals and initiatives are revisited and revised on a quarterly basis. This adaptive approach ensures that the organisation remains agile and can quickly respond to changes.

One of the most compelling examples of situational analysis and adaptive strategy formulation in action is the response of many companies to the COVID-19 pandemic. The pandemic created unprecedented challenges and forced organisations to rethink their strategies. Companies that excelled in adapting their strategies were able to navigate the crisis effectively and even capitalise on new opportunities. For instance, many retailers shifted their focus to e-commerce as physical stores were closed due to lockdowns. By enhancing their online presence, improving logistics, and offering contactless delivery options, these companies were able to meet the surge in online shopping demand and maintain revenue streams.

Implementing remote work policies was another adaptive strategy employed by companies during the pandemic. Organisations quickly transitioned to remote work setups to ensure business continuity while safeguarding employee health. This involved investing in digital collaboration tools, enhancing cybersecurity measures, and providing support for remote work infrastructure. By adopting flexible work arrangements, companies were able to maintain productivity and employee engagement despite the disruption caused by the pandemic.

Developing new product offerings was also a key strategy for many companies during the pandemic. Businesses in various industries pivoted to address the changing needs and preferences of their customers. For example, distilleries and breweries shifted production to create hand sanitisers, while fashion brands started producing face masks. These adaptive strategies allowed companies to stay relevant, contribute to public health efforts, and generate new revenue streams.

The ability to study circumstances and adapt strategies is not limited to crisis situations. Companies must continuously engage in situational analysis and adaptive strategy formulation to thrive in a dynamic business environment. This involves fostering a culture of agility and innovation, where employees are encouraged to experiment with new ideas and embrace change. For instance, a technology company might establish an innovation hub where employees can collaborate on projects that explore emerging technologies and market opportunities. By promoting a mindset of continuous learning and adaptation, companies can remain competitive and resilient in the face of evolving market conditions.

Summary

Sun Tzu's *Manoeuvring* offers timeless insights that are highly relevant to modern strategic management. The principles of leadership, resource harmonisation, strategic flexibility, speed and efficiency, intelligence, discipline, and adaptive strategy formulation provide a robust framework for navigating the complexities of the business world.

CHAPTER 8 – VARIATION OF TACTICS

In hemmed-in situations, you must resort to stratagem.
In a desperate position, you must fight.
Sun Tzu

Sun Tzu's *Variation of Tactics* focuses on the need for flexibility, adaptability, and strategic acumen in response to dynamic conditions. These principles are indispensable in today's volatile and complex business environment.

Flexibility & Adaptability in Strategy

Sun Tzu begins by emphasising that in war, the general must adapt tactics based on the commands from the sovereign and the conditions of the battlefield. This principle translates seamlessly into the modern business world, where flexibility and adaptability are crucial for navigating the ever-changing landscape. Companies must be prepared to adjust their strategies in response to fluctuating market conditions, competitive dynamics, and internal challenges. Being flexible and adaptable means having the ability to pivot quickly and effectively to seize opportunities and mitigate risks.

Strategic flexibility starts with a keen understanding of the external environment. Companies must continuously monitor market trends, economic indicators, technological advancements, and regulatory changes to anticipate shifts that could impact their operations. This proactive approach allows businesses to stay ahead of the curve and be prepared for any eventuality. For instance, a retail company might keep a close eye on emerging consumer trends, such as the growing preference for online shopping, and adjust its strategy to enhance its e-commerce capabilities.

Gathering intelligence is a vital component of strategic flexibility. This involves collecting data from various sources, such as market research, customer feedback, competitor analysis, and industry reports. By analysing this data, companies can gain valuable insights that inform their decision-making processes. For example, a financial services firm might use data analytics to track changes in consumer spending patterns and adjust its product offerings to better meet customer needs. This data-driven approach ensures that decisions are based on solid evidence rather than intuition alone.

Implementing adaptive planning processes is essential for maintaining flexibility. Companies must develop planning frameworks that allow for regular reassessment and adjustments based on new information. This involves setting short-term goals that are regularly reviewed and updated to reflect current conditions. For instance, a manufacturing company might use rolling forecasts to continuously update its production plans based on real-time demand data. This adaptive approach enables the company to respond swiftly to changes in customer demand and optimise its operations.

Adopting agile methodologies is another critical aspect of enhancing strategic flexibility. Agile practices, such as iterative planning, continuous feedback loops, and incremental development, enable companies to quickly adapt to changing circumstances. By breaking down large projects into smaller, manageable tasks, companies can iterate and refine their strategies based on real-time feedback. For example, a software development company might use agile methodologies to deliver incremental updates and enhancements, allowing it to respond quickly to user needs and market demands. This iterative approach fosters a culture of continuous improvement and ensures that the company remains agile and resilient.

Fostering a culture of innovation is paramount for driving strategic flexibility. Companies should create an environment that encourages creativity, experimentation, and risk-taking. This involves providing employees with the resources and autonomy to explore new ideas and develop innovative solutions. For instance, a technology company might establish an innovation lab where employees can collaborate on cutting-edge projects and prototype new products. By promoting a culture of innovation, companies can drive continuous improvement and stay ahead of industry trends.

The COVID-19 pandemic serves as a poignant example of the importance of strategic flexibility and adaptability. Many businesses were forced to rapidly adjust their strategies to address new market realities. Companies across various industries shifted to e-commerce, implemented remote work policies, and developed new product offerings to meet changing customer needs. For example, retail companies that traditionally relied on brick-and-mortar stores quickly expanded their online presence to cater to the surge in online shopping. By leveraging digital technologies and optimising their supply chains, these companies were able to maintain operations and meet customer demand.

Furthermore, businesses in the hospitality industry adapted by introducing contactless services, enhancing hygiene protocols, and offering flexible booking options. These adaptations not only addressed immediate challenges but also positioned these companies for long-term success in a post-pandemic world. The ability to pivot quickly and effectively was a key determinant of success during the pandemic, highlighting the critical importance of strategic flexibility.

Strategic Alliances & Collaboration

Sun Tzu advises joining hands with allies in situations where high roads intersect and avoiding dangerous isolated positions. This timeless principle underscores the critical importance of strategic alliances and collaboration in the modern business landscape. In a world characterised by rapid technological advancements, globalisation, and competitive pressures, companies can significantly enhance their competitiveness by forming strategic partnerships and alliances. These collaborations enable organisations to access new markets, cutting-edge technologies, and valuable resources, fostering an environment where mutual strengths are leveraged for shared success.

Strategic alliances involve more than just a handshake agreement; they represent a formal and mutual commitment to achieving common goals. By partnering with other organisations, companies can pool their resources, share risks, and accelerate the pace of innovation. For instance, technology giants often collaborate to develop new products, enter new markets, or enhance existing services. These alliances are designed to create synergies that benefit all parties involved, allowing each organisation to capitalise on the other's strengths.

One of the primary advantages of strategic alliances is access to new markets. Through collaboration, companies can penetrate regions or customer segments that would otherwise be difficult or costly to reach independently. For example, a domestic company looking to expand internationally might form an alliance with a local company that has established market presence and knowledge. This partnership can provide invaluable insights into local consumer behaviour, regulatory requirements, and cultural nuances, facilitating a smoother market entry and increasing the chances of success. By leveraging the local partner's expertise and network, the company can reduce risks and costs associated with international expansion.

In addition to market access, strategic alliances offer the opportunity to share and develop new technologies. In today's fast-paced technological landscape, staying ahead of the curve requires continuous innovation and access to the latest advancements. By forming alliances with technology leaders, companies can benefit from shared research and development efforts, resulting in faster and more cost-effective innovation. For instance, automotive manufacturers might collaborate with technology firms to develop advanced driver-assistance systems (ADAS) or autonomous driving technologies. These partnerships enable both parties to combine their expertise and resources, driving technological advancements that would be challenging to achieve independently.

Resource sharing is another key benefit of strategic alliances. By pooling resources, companies can achieve economies of scale, reduce costs, and enhance operational efficiency. This can include sharing manufacturing facilities, distribution networks, or research and development capabilities. For example, pharmaceutical companies often form alliances to co-develop and commercialise new drugs. By sharing the costs and risks of clinical trials, manufacturing, and marketing, these companies can bring new treatments to market more efficiently and effectively. This collaborative approach not only accelerates the development process but also maximises the potential for commercial success.

Moreover, strategic alliances can accelerate innovation by fostering a culture of collaboration and knowledge exchange. When companies work together, they can cross-pollinate ideas, learn from each other's best practices, and inspire creativity. This collaborative environment encourages experimentation and risk-taking, leading to breakthrough innovations. For instance, the strategic alliance between Microsoft and LinkedIn has enabled both companies to leverage each other's strengths and create new value propositions for their customers. By integrating LinkedIn's vast professional network with Microsoft's productivity tools, the partnership has created innovative solutions that enhance collaboration, learning, and career development for professionals worldwide.

Effective strategic alliances require careful planning, clear communication, and a shared vision. Companies must align their objectives, establish governance structures, and define the roles and responsibilities of each partner. This ensures that both parties are committed to the alliance's success and are working towards common goals. For example, a strategic alliance between two retail giants might involve joint marketing campaigns, shared customer data, and coordinated product launches. By aligning their strategies and leveraging each other's strengths, the companies can create a unified and compelling value proposition for consumers.

Trust and transparency are also crucial for the success of strategic alliances. Companies must build and maintain trust through open communication, mutual respect, and shared decision-making. This involves regularly assessing the alliance's performance, addressing any issues or conflicts promptly, and making necessary adjustments to the partnership agreement. By fostering a culture of trust and collaboration, companies can ensure the long-term success of their strategic alliances.

Avoiding Unnecessary Risks

Sun Tzu wisely emphasises the importance of avoiding roads that must not be followed, armies that must not be attacked, and towns that must not be besieged. This principle, derived from the art of warfare, directly translates into the business world, underscoring the critical need for prudent risk management and the avoidance of unnecessary risks. Companies must meticulously assess the potential risks and rewards of their strategic initiatives, steering clear of actions that could jeopardise their long-term viability. The essence of this approach lies in making informed decisions that safeguard the organisation's future while allowing for sustainable growth.

Effective risk management is a multifaceted process that begins with the identification of potential risks. This involves conducting a comprehensive risk assessment to uncover various types of risks that could impact the business, including financial, operational, market, regulatory, and reputational risks. For example, a financial services firm might identify risks related to market volatility, regulatory changes, and cyber threats. By understanding these risks, the company can develop strategies to mitigate them effectively.

Once potential risks are identified, companies must assess their impact and likelihood. This involves evaluating the severity of each risk and its probability of occurrence. Tools such as risk matrices and scenario analysis can help quantify risks and prioritise them based on their significance. For instance, a manufacturing company might use a risk matrix to assess the impact of supply chain disruptions on production and identify which suppliers or processes are most vulnerable. This assessment allows the company to focus its risk management efforts on the most critical areas.

Developing mitigation strategies is a crucial step in risk management. Companies must create action plans to reduce the likelihood of risks occurring and minimise their impact if they do. This might involve diversifying suppliers, implementing robust cybersecurity measures, or establishing contingency plans for operational disruptions. For example, a retail company might develop a business continuity plan that includes alternative suppliers, emergency response protocols, and communication strategies to ensure it can continue operations during a crisis. By having these plans in place, the company can respond swiftly and effectively to unexpected events.

Avoiding unnecessary risks means making strategic choices that prioritise high-impact opportunities while steering clear of ventures that offer limited returns or significant threats. This involves conducting thorough due diligence and market analysis before embarking on new initiatives. For instance, a company considering entering a highly competitive market with low profit margins must weigh the potential benefits against the challenges and risks. Instead of pursuing this risky venture, the company might choose to focus on niches where it has a unique competitive advantage, such as specialised products or services that cater to a specific customer segment. This targeted approach can result in higher profitability and reduced exposure to risks.

Moreover, prudent risk management requires continuous monitoring and reassessment. The business environment is dynamic, and risks can evolve over time. Companies must regularly review their risk management strategies and update them as needed to ensure they remain effective. This involves staying informed about industry trends, regulatory changes, and emerging threats. For example, a technology company might monitor developments in cybersecurity threats and adjust its defence mechanisms accordingly. By keeping a pulse on the external environment, companies can proactively manage risks and maintain their resilience.

The COVID-19 pandemic is a poignant example of the importance of avoiding unnecessary risks and focusing on high-impact opportunities. Many companies had to quickly adapt their strategies to navigate the uncertainties brought about by the pandemic. Businesses that successfully avoided unnecessary risks were those that demonstrated agility and foresight. For instance, companies that shifted their focus to e-commerce and digital channels were able to sustain operations and meet changing consumer demands. By avoiding the risks associated with traditional brick-and-mortar operations during lockdowns, these companies capitalised on the growing demand for online shopping.

Another illustrative example is Southwest Airlines, known for its disciplined approach to operations and risk management. The airline has consistently focused on maintaining low operational costs, avoiding unnecessary risks such as entering highly competitive international markets with low margins. Instead, Southwest has concentrated on domestic routes where it has a strong competitive advantage. This strategic focus has enabled the airline to achieve high levels of customer satisfaction and operational efficiency while minimising exposure to unnecessary risks.

Strategic Deception & Competitive Advantage

Sun Tzu advises reducing hostile chiefs by inflicting damage on them, creating trouble, and holding out specious allurements. This principle highlights the crucial importance of strategic deception and the creation of competitive advantage in the business world. Companies can achieve this by shaping perceptions that influence competitor behaviour and market dynamics, thereby securing a strategic edge. Competitive advantage involves crafting unique value propositions that set a company apart from its competitors. Strategic deception entails creating uncertainty and ambiguity to mislead competitors about one's true intentions. By skillfully combining these elements, businesses can outmanoeuvre rivals and capture market share.

Creating a competitive advantage begins with developing a unique value proposition that resonates with customers and differentiates the company from its competitors. This involves understanding customer needs and preferences, analysing market trends, and identifying gaps that the company can fill. By offering products or services that provide exceptional value, companies can attract and retain customers, building a loyal customer base. For example, a technology company might develop a revolutionary new gadget that addresses a common pain point for consumers, such as battery life or ease of use. This unique offering can set the company apart from competitors and drive significant market demand.

Strategic deception, on the other hand, involves creating perceptions that mislead competitors about the company's true intentions. This can be a powerful tool for gaining a competitive edge, as it forces competitors to allocate resources and make decisions based on false information. For instance, a company might signal a future product launch to generate buzz and deter competitors from entering the same market. While competitors are focused on responding to the anticipated launch, the company can secretly work on a different strategic initiative, such as enhancing its existing product line or expanding into new markets. By creating uncertainty and ambiguity, the company can keep competitors off balance and maintain its strategic advantage.

The art of strategic deception requires a deep understanding of the competitive landscape and the ability to anticipate competitors' reactions. Companies must carefully craft their messages and actions to influence competitors' perceptions without revealing their true intentions. This involves a combination of public announcements, strategic leaks, and controlled information dissemination. For example, a fashion brand might announce a collaboration with a high-profile designer to create excitement and distract competitors, while its actual focus is on launching a new sustainable fashion line. This strategic manoeuvring allows the company to capture market attention and maintain a competitive edge.

Furthermore, creating competitive advantages involves continuous innovation and improvement. Companies must invest in research and development, explore new technologies, and enhance their product offerings to stay ahead of competitors. By fostering a culture of innovation and encouraging employees to think creatively, companies can develop groundbreaking solutions that set them apart in the market. For instance, a pharmaceutical company might invest in cutting-edge research to develop new treatments for unmet medical needs, positioning itself as a leader in the industry and attracting significant investment and market interest.

Effective use of strategic deception also requires meticulous planning and execution. Companies must ensure that their deceptive strategies are coherent and aligned with their overall strategic goals. This involves coordinating efforts across different departments and teams to create a seamless and believable narrative. For example, a company planning a strategic deception might involve its marketing, public relations, and product development teams to create a comprehensive plan that includes press releases, social media campaigns, and product demonstrations. By presenting a unified front, the company can enhance the credibility of its deception and achieve its strategic objectives.

A prime example of a company that has successfully employed strategic deception and created competitive advantages is Apple. Apple is known for its ability to generate significant buzz and excitement around its product launches, often through strategic deception. The company has mastered the art of creating ambiguity and misdirecting competitors about its true intentions. For instance, Apple might leak information about an upcoming iPhone model, generating anticipation and diverting competitors' focus, while secretly working on a major software update or a new product category. This strategic deception keeps competitors guessing and allows Apple to maintain its competitive edge.

Apple's competitive advantage is also rooted in its unique value propositions, which include innovative design, seamless user experience, and ecosystem integration. The company's commitment to continuous innovation and improvement has resulted in a loyal customer base and strong brand equity. By consistently delivering high-quality products and creating exceptional customer experiences, Apple has set itself apart from competitors and captured significant market share.

Moreover, Apple's strategic deception and competitive advantage extend to its marketing and public relations efforts. The company carefully orchestrates its product launches, creating an aura of mystery and excitement that drives consumer demand. Apple's ability to create compelling narratives and generate media coverage has been instrumental in building its brand and maintaining its market leadership. This strategic approach not only deters competitors but also captivates consumers, creating a virtuous cycle of innovation and growth.

Preparedness & Resilience

Sun Tzu emphasises the paramount importance of relying not on the enemy's actions but on one's own readiness to face any eventualities. This principle is profoundly relevant in the business world, underscoring the critical need for preparedness and resilience. Companies must build robust capabilities and infrastructure to withstand market fluctuations, economic downturns, and competitive pressures. By focusing on preparedness and resilience, organisations can ensure their long-term viability and success in a dynamic and often unpredictable environment.

Preparedness in business involves a comprehensive approach to planning and risk management. Developing contingency plans is a fundamental aspect of preparedness. These plans provide a roadmap for responding to potential disruptions, such as supply chain interruptions, technological failures, or market crises. For example, a company might create a detailed business continuity plan that outlines steps for maintaining operations during a natural disaster. This plan could include alternative suppliers, remote work arrangements, and emergency communication protocols. By having contingency plans in place, companies can quickly and effectively respond to unexpected events, minimising their impact on operations.

Building strong operational capabilities is another critical component of preparedness. Companies must ensure that their processes, systems, and resources are optimised for efficiency and effectiveness. This involves investing in technology, training employees, and continuously improving operations. For instance, a manufacturing company might implement advanced automation technologies to enhance production efficiency and reduce the risk of human error. By building robust operational capabilities, companies can maintain high levels of productivity and quality, even in the face of challenges.

Financial stability is also essential for preparedness. Companies must maintain healthy financial reserves and manage their cash flow effectively to ensure they can weather economic downturns or unexpected expenses. This involves prudent financial planning, budgeting, and cost management. For example, a retail company might establish a financial buffer by setting aside a portion of its profits each year, creating a reserve fund that can be used in times of need. Additionally, the company might diversify its revenue streams to reduce reliance on a single market or product line, enhancing its financial resilience.

Resilience, on the other hand, involves the ability to recover from setbacks and adapt to changing conditions. Companies must cultivate a mindset of agility and flexibility, enabling them to pivot quickly in response to new challenges or opportunities. This requires a culture of continuous improvement, where employees are encouraged to identify areas for enhancement and suggest innovative solutions. For instance, a technology company might regularly review its product development processes, seeking ways to accelerate time-to-market and improve product quality. By fostering a culture of resilience, companies can stay ahead of competitors and remain relevant in a rapidly evolving marketplace.

Adaptability is a key aspect of resilience. Companies must be willing to adjust their strategies, operations, and business models in response to external changes. This involves staying attuned to market trends, customer preferences, and regulatory developments. For example, during the COVID-19 pandemic, many businesses quickly adapted their strategies to address changing market conditions. Companies that successfully navigated the pandemic were those that shifted their focus to e-commerce, implemented remote work policies, and developed new product offerings to meet emerging customer needs. This adaptability allowed them to maintain operations and continue serving their customers despite the disruptions.

Toyota exemplifies the principles of preparedness and resilience in its approach to supply chain management. The company has built resilience into its supply chains by diversifying suppliers, implementing risk management practices, and maintaining operational flexibility. By working with multiple suppliers and sourcing materials from different regions, Toyota reduces its vulnerability to supply chain disruptions. The company also conducts regular risk assessments to identify potential threats and develop mitigation strategies. This proactive approach ensures that Toyota can quickly respond to supply chain interruptions and continue production with minimal impact.

In addition to supply chain resilience, Toyota's commitment to continuous improvement, known as the Toyota Production System (TPS), further enhances its preparedness and resilience. TPS emphasises the elimination of waste, efficient resource utilisation, and continuous process optimisation. This disciplined approach to operations allows Toyota to maintain high levels of productivity and quality, even in challenging conditions. By fostering a culture of continuous improvement, Toyota ensures that its operations remain robust and adaptable, positioning the company for long-term success.

Moreover, resilience is not just about responding to crises; it also involves proactively seeking opportunities for growth and innovation. Companies must be willing to take calculated risks and explore new markets or technologies. This involves investing in research and development, exploring strategic partnerships, and leveraging emerging trends. For example, a pharmaceutical company might invest in the development of new therapies and treatments, positioning itself as a leader in the healthcare industry. By continuously seeking opportunities for innovation, companies can drive growth and stay ahead of competitors.

Avoiding Dangerous Faults

Sun Tzu identifies five dangerous faults that can affect a general: recklessness, cowardice, a hasty temper, a delicate sense of honour, and over-solicitude for subordinates. Translated into the context of modern strategic management, these faults can represent common leadership pitfalls that, if unchecked, may significantly undermine organisational success.

Recklessness:

Taking unnecessary risks without thorough analysis can lead to disastrous consequences. In the business context, this translates to making hasty decisions or entering markets without proper research. Leaders must balance boldness with prudence, ensuring that every major move is backed by comprehensive data and strategic insights. For instance, before launching a new product, a company should conduct market research, feasibility studies, and risk assessments. This thorough approach helps mitigate risks and aligns initiatives with the organisation's overall strategy, ensuring sustainable growth.

Cowardice:

Avoiding necessary risks and failing to seize opportunities can lead to stagnation and lost potential. In today's fast-paced business environment, leaders must be willing to take calculated risks to drive growth and innovation. This means being open to new ideas, exploring uncharted territories, and investing in emerging technologies. For example, a company that avoids digital transformation risks falling behind competitors who embrace new technologies. Leaders must recognise the importance of calculated risk-taking as a catalyst for progress and innovation, pushing the boundaries while maintaining a safety net through careful planning and contingency measures.

Hasty Temper:

Reacting impulsively to challenges and setbacks can undermine strategic initiatives and destabilise the organisation. Leaders must cultivate the ability to maintain composure under pressure, think critically, and make deliberate decisions. This involves taking a step back to assess the situation, gathering relevant information, and consulting with key stakeholders before acting. For instance, during a financial downturn, a leader who impulsively cuts critical investments might harm long-term growth prospects. By maintaining a level head and considering the broader impact of their decisions, leaders can navigate crises more effectively and maintain organisational stability.

Delicate Sense of Honour:

Being overly sensitive to criticism and reputation can lead to defensive behaviour and missed learning opportunities. Leaders must be open to feedback, learn from mistakes, and continuously improve. This involves fostering a culture of transparency where constructive criticism is welcomed and viewed as a pathway to growth. For example, a leader who responds defensively to employee feedback may stifle open communication and innovation. Instead, leaders should encourage honest dialogue, acknowledge areas for improvement, and demonstrate a commitment to personal and organisational development. This openness not only builds trust but also drives a culture of continuous improvement.

Over-Solicitude for Subordinates:

Overprotecting employees and avoiding difficult decisions can create inefficiencies and hinder performance. Leaders must balance empathy with accountability, ensuring that decisions are made in the best interest of the organisation. This involves setting clear expectations, providing support and resources, and holding team members accountable for their performance. For example, a leader who consistently shields underperforming employees from consequences may demotivate high performers and reduce overall productivity. By fostering a culture of accountability, leaders can drive higher performance standards and ensure that all employees are aligned with organisational goals. This balance of empathy and accountability creates a motivated and high-performing workforce.

To illustrate these principles in action, consider the leadership approach at Amazon. Under Jeff Bezos, Amazon has demonstrated a keen ability to avoid these dangerous faults, striking a balance between bold innovation and prudent risk management. Bezos has fostered a culture that values calculated risk-taking, continuous improvement, and accountability. Amazon's strategic initiatives, from expanding into cloud computing with AWS to revolutionising logistics and delivery, reflect a careful balance of bold vision and meticulous planning. This approach has enabled Amazon to maintain its market leadership and drive sustained growth.

Recklessness is mitigated through Amazon's data-driven decision-making processes, ensuring that strategic moves are informed by comprehensive analysis and insights. The company's bold investments in emerging technologies, such as artificial intelligence and robotics, are supported by thorough research and feasibility studies. This balance of boldness and prudence has driven Amazon's innovation while managing risks effectively.

Avoiding cowardice, Amazon has consistently embraced new opportunities and expanded into various sectors. The company's entry into cloud computing with AWS and its foray into the grocery market with the acquisition of Whole Foods exemplify calculated risk-taking. These strategic moves were based on careful analysis and have positioned Amazon as a leader in multiple industries.

Maintaining composure under pressure, Amazon's leadership has navigated challenges such as antitrust scrutiny and market competition with a strategic and deliberate approach. Bezos's focus on long-term growth rather than short-term gains has ensured that decisions are made with a broader perspective, fostering stability and resilience.

Addressing a delicate sense of honour, Amazon encourages a culture of feedback and continuous improvement. The company's Leadership Principles, such as "Earn Trust" and "Learn and Be Curious," emphasise the importance of transparency, feedback, and personal development. This openness drives innovation and fosters a culture of trust and collaboration.

Balancing empathy with accountability, Amazon's performance management system sets clear expectations and holds employees accountable for their contributions. The company provides support and resources to help employees succeed while ensuring that performance standards are met. This balance drives high performance and aligns employees with the organisation's strategic goals.

Summary

Sun Tzu's *Variation of Tactics* offers timeless insights that are highly relevant to modern strategic management. The principles of flexibility, strategic alliances, risk management, competitive advantage, preparedness, and resilient leadership provide a robust framework for navigating the complexities of the business world.

CHAPTER 9 – THE ARMY ON THE MARCH

> *To begin by bluster, but afterwards to take fright at the enemy's numbers, shows a supreme lack of intelligence.*
>
> Sun Tzu

Sun Tzu's *The Army on the March* delves into the intricacies of positioning, observation, and adaptability. These principles are highly relevant to modern strategic management, where businesses must navigate competitive landscapes, anticipate market changes, and leverage their strengths.

Strategic Positioning & Environmental Awareness

Sun Tzu begins The Army on the March by emphasising the paramount importance of strategic positioning and environmental awareness. He advises passing quickly over mountains, camping in high places, and avoiding heights during combat. This ancient wisdom underscores the necessity for companies to position themselves advantageously and remain keenly aware of their environment. In the business realm, strategic positioning and environmental awareness are critical for achieving competitive advantage and sustaining long-term success.

Strategic positioning involves identifying and occupying a unique market position that leverages a company's strengths while mitigating its weaknesses. This process requires a deep understanding of the company's core competencies, market dynamics, and competitive landscape. Companies must continuously assess their market environment, analysing factors such as customer preferences, technological advancements, and regulatory changes. By doing so, they can identify opportunities for differentiation and craft strategies that set them apart from competitors. For instance, a technology company might position itself as a leader in innovation by investing heavily in research and development, fostering a culture of creativity, and continuously bringing groundbreaking products to market. This strategic focus allows the company to establish itself as an industry pioneer, attracting customers who seek cutting-edge solutions.

Effective strategic positioning also involves the deliberate selection of target markets and customer segments. Companies must identify the most lucrative and strategically important markets to focus their efforts. This requires conducting thorough market research to understand the needs, preferences, and behaviours of different customer segments. For example, a luxury brand might target affluent consumers who value exclusivity and premium quality. By tailoring its marketing efforts and product offerings to this specific audience, the brand can create a strong emotional connection with customers and build lasting brand loyalty.

Furthermore, strategic positioning entails developing a compelling value proposition that clearly communicates the unique benefits of the company's products or services. This value proposition should resonate with customers and address their specific pain points and desires. For instance, a company that offers eco-friendly products might emphasise its commitment to sustainability and environmental stewardship in its marketing messaging. This appeals to environmentally conscious consumers and differentiates the company from competitors that may not prioritise sustainability.

Environmental awareness is equally crucial for business success. Companies must stay attuned to market trends, customer preferences, and competitor actions to anticipate changes and adapt their strategies accordingly. This involves continuously monitoring the external environment through market intelligence, data analytics, and industry analysis. By keeping a finger on the pulse of the market, companies can identify emerging trends, potential threats, and new opportunities. For example, a retail company might use data analytics to track shifts in consumer purchasing behaviour, allowing it to adjust its inventory and marketing strategies in real-time. This proactive approach ensures that the company remains responsive to changing market conditions and maintains its competitive edge.

Environmental awareness also involves understanding the broader economic, social, and technological context in which the company operates. Companies must consider factors such as economic cycles, demographic shifts, and technological disruptions that can impact their business. For example, a company that recognises the growing trend towards digital transformation might invest in developing digital solutions and expanding its online presence. By staying ahead of technological advancements, the company can capture new market opportunities and enhance its competitive positioning.

Netflix serves as a prime example of a company that has successfully leveraged strategic positioning and environmental awareness to achieve sustained success. Originally a DVD rental service, Netflix recognised the shifting consumer preferences towards on-demand digital content and strategically adapted its business model to focus on streaming services. By investing in technology and content creation, Netflix positioned itself as a leader in the entertainment industry. The company continuously monitors consumer preferences and uses data analytics to inform its content strategy, ensuring that it offers a diverse and appealing library of shows and movies. This ability to anticipate and respond to changing market dynamics has enabled Netflix to stay ahead of the competition and capture significant market share.

In addition to adapting its business model, Netflix's strategic positioning is further reinforced by its commitment to original content production. By creating exclusive and high-quality content, Netflix differentiates itself from competitors and builds strong brand loyalty. The company's investment in original programming, such as critically acclaimed series and movies, has attracted millions of subscribers worldwide. This strategic focus on content creation not only enhances Netflix's value proposition but also strengthens its competitive advantage in a crowded market.

Moreover, Netflix's environmental awareness extends to its global expansion strategy. The company carefully analyses local market conditions, cultural preferences, and regulatory requirements to tailor its offerings to different regions. For example, Netflix produces localised content that resonates with audiences in specific countries, enhancing its appeal and market penetration. By understanding and adapting to the unique characteristics of each market, Netflix successfully navigates the complexities of international expansion and solidifies its position as a global entertainment leader.

Adaptability & Flexibility

Sun Tzu advises adapting tactics based on the terrain and circumstances, emphasising the importance of moving quickly through salt marshes, avoiding precipitous cliffs, and waiting for rivers to subside before crossing. This ancient wisdom translates directly to modern strategic management, highlighting the critical need for adaptability and flexibility in response to changing conditions. In today's rapidly evolving business environment, the ability to pivot strategies, processes, and operations in response to market dynamics and emerging opportunities is essential for sustaining competitive advantage and achieving long-term success.

Adaptability involves the capacity to pivot strategies and operational approaches swiftly in response to external changes. This requires an organisational culture that values agility and encourages continuous learning and innovation. By fostering an adaptable mindset, companies can respond proactively to market trends, technological advancements, and shifts in customer preferences. For example, during the COVID-19 pandemic, many businesses had to rapidly adapt their strategies to address new market realities. Companies that successfully navigated the pandemic were those that embraced e-commerce, implemented remote work policies, and developed new product offerings tailored to changing consumer needs. By being adaptable, these companies not only survived the crisis but also positioned themselves for future growth.

Agile methodologies are a key enabler of adaptability. Agile practices, such as iterative planning, cross-functional collaboration, and continuous feedback loops, allow companies to respond quickly to changing circumstances. This approach involves breaking down large projects into smaller, manageable tasks that can be adjusted based on real-time feedback. For instance, a software development company might use agile methodologies to deliver incremental updates and enhancements, ensuring that the final product meets evolving customer requirements. By adopting agile practices, companies can enhance their responsiveness and remain competitive in a fast-paced market.

Implementing flexible planning processes is also essential for enhancing adaptability. Companies must develop strategic plans that are flexible and allow for adjustments based on changing conditions. This involves setting clear objectives, identifying key performance indicators, and regularly reviewing progress to ensure alignment with strategic goals. For example, a manufacturing company might adopt a rolling planning process, where strategic plans are revisited and updated quarterly based on market conditions and operational performance. By maintaining flexible planning processes, companies can stay agile and responsive, making timely adjustments to their strategies as needed.

Fostering a culture of innovation is critical for driving adaptability and flexibility. Companies should create an environment that encourages creativity, experimentation, and risk-taking. This involves providing employees with the resources and autonomy to explore new ideas and develop innovative solutions. For example, a technology company might establish an innovation lab where employees can collaborate on cutting-edge projects and prototype new products. By promoting a culture of innovation, companies can drive continuous improvement and stay ahead of industry trends.

Furthermore, adaptability requires a keen awareness of the external environment. Companies must continuously monitor market trends, customer preferences, and competitor actions to anticipate changes and adapt their strategies accordingly. This involves leveraging market intelligence, data analytics, and industry analysis to gain insights into emerging opportunities and potential threats. For example, a retail company might use data analytics to track shifts in consumer purchasing behaviour, allowing it to adjust its inventory and marketing strategies in real-time. This proactive approach ensures that the company remains responsive to changing market conditions and maintains its competitive edge.

Netflix serves as a prime example of a company that has successfully leveraged adaptability and flexibility to achieve sustained success. Originally a DVD rental service, Netflix recognised the shifting consumer preferences towards on-demand digital content and strategically adapted its business model to focus on streaming services. By investing in technology and content creation, Netflix positioned itself as a leader in the entertainment industry. The company continuously monitors consumer preferences and uses data analytics to inform its content strategy, ensuring that it offers a diverse and appealing library of shows and movies. This ability to anticipate and respond to changing market dynamics has enabled Netflix to stay ahead of the competition and capture significant market share.

In addition to adapting its business model, Netflix's strategic flexibility is further reinforced by its commitment to original content production. By creating exclusive and high-quality content, Netflix differentiates itself from competitors and builds strong brand loyalty. The company's investment in original programming, such as critically acclaimed series and movies, has attracted millions of subscribers worldwide. This strategic focus on content creation not only enhances Netflix's value proposition but also strengthens its competitive advantage in a crowded market.

Moreover, Netflix's adaptability extends to its global expansion strategy. The company carefully analyses local market conditions, cultural preferences, and regulatory requirements to tailor its offerings to different regions. For example, Netflix produces localised content that resonates with audiences in specific countries, enhancing its appeal and market penetration. By understanding and adapting to the unique characteristics of each market, Netflix successfully navigates the complexities of international expansion and solidifies its position as a global entertainment leader.

Observation & Intelligence

Sun Tzu emphasises the critical importance of observing signs of the enemy and interpreting their meaning. He advises that interpreting movements, dust patterns, and other subtle indicators can provide valuable insights into enemy actions and intentions. In the business world, this principle translates into the crucial role of observation and intelligence in strategic decision-making. Companies must develop robust mechanisms to gather, analyse, and interpret market intelligence to stay ahead in a competitive landscape.

Market intelligence involves systematically collecting and analysing data on various aspects of the market, including trends, customer behaviours, and competitor actions. This data-driven approach enables businesses to make informed decisions, anticipate competitive threats, and identify new opportunities. For instance, a retail company might use market intelligence to understand seasonal shopping trends, allowing it to adjust its inventory and marketing strategies to meet customer demand more effectively. This proactive approach ensures that the company remains responsive to market dynamics and maximises its competitive advantage.

Understanding market trends is a fundamental aspect of market intelligence. Companies need to track and analyse changes in consumer preferences, technological advancements, and industry developments. By doing so, they can identify emerging trends and adjust their strategies accordingly. For example, a technology company might monitor the increasing demand for smart home devices and decide to invest in developing new products in this category. By staying attuned to market trends, the company can capitalise on new opportunities and maintain its relevance in a rapidly evolving market.

Customer behaviour analysis is another critical component of market intelligence. Companies must gather data on customer preferences, purchasing patterns, and feedback to gain insights into their needs and expectations. This information allows businesses to tailor their products, services, and marketing efforts to better meet customer demands. For instance, an e-commerce company might analyse customer browsing and purchasing behaviour to recommend personalised products and enhance the shopping experience. By understanding and addressing customer needs, the company can build stronger relationships and drive customer loyalty.

Competitor analysis is essential for anticipating competitive threats and formulating effective strategies. Companies must keep a close eye on their competitors' actions, such as product launches, marketing campaigns, and strategic initiatives. This involves analysing competitors' strengths, weaknesses, opportunities, and threats (SWOT analysis) to identify potential areas of advantage. For example, a pharmaceutical company might track its competitors' drug development pipelines and regulatory approvals to anticipate market movements and adjust its research and development priorities. By staying informed about competitors' activities, the company can proactively defend its market position and explore new growth opportunities.

Investing in data analytics is crucial for leveraging market intelligence effectively. Advanced data analytics tools and technologies enable companies to process vast amounts of data and extract actionable insights. Companies like Amazon and Google are exemplary in their use of data analytics to gain deep insights into customer preferences and market trends. Amazon, for instance, utilises data analytics to personalise the shopping experience, recommend products, and optimise its supply chain operations. By leveraging data-driven insights, Amazon can make informed strategic decisions that enhance customer satisfaction and drive sales growth.

Google, on the other hand, uses data analytics to understand user behaviour and improve its search algorithms, advertising platforms, and product offerings. By analysing search patterns, user interactions, and feedback, Google can continuously refine its services to deliver more relevant and valuable experiences to users. This data-driven approach not only strengthens Google's competitive position but also fuels innovation and growth.

Furthermore, observation and intelligence extend beyond market data to include environmental scanning and scenario planning. Companies must monitor the broader economic, social, and regulatory environment to anticipate changes that could impact their business. This involves staying informed about economic indicators, regulatory developments, and geopolitical trends. For example, a manufacturing company might monitor trade policies and tariffs to assess their impact on supply chain costs and adjust sourcing strategies accordingly. By considering the broader environment, companies can develop robust strategies that navigate uncertainties and enhance their resilience.

Scenario planning is another valuable tool for strategic decision-making. This involves creating and analysing multiple scenarios based on different assumptions about the future. Companies can use scenario planning to explore potential outcomes and develop contingency plans for various situations. For instance, a financial services firm might create scenarios based on different interest rate environments to assess their impact on investment portfolios and develop strategies to mitigate risks. By preparing for multiple scenarios, the firm can enhance its ability to adapt to changing conditions and seize opportunities.

Managing Resources & Logistics

Sun Tzu astutely highlights the importance of managing resources and logistics to ensure the army's effectiveness. He advises ensuring the availability of water and grass when fighting in a salt-marsh and camping in sunny places to prevent disease. In the business world, this principle underscores the critical importance of effective resource management and logistics, which are essential for maintaining operational efficiency and achieving strategic objectives. Companies must optimise the use of financial, human, and physical resources to ensure that their operations run smoothly and that they can respond agilely to market demands and competitive pressures.

Effective resource management begins with the efficient allocation of financial resources. This involves prudent budgeting, rigorous financial planning, and continuous monitoring of expenses. Companies must ensure that their financial resources are allocated in a way that maximises return on investment and supports strategic initiatives. For example, a company planning to expand its product line might allocate funds towards research and development, marketing, and production capacity. By strategically investing financial resources, the company can drive innovation, enhance its market position, and achieve long-term growth.

Human resource management is another critical aspect of resource optimisation. Companies must attract, develop, and retain talented employees who can contribute to achieving organisational goals. This involves implementing effective recruitment processes, providing opportunities for professional development, and fostering a positive work environment. For instance, a technology company might invest in training programmes to upskill its workforce, ensuring that employees have the latest knowledge and skills to drive innovation. By nurturing talent and creating a supportive culture, companies can enhance employee engagement and productivity.

Physical resource management encompasses the efficient use of facilities, equipment, and materials. Companies must ensure that their physical resources are utilised optimally to minimise waste and maximise productivity. This involves implementing maintenance programmes, optimising inventory levels, and leveraging technology to streamline operations. For example, a manufacturing company might use predictive maintenance technologies to monitor equipment performance and prevent breakdowns, thereby reducing downtime and maintaining production efficiency. By effectively managing physical resources, companies can improve operational efficiency and reduce costs.

Logistics management plays a crucial role in ensuring that resources are available when and where they are needed. This involves coordinating the movement of goods, managing supply chains, and optimising distribution networks. Companies must ensure that their logistics processes are streamlined to support timely delivery and meet customer expectations. For instance, a retail company might use advanced logistics software to track inventory levels, forecast demand, and optimise delivery routes. By enhancing logistics efficiency, companies can reduce lead times, lower transportation costs, and improve service levels.

Toyota and Walmart are exemplary models of companies that have built their competitive advantage on efficient supply chain management. Toyota's adoption of the lean manufacturing system, also known as the Toyota Production System (TPS), emphasises continuous improvement, waste reduction, and efficient resource utilisation. TPS involves practices such as just-in-time (JIT) inventory management, where materials are delivered exactly when needed, reducing inventory costs and minimising waste. Toyota's commitment to lean principles has enabled the company to achieve high levels of operational efficiency, product quality, and customer satisfaction.

Walmart's success is also deeply rooted in its efficient supply chain management. The company's logistics strategy focuses on optimising the flow of goods from suppliers to stores, ensuring that products are available to customers at the right time and place. Walmart leverages advanced technology, such as radio-frequency identification (RFID) and data analytics, to track inventory, forecast demand, and manage replenishment processes. The company's investment in an extensive distribution network, including strategically located distribution centres and a fleet of transportation vehicles, ensures seamless logistics operations. By maintaining tight control over its supply chain, Walmart can reduce costs, offer competitive prices, and deliver a superior shopping experience to customers.

Moreover, effective resource management and logistics involve continuous monitoring and improvement. Companies must regularly assess their resource allocation and logistics processes to identify areas for enhancement. This involves analysing performance metrics, gathering feedback, and implementing best practices. For example, a company might conduct regular supply chain audits to assess efficiency, identify bottlenecks, and implement corrective actions.

By fostering a culture of continuous improvement, companies can ensure that their resource management and logistics processes remain agile and responsive to changing market conditions.

Maintaining Discipline & Morale

Sun Tzu emphasises the crucial importance of maintaining discipline and morale within the army, advising that soldiers be treated with humanity while enforcing discipline through firm control. In the business context, this principle underscores the dual necessity of strict adherence to established processes and the cultivation of a positive organisational culture. Companies that successfully balance discipline and morale are better positioned to enhance productivity, drive innovation, and achieve sustained high performance.

Discipline in the business world involves a rigorous commitment to established processes, operational excellence, and consistent performance. This requires a well-defined set of policies, procedures, and standards that guide employees' actions and decisions. Companies must ensure that these processes are clearly communicated and understood by all employees, fostering a culture of accountability and consistency. For example, a manufacturing company might implement lean production methodologies to streamline operations, reduce waste, and enhance efficiency. By adhering to these disciplined practices, the company can maintain high-quality standards and optimise resource utilisation, resulting in improved productivity and reduced costs.

Operational excellence is a key component of discipline. It involves continuously seeking ways to improve processes, enhance efficiency, and deliver superior value to customers. This requires a commitment to continuous improvement and the adoption of best practices across the organisation. For instance, a healthcare provider might implement evidence-based practices and quality improvement initiatives to enhance patient care and outcomes. By fostering a culture of excellence, the organisation can ensure consistent performance and high standards of service delivery.

Performance management is another critical aspect of maintaining discipline. Companies must establish clear performance metrics and regularly assess employee performance against these benchmarks. This involves setting specific, measurable, achievable, relevant, and time-bound (SMART) goals, providing regular feedback, and conducting performance reviews. For example, a sales team might have clear targets for revenue growth, customer acquisition, and market penetration, with regular reviews to track progress and provide constructive feedback. By maintaining a disciplined approach to performance management, companies can drive accountability, motivate employees, and achieve strategic objectives.

Morale involves fostering a positive organisational culture that values and supports employees. This requires creating an environment where employees feel valued, respected, and motivated to contribute their best efforts. Companies must provide opportunities for growth and development, recognising and rewarding employees' contributions. For example, a technology company might offer professional development programmes, mentorship opportunities, and career advancement pathways to help employees develop their skills and achieve their career goals. By investing in employee development, companies can enhance engagement, retention, and overall job satisfaction.

Creating a positive work culture involves promoting work-life balance, fostering collaboration, and encouraging open communication. Companies should implement policies and initiatives that support employees' well-being, such as flexible work arrangements, wellness programmes, and mental health support. For instance, a company might offer remote work options, on-site fitness facilities, and employee assistance programmes to support work-life balance and overall well-being. By prioritising employees' well-being, companies can enhance morale and create a more engaged and productive workforce.

Recognition and rewards are essential for maintaining high morale. Companies must implement recognition programmes that celebrate employees' achievements and contributions. This can include monetary rewards, promotions, public recognition, and non-monetary incentives such as extra time off or special projects. For example, a company might establish an "Employee of the Month" programme to highlight outstanding performance and inspire others. Recognising and rewarding employees not only boosts morale but also reinforces desired behaviours and motivates employees to continue striving for excellence.

Employee engagement is a critical factor in maintaining morale. Engaged employees are more committed, motivated, and productive. Companies must actively seek to engage employees through meaningful work, opportunities for growth, and a supportive work environment. For example, a company might conduct regular employee engagement surveys to gather feedback and identify areas for improvement. By acting on this feedback and implementing changes that address employees' needs and concerns, companies can enhance engagement and create a more positive work environment.

Leadership plays a vital role in maintaining discipline and morale. Leaders must set the tone for the organisation, modelling the behaviours and values that they expect from employees. This involves demonstrating integrity, transparency, and empathy in their interactions with employees. Leaders must also provide clear direction, support, and resources to help employees achieve their goals. For example, a leader who actively listens to employees' concerns, provides regular feedback, and offers guidance and support can build trust and foster a positive work culture. By embodying the principles of discipline and morale, leaders can inspire and motivate employees to perform at their best.

Companies like Google and Microsoft exemplify the successful balance of discipline and morale in their organisational cultures. Google emphasises employee engagement and satisfaction, fostering a culture of innovation and excellence. The company offers a wide range of benefits and programmes to support employees' well-being, including flexible work arrangements, wellness programmes, and professional development opportunities. By prioritising employee satisfaction and fostering a positive work environment, Google has created a highly engaged and productive workforce that drives innovation and success.

Microsoft, under the leadership of Satya Nadella, has also placed a strong emphasis on employee engagement and satisfaction. Nadella's focus on a growth mindset, continuous learning, and collaboration has transformed the company's culture and driven significant advancements in technology and market leadership. Microsoft provides opportunities for professional development, recognises and rewards employees' contributions, and fosters a culture of innovation and excellence. By maintaining discipline and morale, Microsoft has achieved high levels of employee engagement and organisational performance.

Anticipating & Responding to Competitor Actions

Sun Tzu provides meticulous guidance on interpreting enemy actions and responding effectively. He advises recognising signs of ambush, interpreting dust patterns, and understanding when the enemy is likely to advance or retreat. Translated into the business world, this principle emphasises the critical importance of anticipating and responding to competitor actions. Companies must develop robust mechanisms to monitor, analyse, and proactively address competitors' strategies, product launches, and market moves.

Anticipating competitor actions begins with continuous and comprehensive monitoring. Companies must keep a vigilant eye on their competitors by tracking their strategic initiatives, new product developments, marketing campaigns, and market expansions. This involves utilising various tools and sources, such as industry reports, press releases, social media, and market research, to gather relevant data. For example, a consumer electronics company might subscribe to industry publications, attend trade shows, and monitor competitors' social media channels to stay informed about their latest activities. This systematic approach to intelligence gathering allows companies to build a detailed understanding of their competitors' actions and intentions.

Understanding competitors' strengths and weaknesses is a fundamental aspect of developing effective counter-strategies. This involves conducting a thorough analysis of competitors' capabilities, market positions, and potential vulnerabilities. Companies can use frameworks such as SWOT (Strengths, Weaknesses, Opportunities, Threats) analysis to systematically evaluate their competitors. For instance, a software company might analyse a competitor's product features, customer reviews, and market performance to identify areas where the competitor excels and where it falls short. By gaining insights into competitors' strengths and weaknesses, the company can craft strategies that leverage its own strengths to exploit competitors' vulnerabilities and counter their moves effectively.

Competitive benchmarking is another valuable tool for anticipating and responding to competitor actions. Companies can compare their own performance, processes, and products against those of their competitors to identify gaps and areas for improvement. This involves collecting data on key performance indicators (KPIs) such as market share, customer satisfaction, product quality, and innovation. For example, an automotive manufacturer might benchmark its vehicle performance metrics against those of leading competitors to identify opportunities for enhancing fuel efficiency, safety, and customer features. By continuously benchmarking against competitors, companies can ensure that they remain competitive and responsive to market dynamics.

Developing proactive strategies to counter competitors' actions is essential for gaining a competitive edge. Companies must be agile and innovative in their approach, ready to pivot and adapt their strategies in response to competitors' moves. This might involve launching new products, enhancing existing offerings, adjusting pricing strategies, or entering new markets. For instance, a pharmaceutical company might respond to a competitor's launch of a new drug by accelerating its own drug development timeline or introducing a new treatment option. By being proactive and responsive, companies can effectively counter competitors' initiatives and capture market share.

An illustrative example of successful anticipation and response to competitor actions is Apple's strategic approach. Apple continuously monitors its competitors' product launches, market strategies, and technological advancements. By closely observing competitors' actions, Apple can anticipate market trends and identify opportunities for innovation. For example, when competitors introduced smartphones with larger screens and advanced camera features, Apple responded by launching the iPhone Plus series, which incorporated these features while maintaining Apple's signature design and user experience. This proactive approach enabled Apple to capture consumer interest and maintain its market leadership.

Apple's ability to anticipate and respond to competitor actions is further reinforced by its commitment to continuous innovation. The company invests heavily in research and development to stay ahead of technological advancements and deliver groundbreaking products. By fostering a culture of creativity and experimentation, Apple can quickly adapt to changing market dynamics and introduce innovative solutions that set it apart from competitors. For example, the launch of the Apple Watch demonstrated Apple's ability to diversify its product portfolio and enter new market segments, capturing significant market share in the wearable technology industry.

Moreover, Apple's strategic use of competitive intelligence and data analytics enhances its ability to make informed decisions. The company leverages advanced analytics tools to gather insights into customer preferences, market trends, and competitor activities. This data-driven approach informs Apple's product development, marketing, and pricing strategies, ensuring that the company remains responsive and competitive. For instance, Apple uses customer feedback and market research to continuously refine its products and enhance the user experience, driving customer loyalty and satisfaction.

In addition to monitoring and responding to competitors, Apple employs strategic alliances and collaborations to strengthen its market position. The company partners with other industry leaders to enhance its product offerings and expand its market reach. For example, Apple's collaboration with Nike on the Apple Watch Nike+ edition combined the strengths of both brands to create a product tailored for fitness enthusiasts. This strategic partnership allowed Apple to tap into Nike's extensive customer base and expertise in the fitness industry, further enhancing its competitive advantage.

Strategic Patience & Timing

Sun Tzu emphasises the crucial importance of strategic patience and timing, advising that one should wait for the right moment to deliver an attack and avoid unnecessary confrontations. This principle is profoundly relevant in the business world, underscoring the need for strategic patience and timing in decision-making. Companies that master the art of waiting for the most opportune moment to execute strategic initiatives, launch new products, or enter new markets are better positioned to maximise their impact and ensure success.

Strategic patience involves a disciplined approach to decision-making, where companies carefully evaluate the timing and potential impact of their actions. This requires a deep understanding of market dynamics, customer behaviours, and competitive landscape. Companies must resist the urge to rush into decisions and instead wait for the optimal conditions that will enhance their chances of success. For example, a technology company planning to launch a new product might conduct extensive market research to identify the best time for release, considering factors such as seasonal demand, competitor activity, and economic conditions. By exercising strategic patience, the company can ensure that its product launch generates maximum interest and achieves strong market penetration.

Timing is a critical element in strategic decision-making. It involves identifying the precise moment when conditions are most favourable for executing a strategic action. This requires continuous monitoring of the external environment and staying attuned to shifts in market trends, customer preferences, and industry developments. For instance, a retail company might decide to introduce a new clothing line at the start of the holiday shopping season, capitalising on increased consumer spending and heightened market activity. By aligning strategic actions with the most opportune timing, companies can maximise their impact and drive significant results.

Successful companies recognise that timing is not just about launching new products or entering new markets; it also involves knowing when to pause, observe, and adjust strategies. This adaptive approach ensures that companies remain agile and responsive to changing conditions. For example, during an economic downturn, a company might delay a planned expansion to conserve resources and focus on strengthening its core operations. By waiting for more stable economic conditions, the company can mitigate risks and position itself for long-term growth.

Anticipating market trends and aligning strategic actions with these trends is essential for maximising the impact of timing. Companies must leverage data analytics, market research, and industry insights to forecast future trends and identify emerging opportunities. For example, a pharmaceutical company might track advancements in biotechnology and regulatory developments to determine the best time to introduce a new drug. By staying ahead of market trends, the company can capture market share and establish itself as a leader in innovation.

Strategic patience and timing also involve recognising and seizing opportunistic moments. Companies must be ready to act swiftly when the right opportunities arise, even if it means deviating from planned strategies. This requires a balance between patience and agility, where companies remain vigilant and prepared to capitalise on unexpected opportunities. For instance, a financial services firm might take advantage of a sudden market dip to acquire undervalued assets, positioning itself for future gains. By maintaining strategic flexibility and readiness, companies can turn challenges into opportunities and drive growth.

Tesla's success in the electric vehicle (EV) market exemplifies the power of strategic patience and timing. Tesla strategically timed its introduction of electric vehicles to coincide with growing consumer interest in sustainable transportation and advancements in battery technology. By patiently waiting for the market conditions to be favourable, Tesla was able to capture significant consumer interest and establish itself as a leader in the EV market. The company's timing was further reinforced by its investment in building a comprehensive charging infrastructure, ensuring that its customers had access to convenient charging options, thereby enhancing the overall ownership experience.

Tesla's strategic timing extended to its expansion plans and product line diversification. The company introduced the Model S, a high-performance electric sedan, at a time when there was increasing demand for luxury electric vehicles. This was followed by the launch of the Model 3, a more affordable option that targeted the mass market. By carefully timing these product launches, Tesla was able to capture a broad customer base and drive substantial sales growth. Additionally, Tesla's entry into energy solutions, such as solar panels and energy storage systems, was timed to align with the growing focus on renewable energy. This strategic diversification not only reinforced Tesla's commitment to sustainability but also created new revenue streams and growth opportunities.

Moreover, Tesla's approach to strategic patience and timing is evident in its handling of market expansions. The company has gradually expanded its presence in international markets, carefully assessing local conditions and regulatory environments before making significant investments. For example, Tesla's entry into the Chinese market was strategically timed to leverage the country's support for electric vehicles and growing consumer demand. By building a Gigafactory in Shanghai, Tesla was able to produce vehicles locally, reduce costs, and enhance its competitiveness in the Chinese market.

Strategic partnerships and collaborations are also part of Tesla's timing strategy. The company has formed alliances with key suppliers and technology partners to ensure a steady supply of components and access to cutting-edge innovations. For instance, Tesla's partnership with Panasonic for battery production has been instrumental in supporting its ambitious production targets and ensuring the quality and performance of its vehicles. By timing these partnerships to coincide with product launches and market expansions, Tesla has strengthened its market position and operational capabilities.

Summary

Sun Tzu's *The Army on the March* offers timeless insights that are highly relevant to modern strategic management. The principles of strategic positioning, adaptability, observation, resource management, discipline, anticipation, and strategic patience provide a robust framework for navigating the complexities of the business world.

CHAPTER 10 – TERRAIN

*Regard your soldiers as your children,
and they will follow you into the deepest valleys;
look on them as your own beloved sons,
and they will stand by you even unto death.*

Sun Tzu

Sun Tzu's *Terrain* focuses on understanding and leveraging different types of terrain to gain strategic advantage. These principles are highly applicable to modern strategic management, where businesses must navigate complex market landscapes, adapt to changing conditions, and optimise their resources.

Understanding & Navigating Different Market Conditions

Sun Tzu distinguishes six types of terrain: accessible ground, entangling ground, temporising ground, narrow passes, precipitous heights, and positions at a great distance from the enemy. In the business context, these terrains can be seen as different market conditions and competitive landscapes that companies must navigate. By understanding these terrains and developing appropriate strategies, companies can effectively position themselves and achieve long-term success.

Accessible Ground:

Ground that can be freely traversed by both sides represents markets that are easily accessible to all competitors. In such markets, the barriers to entry are low, and many companies can participate without significant restrictions. To succeed in these markets, companies must focus on occupying advantageous positions that allow them to stand out from the competition. This involves establishing a strong brand presence, developing a loyal customer base, and securing reliable supply chains. By positioning themselves strategically and leveraging their strengths, companies can gain a competitive edge and capitalise on market opportunities. For instance, a consumer goods company operating in a highly competitive market might invest in brand building and customer loyalty programmes to differentiate itself from rivals and secure a significant market share.

Entangling Ground:

Ground that is easy to abandon but hard to re-occupy represents markets with high entry and exit barriers. These markets require companies to invest substantial resources to enter, but exiting can be relatively easy. However, re-entering the market once exited can be challenging and costly. Companies must be cautious when entering such markets and ensure they have a clear strategy for gaining and maintaining a competitive position. This involves conducting thorough market research, assessing the competitive landscape, and developing a robust business plan. If a competitor is unprepared, a company may seize the opportunity to gain market share by offering superior products or services. However, if the competitor is well-prepared and entrenched, attempting to enter or re-enter the market can lead to disaster. For example, a technology firm considering entering the semiconductor market must carefully evaluate the high capital investment required and the presence of established players before making a decision.

Temporising Ground:

Ground where neither side gains by making the first move represents markets with uncertain or fluctuating conditions. In such markets, the environment is volatile, and making premature moves can result in significant risks. Companies should avoid taking hasty actions and instead adopt a wait-and-see approach. By monitoring the market, gathering intelligence, and analysing competitors' actions, companies can entice competitors to make the first move and then capitalise on their weaknesses. This strategic patience allows companies to gain a strategic advantage by positioning themselves to respond effectively to changing conditions. For instance, during an economic downturn, a financial services company might wait to see how competitors adjust their strategies before launching new products or services, enabling it to learn from others' mistakes and seize opportunities as the market stabilises.

Narrow Passes:

Ground that is difficult to traverse and easily defensible represents niche markets or market segments with specific entry barriers. These markets often have specialised requirements or limited customer bases, making it challenging for new entrants to establish a foothold. Companies that can occupy these positions first should fortify their presence and defend against competitors by continuously innovating and improving their offerings. This involves focusing on quality, customer relationships, and unique value propositions. If a competitor occupies these positions, companies should only challenge them if the competitor's defences are weak and there is a clear opportunity for success. For example, a pharmaceutical company operating in a niche market for rare disease treatments must invest in research and development to maintain its competitive edge and defend its market position.

Precipitous Heights:

Ground that is advantageous due to its elevation represents markets with inherent advantages, such as technological leadership, regulatory protection, or unique intellectual property. Companies that can secure these positions should leverage their advantages and wait for competitors to approach. This involves investing in research and development, protecting intellectual property, and capitalising on regulatory advantages. If a competitor holds these positions, companies should avoid direct confrontation and instead attempt to lure the competitor away by offering alternative solutions or targeting different market segments. For example, a company with a patented technology that provides a significant competitive edge should focus on maximising its market potential while deterring competitors from entering the space through continuous innovation and strategic partnerships.

Distant Positions:

Ground that is far from the enemy represents markets with low competitive intensity or low relevance to the core business. Engaging in these markets may not be advantageous, especially if the competition is strong and the potential gains are limited. Companies should carefully assess the value of entering such markets and prioritise their resources accordingly. This involves conducting a cost-benefit analysis to determine whether the potential returns justify the investment and effort required. For example, a company specialising in consumer electronics might decide to avoid entering the highly competitive and low-margin home appliance market, instead focusing on its core strengths and expanding its product line within the consumer electronics segment.

By understanding and navigating these different market conditions, companies can develop strategies that align with their strengths and market opportunities. Sun Tzu's wisdom in distinguishing various types of terrain provides valuable insights for businesses to effectively position themselves, anticipate challenges, and capitalise on opportunities. By adopting a strategic approach and being mindful of the unique characteristics of each market, companies can achieve sustained success and maintain a competitive edge in the dynamic business landscape.

Strategic Decision-Making & Risk Management

Sun Tzu underscores the critical importance of understanding the principles connected with terrain and their implications for strategic decision-making. This principle, steeped in ancient wisdom, is profoundly relevant to modern strategic management, where comprehensive market analysis and robust risk management are essential for navigating complex business landscapes. Companies must conduct thorough research to grasp the competitive landscape, assess market conditions, and identify potential risks. By doing so, they can make well-informed decisions that drive success while avoiding strategic pitfalls.

Effective risk management starts with identifying potential threats. This involves a systematic approach to uncovering various risks that could impact the business. These risks can be financial, operational, market-based, or even reputational. Companies need to establish mechanisms for ongoing risk identification, including the use of advanced technologies like artificial intelligence and data analytics to detect potential threats early. For instance, a manufacturing company might utilise IoT (Internet of Things) devices to monitor equipment and predict failures before they occur. This proactive approach allows companies to address risks promptly, reducing the likelihood of significant disruptions.

Once potential risks are identified, the next step is to assess their impact and likelihood. This process involves evaluating the severity of each risk and its probability of occurrence. Tools such as risk matrices and scenario analysis can help quantify these risks and prioritise them based on their significance. For example, a financial services firm might use scenario planning to assess the potential impact of regulatory changes on its operations and develop strategies to mitigate those risks. By understanding the potential impact and likelihood of risks, companies can allocate resources effectively to address the most critical threats.

Developing mitigation strategies is a crucial component of effective risk management. Companies must create comprehensive plans to reduce the likelihood of risks occurring and minimise their impact if they do. This might involve diversifying suppliers, implementing robust cybersecurity measures, or establishing contingency plans for operational disruptions. For instance, a retail company might develop a business continuity plan that includes alternative suppliers, remote work arrangements, and emergency communication protocols. By having these plans in place, the company can respond swiftly and effectively to unexpected events, minimising their impact on operations.

A SWOT analysis (Strengths, Weaknesses, Opportunities, Threats) is a valuable tool for evaluating a company's market position and developing strategies to mitigate risks and capitalise on opportunities. Conducting a SWOT analysis involves a comprehensive assessment of both internal and external factors that influence the business. By identifying strengths, companies can leverage their core competencies to gain a competitive edge. For example, a tech company might highlight its innovative R&D capabilities as a key strength. Understanding weaknesses allows companies to address vulnerabilities and improve their market position. For instance, a company with outdated technology might invest in modernising its IT infrastructure to enhance efficiency.

Opportunities identified in the SWOT analysis can guide strategic initiatives. These opportunities might include emerging market trends, technological advancements, or regulatory changes that can be leveraged for growth. For example, a pharmaceutical company might identify the growing demand for personalised medicine as an opportunity and invest in developing tailored treatments.

Threats identified in the SWOT analysis can inform risk mitigation strategies. These threats might include competitive pressures, economic downturns, or supply chain disruptions. By understanding these threats, companies can develop strategies to mitigate their impact, such as diversifying markets or enhancing supply chain resilience.

Comprehensive market analysis is essential for informed strategic decision-making. Companies must conduct thorough research to understand the competitive landscape, assess market conditions, and identify potential risks. This involves analysing market trends, customer preferences, and competitor actions. For instance, a consumer goods company might conduct market research to understand shifting consumer preferences and adjust its product offerings accordingly. By staying attuned to market dynamics, companies can anticipate changes and proactively adjust their strategies.

In addition to market analysis, companies must also consider the broader economic, social, and regulatory environment. Understanding these external factors can provide valuable insights for strategic decision-making. For example, a company considering expanding into a new geographic market might analyse the region's economic conditions, regulatory environment, and cultural nuances to ensure a successful entry. By considering the broader environment, companies can develop robust strategies that navigate uncertainties and enhance their resilience.

Risk management and strategic decision-making are interrelated processes that require continuous monitoring and adaptation. Companies must regularly review their risk management strategies and update them as needed to ensure they remain effective. This involves staying informed about industry trends, regulatory changes, and emerging threats. For example, a technology company might monitor developments in cybersecurity threats and adjust its defence mechanisms accordingly. By keeping a pulse on the external environment, companies can proactively manage risks and maintain their resilience.

A prime example of effective strategic decision-making and risk management is seen in the practices of global retail giant Walmart. Walmart's competitive advantage is deeply rooted in its efficient supply chain management and rigorous risk management practices. The company conducts extensive market analysis to understand consumer behaviour, market trends, and competitive dynamics. Walmart leverages advanced data analytics to gain insights into customer preferences and optimise inventory levels. This data-driven approach informs strategic decisions, such as product assortment, pricing strategies, and store locations.

Walmart's risk management practices include diversifying suppliers, implementing robust contingency plans, and investing in advanced logistics technology. The company's extensive distribution network and strategic partnerships with suppliers ensure a steady flow of goods, even during disruptions. For example, during the COVID-19 pandemic, Walmart quickly adapted its supply chain operations to meet the surge in demand for essential goods. The company's strategic decision-making and risk management practices enabled it to navigate the challenges effectively and maintain operational continuity.

Leadership & Organisational Dynamics

Sun Tzu identifies six potential calamities that can affect an army: flight, insubordination, collapse, ruin, disorganisation, and rout. In the context of modern business, these calamities can be seen as challenges arising from poor leadership and organisational dynamics. Effective leaders must proactively address these challenges to ensure organisational success and resilience.

Flight:

Sun Tzu states that when one force is hurled against another ten times its size, the result is flight. In the business context, this represents situations where companies take on challenges that far exceed their capabilities and resources. This often occurs when companies overextend themselves by entering markets that are too competitive or launching products without sufficient preparation. To avoid such overwhelming challenges, leaders must ensure that their strategies align with the company's strengths and resources. This involves conducting thorough market research, assessing the company's core competencies, and setting realistic goals. For instance, a start-up in the tech industry should focus on perfecting its initial product offering before attempting to diversify into multiple markets simultaneously. By aligning their strategic initiatives with their available resources, companies can build a solid foundation for sustainable growth.

Insubordination:

Sun Tzu warns that when common soldiers are too strong and their officers too weak, the result is insubordination. In a business setting, this reflects situations where frontline employees lack respect for leadership, leading to a breakdown in authority and operational inefficiencies. This can occur when leaders fail to establish clear authority, communicate effectively, or build trust with their teams. To mitigate this challenge, leaders must demonstrate strong, decisive leadership while fostering a culture of respect and collaboration. This involves setting clear expectations, providing consistent feedback, and actively engaging with employees. For example, a retail company can implement regular team meetings where managers and frontline staff discuss performance, share updates, and address concerns. By establishing clear authority and open communication channels, leaders can build trust and ensure alignment with organisational goals.

Collapse:

Sun Tzu identifies collapse as a result of officers being too strong and common soldiers too weak. In business, this represents situations where leadership is disconnected from frontline employees, leading to disengagement and lack of empowerment among the workforce. This can occur when leaders are overly authoritative or fail to delegate responsibilities effectively. To prevent collapse, leaders must ensure that all employees are empowered, supported, and aligned with organisational objectives. This involves providing opportunities for professional development, encouraging collaboration, and recognising employee contributions. For instance, a software development company can implement mentorship programmes where senior developers mentor junior staff, fostering knowledge transfer and career growth. By empowering employees and fostering a supportive work environment, leaders can enhance engagement and drive organisational success.

Ruin:

Sun Tzu warns that ruin occurs when higher officers act out of resentment and give battle on their own account. In business, this reflects situations where leaders act impulsively or out of personal motivations without considering the broader strategic context. Such actions can lead to misaligned priorities and organisational chaos. Effective leaders must make decisions based on data, analysis, and strategic priorities rather than personal biases or emotions. This involves conducting thorough analysis, consulting with key stakeholders, and aligning decisions with the company's long-term goals. For example, a financial services firm should base its investment decisions on comprehensive market analysis and risk assessments rather than individual preferences. By making data-driven decisions, leaders can ensure strategic alignment and prevent actions that could jeopardise the organisation's success.

Disorganisation:

Sun Tzu highlights disorganisation as a result of unclear orders, unassigned duties, and haphazard ranks. In the business context, this represents situations where companies lack clear processes, organisational structure, and role definitions. Such disorganisation can lead to inefficiencies, confusion, and decreased productivity. Leaders must establish clear roles, responsibilities, and processes to ensure operational efficiency and effectiveness. This involves defining job descriptions, setting performance standards, and implementing structured workflows. For instance, a healthcare organisation can enhance operational efficiency by defining roles for each team member, standardising patient care protocols, and implementing electronic health records for streamlined communication. By creating a well-organised structure, leaders can ensure that employees understand their responsibilities and contribute effectively to organisational goals.

Rout:

Sun Tzu states that rout occurs when a general allows an inferior force to engage a larger one without proper planning. In business, this represents situations where companies take on competitors without adequate preparation, leading to strategic failures and market losses. Leaders must conduct thorough analysis, develop robust strategies, and ensure that their initiatives are well-planned and executed. This involves assessing the competitive landscape, identifying key differentiators, and leveraging the company's strengths. For example, a telecommunications company planning to enter a new market should conduct a comprehensive market analysis to understand the competitive environment, regulatory landscape, and customer needs. By developing a well-researched market entry strategy, the company can effectively compete and capture market share.

Building Strong Relationships & Morale

Sun Tzu emphasises the importance of treating soldiers with humanity while maintaining discipline. Translated into the business world, this principle highlights the critical need for leaders to build strong relationships with employees and foster a positive organisational culture. Effective leaders must show empathy, provide support, and recognise contributions, all while maintaining high standards of performance. This balanced approach not only enhances morale but also drives higher levels of engagement and productivity, ultimately contributing to the organisation's success.

Building strong relationships with employees begins with creating a culture of trust. Trust is the foundation of any successful relationship and is crucial in the workplace. Leaders must be transparent in their communication, honest in their actions, and consistent in their decisions to build and maintain trust. For instance, a leader who regularly updates their team on company performance, future plans, and any changes helps to build a sense of security and trust among employees. Trust fosters an environment where employees feel safe to express their ideas, take risks, and make decisions, knowing they have the support of their leaders.

Collaboration is another key element of building strong relationships. Leaders should encourage teamwork and provide opportunities for cross-functional collaboration. This can be achieved through team-building activities, collaborative projects, and open communication channels. By promoting a collaborative culture, leaders can harness the diverse skills and perspectives of their employees, leading to more innovative solutions and improved problem-solving capabilities. For example, a company might implement regular brainstorming sessions where employees from different departments can collaborate on new ideas and projects. This not only strengthens relationships but also drives creativity and innovation within the organisation.

Mutual respect is essential for fostering a positive organisational culture. Leaders must demonstrate respect for their employees by valuing their contributions, listening to their concerns, and treating them with dignity. This involves recognising and appreciating employees' efforts, providing constructive feedback, and addressing any issues promptly and fairly. For instance, a leader who acknowledges an employee's hard work and publicly celebrates their achievements fosters a culture of respect and recognition. This not only boosts morale but also encourages other employees to strive for excellence.

Providing opportunities for growth and development is crucial for enhancing morale and engagement. Employees who feel that they have opportunities to learn and advance within the organisation are more likely to be motivated and committed. Leaders should invest in professional development programmes, mentorship opportunities, and career advancement pathways. For example, a company might offer training workshops, leadership development programmes, and access to online learning platforms to help employees develop new skills and advance their careers. By supporting employees' growth, leaders demonstrate their commitment to their team's success and well-being.

Recognition and rewards play a significant role in maintaining high morale. Leaders must implement recognition programmes that celebrate employees' achievements and contributions. This can include monetary rewards, promotions, public recognition, and non-monetary incentives such as extra time off or special projects. For example, a company might establish an "Employee of the Month" programme to highlight outstanding performance and inspire others. Recognising and rewarding employees not only boosts morale but also reinforces desired behaviours and motivates employees to continue striving for excellence.

Empathy is a critical quality for leaders in building strong relationships. Leaders must show genuine care and concern for their employees' well-being, both personally and professionally. This involves being approachable, actively listening to employees' concerns, and providing support when needed. For instance, a leader who takes the time to check in with employees regularly, offer support during challenging times, and celebrate personal milestones fosters a culture of empathy and connection. This not only strengthens relationships but also creates a supportive and inclusive work environment.

Maintaining high standards of performance is essential for achieving organisational success. Leaders must set clear expectations, provide regular feedback, and hold employees accountable for their performance. This involves setting specific, measurable, achievable, relevant, and time-bound (SMART) goals, conducting performance reviews, and providing constructive feedback. For example, a sales team might have clear targets for revenue growth, customer acquisition, and market penetration, with regular reviews to track progress and provide feedback. By maintaining high standards, leaders ensure that employees are aligned with organisational goals and motivated to perform at their best.

Companies like Google and Microsoft exemplify the successful balance of building strong relationships and maintaining high morale. Google emphasises employee well-being and professional development, fostering a culture of innovation and excellence. The company offers a wide range of benefits and programmes to support employees' well-being, including flexible work arrangements, wellness programmes, and professional development opportunities. By prioritising employee satisfaction and fostering a positive work environment, Google has created a highly engaged and productive workforce that drives innovation and success.

Microsoft, under the leadership of Satya Nadella, has also placed a strong emphasis on employee engagement and satisfaction. Nadella's focus on a growth mindset, continuous learning, and collaboration has transformed the company's culture and driven significant advancements in technology and market leadership. Microsoft provides opportunities for professional development, recognises and rewards employees' contributions, and fosters a culture of innovation and excellence. By maintaining discipline and morale, Microsoft has achieved high levels of employee engagement and organisational performance.

Summary

Sun Tzu's *Terrain* offers timeless insights that are highly relevant to modern strategic management. The principles of understanding and navigating different market conditions, strategic decision-making, risk management, leadership, and organisational dynamics provide a robust framework for navigating the complexities of the business world.

CHAPTER 11 – THE NINE SITUATIONS

*If the enemy leaves a door open,
you must rush in.*

Sun Tzu

Sun Tzu's *The Nine Situations* outlines various types of terrain and strategic positions that an army might encounter, providing guidance on how to navigate each scenario. These principles are highly relevant to modern strategic management, where businesses must adapt to dynamic market conditions, anticipate challenges, and leverage their strengths to achieve success.

Understanding Different Market Conditions

Sun Tzu identifies nine varieties of ground: dispersive ground, facile ground, contentious ground, open ground, ground of intersecting highways, serious ground, difficult ground, hemmed-in ground, and desperate ground. In the business context, these terrains can be seen as different market conditions and competitive landscapes that companies must navigate. By understanding these terrains and developing appropriate strategies, companies can effectively position themselves and achieve long-term success.

Dispersive Ground:

Dispersive ground represents situations where a company is operating within its core markets and territories, akin to a familiar battleground. The key is to consolidate resources and avoid unnecessary conflicts that could deplete these resources. Companies should focus on strengthening their market position by enhancing product quality, building strong customer relationships, and investing in brand loyalty programmes. For instance, a retail company operating in its established market should work on retaining its existing customer base through exceptional customer service, loyalty rewards, and consistent product offerings. By fortifying their presence in core markets, companies can create a stable foundation for growth and better withstand competitive pressures.

Facile Ground:

Facile ground represents initial forays into new and potentially lucrative markets. Companies must act swiftly to establish a foothold and avoid prolonged engagements that could exhaust resources. Early wins in these new markets can help build momentum and establish a strong market presence. For example, a tech startup entering the wearable technology market should focus on launching a unique, high-quality product that addresses a gap in the market. Quick and decisive action can help the company gain early adopters and build a loyal customer base, setting the stage for long-term success. Strategic marketing campaigns, partnerships with key industry players, and a robust online presence can further enhance the company's position in the new market.

Contentious Ground:

Contentious ground refers to markets where control provides a significant advantage, often characterised by high stakes and intense competition. Companies should carefully assess the risks and rewards before engaging in direct competition. In such scenarios, strategic alliances and partnerships can be invaluable in securing critical positions. For example, a pharmaceutical company aiming to enter a market dominated by a few large players might form strategic alliances with research institutions and smaller biotech firms to develop and co-market innovative treatments. By leveraging the strengths of its partners, the company can enhance its competitive position and reduce the risks associated with direct confrontation. This collaborative approach allows companies to pool resources, share expertise, and accelerate innovation.

Open Ground:

Open ground represents markets with no significant barriers to entry, where competition is fierce and fluid. Companies operating in such markets must remain flexible and responsive to changes, ensuring they can capitalise on opportunities and mitigate risks. For instance, an online retailer in a highly competitive e-commerce market should continuously innovate its product offerings, optimise its supply chain, and enhance the customer shopping experience. By staying agile and adaptable, the company can respond quickly to market trends and customer demands, maintaining a competitive edge. Data analytics, customer feedback, and market research can provide valuable insights for making informed strategic decisions and staying ahead of the competition.

Ground of Intersecting Highways:

Ground of intersecting highways refers to strategic positions that provide access to multiple markets or customer segments, akin to key crossroads. Companies should secure these positions and leverage their advantages to expand their reach and influence. For example, a logistics company with a strategically located distribution centre can serve multiple regions efficiently, reducing delivery times and costs. By optimising their supply chain network and leveraging technology, such as advanced routing algorithms and real-time tracking, companies can enhance their operational efficiency and customer satisfaction. Additionally, partnerships with local carriers and suppliers can further strengthen their market position and expand their service offerings.

Serious Ground:

Serious ground represents deep penetration into hostile or highly competitive markets. Companies must be prepared for sustained efforts and secure their supply chains to ensure continuous operations. For instance, a consumer electronics company entering the smartphone market, which is dominated by established giants, must invest in cutting-edge research and development, build a robust supply chain, and establish strong distribution channels. By committing to long-term strategic initiatives and maintaining operational resilience, the company can gradually build market share and challenge incumbents. Strong marketing campaigns, product differentiation, and exceptional customer support are essential for success in these highly competitive markets.

Difficult Ground:

Difficult ground refers to markets with significant barriers to entry, such as regulatory challenges or high competition. Companies should proceed with caution, continuously assessing the risks and adapting their strategies. For example, an international food manufacturer considering expansion into a new country must navigate complex regulatory requirements, local tastes, and strong competition from local brands. By conducting thorough market research, engaging with local stakeholders, and customising products to meet local preferences, the company can mitigate risks and enhance its chances of success. Continuous monitoring of the regulatory landscape and proactive compliance efforts are essential for maintaining a strong market presence.

Hemmed-In Ground:

Hemmed-in ground represents situations where a company faces significant constraints and must rely on strategic manoeuvres to survive and thrive. Companies should use creative tactics to navigate these challenges and avoid direct confrontations. For instance, a startup in a highly regulated industry might leverage technology and innovation to disrupt traditional business models and find a niche market. By offering unique solutions, focusing on customer needs, and utilising digital marketing strategies, the company can carve out a distinct market position. Strategic collaborations with industry experts, regulatory compliance, and customer-centric approaches are crucial for overcoming constraints and achieving success.

Desperate Ground:

Desperate ground represents dire situations where immediate and decisive action is required to avoid failure. Companies should rally their resources, focus on critical objectives, and execute turnaround strategies to transform the situation. For example, a retail chain facing significant financial difficulties might implement cost-cutting measures, restructure debt, and revamp its product offerings to revive its business. Engaging with key stakeholders, such as employees, customers, and investors, and communicating a clear vision for the future are essential for rallying support and driving successful turnaround efforts. Innovative marketing campaigns, operational efficiency, and customer engagement can help the company regain market confidence and achieve long-term stability.

Strategic Decision-Making & Adaptability

Sun Tzu emphasises the importance of understanding the nature of the terrain and adapting strategies accordingly. In the realm of modern strategic management, this principle underscores the need for comprehensive market analysis and adaptive decision-making. Companies must conduct thorough research to grasp the competitive landscape, assess market conditions, and identify potential risks and opportunities. By doing so, they can develop agile strategies that respond to dynamic business environments and drive sustained success.

Comprehensive market analysis is the foundation of effective strategic decision-making. Companies must gather extensive data on market trends, customer behaviours, and competitive dynamics. This involves utilising various research methods, such as surveys, focus groups, and data analytics, to gain insights into the external environment. For example, a consumer electronics company might conduct market research to understand the latest technological advancements and shifting consumer preferences. By analysing this data, the company can identify emerging trends, anticipate changes, and develop strategies that align with market demands.

Adaptive decision-making requires companies to continuously monitor the external environment and gather intelligence on potential risks and opportunities. This involves staying attuned to economic, social, and technological factors that could impact the business. For instance, a financial services firm might monitor regulatory changes, economic indicators, and technological advancements to assess their potential impact on the industry. By staying informed, the company can make data-driven decisions that enhance its resilience and competitiveness.

Companies can enhance their adaptability by adopting agile methodologies. Agile methodologies emphasise flexibility, collaboration, and iterative development. By breaking down large projects into smaller, manageable tasks, companies can quickly respond to changing conditions and make adjustments based on real-time feedback. For example, a software development company might implement agile practices to deliver incremental updates and improvements to its products. This iterative approach allows the company to adapt to customer feedback and market changes, ensuring that its offerings remain relevant and competitive.

Implementing flexible planning processes is another critical aspect of adaptive decision-making. Traditional long-term planning can be rigid and slow to respond to dynamic market conditions. Instead, companies should adopt rolling planning processes that allow for regular review and adjustment of strategic plans. For example, a retail company might conduct quarterly planning sessions to reassess market conditions, evaluate performance, and adjust its strategies accordingly. This flexible approach ensures that the company remains agile and can quickly pivot in response to new opportunities or threats.

Fostering a culture of innovation is essential for driving adaptability and continuous improvement. Companies must create an environment that encourages creativity, experimentation, and risk-taking. This involves providing employees with the resources and autonomy to explore new ideas and develop innovative solutions. For example, a technology company might establish an innovation lab where employees can collaborate on cutting-edge projects and prototype new products. By promoting a culture of innovation, companies can drive continuous improvement and stay ahead of industry trends.

The COVID-19 pandemic provides a compelling example of the importance of adaptive decision-making and strategic flexibility. During the pandemic, many businesses rapidly adapted their strategies to address new market realities. For instance, brick-and-mortar retailers quickly pivoted to e-commerce platforms to continue serving customers during lockdowns. Companies implemented remote work policies to ensure employee safety and business continuity. Additionally, businesses developed new product offerings to meet changing consumer needs, such as sanitisation products and home office supplies. These adaptive strategies allowed companies to navigate the challenges of the pandemic and maintain operations.

A prime example of successful adaptive decision-making is seen in the practices of global logistics giant DHL. Faced with the challenges of the COVID-19 pandemic, DHL rapidly adapted its operations to ensure the continued flow of goods and services. The company leveraged its extensive logistics network, advanced technology, and agile methodologies to respond to changing market conditions. DHL implemented flexible planning processes, allowing for quick adjustments to routes, schedules, and resource allocation. By fostering a culture of innovation, DHL developed new solutions, such as contactless delivery and digital tracking, to enhance customer experience and ensure safety. This adaptive approach enabled DHL to maintain operational efficiency and meet increased demand during the pandemic.

Leveraging Strategic Alliances & Partnerships

Sun Tzu advises forming alliances and partnerships in strategic positions, such as the ground of intersecting highways. In the business world, this principle translates into the importance of leveraging strategic alliances and partnerships to achieve organisational goals. These collaborations can provide companies with access to new markets, shared resources, and complementary strengths, enabling them to pool resources, share risks, and accelerate innovation. By joining forces with other organisations, companies can create synergies that enhance their competitive advantage and drive long-term success.

Strategic alliances involve working closely with partners to achieve common goals while leveraging each other's strengths. This collaboration can take various forms, including joint ventures, co-marketing agreements, technology partnerships, and research and development collaborations. Each type of alliance offers unique benefits and opportunities for growth.

Access to New Markets:

One of the primary benefits of strategic alliances is the ability to enter new markets more effectively. By partnering with organisations that have established presence and expertise in target markets, companies can navigate market entry barriers and accelerate their expansion efforts. For instance, a company looking to expand internationally might form an alliance with a local firm that understands the cultural, regulatory, and consumer dynamics of the new market. This partnership can provide invaluable insights and resources, facilitating a smoother and more successful market entry.

For example, a global beverage company might partner with a local distributor in a new region to leverage the distributor's established network and market knowledge. This partnership allows the beverage company to reach new customers quickly, streamline distribution, and enhance its brand presence in the region. By leveraging the local partner's strengths, the company can reduce the risks and costs associated with market entry and achieve faster growth.

Sharing Resources:

Strategic alliances enable companies to share resources, such as technology, infrastructure, and expertise, to achieve mutual benefits. By pooling resources, partners can reduce costs, enhance operational efficiency, and accelerate innovation. For example, two technology companies might form an alliance to co-develop a new product, sharing research and development costs, technical expertise, and intellectual property. This collaboration allows both companies to leverage their combined strengths and bring innovative solutions to market faster.

Consider the partnership between pharmaceutical companies for drug development. Developing a new drug requires significant investment in research, clinical trials, and regulatory approvals. By forming alliances, pharmaceutical companies can share these costs and risks, leveraging each other's expertise and resources to bring new treatments to market more efficiently. This collaborative approach not only accelerates innovation but also increases the likelihood of success by combining complementary strengths.

Leveraging Complementary Strengths:

Strategic alliances are particularly effective when partners have complementary strengths that can be leveraged to achieve common goals. By combining their unique capabilities, companies can create synergies that enhance their competitive advantage. For instance, a technology company with advanced research and development capabilities might partner with a manufacturing firm that excels in production and distribution. This partnership allows the technology company to focus on innovation while leveraging the manufacturing firm's expertise to bring products to market efficiently.

A compelling example of leveraging complementary strengths is the strategic alliance between Microsoft and LinkedIn. Microsoft, a global leader in software and technology solutions, partnered with LinkedIn, a leading professional networking platform, to create new value propositions for their customers. This alliance enabled both companies to integrate their services, offering enhanced solutions for professionals and businesses. By combining Microsoft's productivity tools with LinkedIn's networking capabilities, the partnership provided a seamless experience for users, driving greater engagement and value.

Accelerating Innovation:

Collaborative partnerships can significantly accelerate the pace of innovation. By working together, companies can share ideas, knowledge, and technologies, leading to the development of innovative solutions that might not have been possible independently. For example, two companies in the renewable energy sector might collaborate on research and development projects to advance solar panel technology. By combining their expertise and resources, they can accelerate the development of more efficient and cost-effective solar panels, driving the adoption of renewable energy solutions.

Strategic alliances also foster a culture of innovation by promoting cross-functional collaboration and knowledge exchange. When employees from different organisations work together, they bring diverse perspectives and ideas, leading to creative problem-solving and breakthrough innovations. For example, a collaboration between a healthcare provider and a technology company can result in the development of advanced telemedicine solutions, improving patient care and expanding access to healthcare services.

Risk Sharing:

One of the key advantages of strategic alliances is the ability to share risks. By partnering with other organisations, companies can distribute the risks associated with new ventures, reducing their individual exposure. This is particularly valuable in industries characterised by high levels of uncertainty and volatility. For instance, a company entering a new market with significant regulatory challenges might form an alliance with a local partner to navigate these complexities. By sharing the risks and benefits, both companies can achieve their objectives while minimising potential downsides.

An example of risk sharing can be seen in joint ventures between automobile manufacturers for developing electric vehicles (EVs). The development and production of EVs require substantial investment in research, infrastructure, and technology. By forming joint ventures, automobile manufacturers can share the financial and operational risks, pooling their resources and expertise to accelerate the development and commercialisation of EVs. This collaborative approach not only reduces individual risks but also enhances the competitiveness of the partners in the evolving automotive market.

Strategic Flexibility:

Strategic alliances provide companies with the flexibility to adapt to changing market conditions and emerging opportunities. By forming alliances, companies can quickly respond to shifts in consumer demand, technological advancements, and competitive pressures. For example, a company in the technology sector might form an alliance with a startup to explore new markets or develop innovative solutions. This strategic flexibility allows the company to remain agile and responsive, positioning itself for long-term success.

Managing Resources & Logistics

Sun Tzu highlights the critical importance of managing resources and logistics to ensure the army's effectiveness. This ancient wisdom is equally pertinent in the modern business context, where effective resource management is vital for achieving strategic objectives and maintaining a competitive edge. Companies must optimise the use of financial, human, and physical resources to maximise efficiency and productivity. This requires a holistic approach that encompasses strategic planning, continuous improvement, and technological innovation.

Financial Resource Management:

Effective financial resource management begins with prudent budgeting and financial planning. Companies must allocate their financial resources in a way that maximises return on investment and supports strategic initiatives. This involves setting clear financial goals, developing detailed budgets, and monitoring expenditures to ensure alignment with strategic priorities. For instance, a company planning to expand its product line might allocate funds towards research and development, marketing, and production capacity. By strategically investing financial resources, the company can drive innovation, enhance its market position, and achieve long-term growth.

Financial resource management also involves implementing robust financial controls to prevent fraud and mismanagement. Companies must establish internal controls, conduct regular audits, and enforce strict compliance with financial regulations. For example, a retail company might implement a comprehensive financial control system that includes segregation of duties, regular reconciliations, and periodic financial reviews. By maintaining strong financial discipline, the company can safeguard its assets and ensure financial stability.

Human Resource Management:

Human resources are the backbone of any organisation, and effective human resource management is essential for achieving strategic objectives. This begins with attracting and retaining top talent. Companies must implement effective recruitment processes, offer competitive compensation packages, and create a positive work environment. For instance, a technology company might develop an employer branding strategy that highlights its innovative culture, career development opportunities, and commitment to employee well-being. By positioning itself as an employer of choice, the company can attract high-caliber candidates and build a strong, motivated workforce.

Employee development is another critical aspect of human resource management. Companies must invest in training and development programmes to enhance employees' skills and capabilities. This involves offering workshops, online courses, mentorship programmes, and leadership development initiatives. For example, a manufacturing company might offer Lean Six Sigma training to its employees, equipping them with the skills to improve operational efficiency and drive continuous improvement. By investing in employee development, companies can enhance engagement, productivity, and retention.

Performance management is also crucial for human resource management. Companies must establish clear performance metrics, set specific, measurable, achievable, relevant, and time-bound (SMART) goals, and conduct regular performance reviews. This involves providing constructive feedback, recognising achievements, and addressing performance issues promptly. For example, a sales team might have clear targets for revenue growth, customer acquisition, and market penetration, with regular reviews to track progress and provide feedback. By maintaining a disciplined approach to performance management, companies can drive accountability and achieve strategic goals.

Physical Resource Management:

Effective management of physical resources, such as facilities, equipment, and materials, is essential for maximising productivity and efficiency. Companies must ensure that their physical resources are utilised optimally, minimising waste and reducing costs. This involves implementing maintenance programmes, optimising inventory levels, and leveraging technology to streamline operations. For example, a manufacturing company might use predictive maintenance technologies to monitor equipment performance and prevent breakdowns, reducing downtime and maintaining production efficiency. By effectively managing physical resources, companies can improve operational efficiency and enhance product quality.

Logistics Management:

Logistics management plays a crucial role in ensuring that resources are available when and where they are needed, supporting timely delivery and meeting customer expectations. Companies must coordinate the movement of goods, manage supply chains, and optimise distribution networks. This involves developing efficient logistics processes, leveraging technology, and collaborating with supply chain partners. For instance, a retail company might use advanced logistics software to track inventory levels, forecast demand, and optimise delivery routes. By enhancing logistics efficiency, companies can reduce lead times, lower transportation costs, and improve service levels.

Toyota and Walmart are exemplary models of companies that have built their competitive advantage on efficient supply chain management. Toyota's adoption of the Lean Manufacturing System, also known as the Toyota Production System (TPS), emphasises continuous improvement, waste reduction, and efficient resource utilisation. TPS involves practices such as just-in-time (JIT) inventory management, where materials are delivered exactly when needed, reducing inventory costs and minimising waste. Toyota's commitment to lean principles has enabled the company to achieve high levels of operational efficiency, product quality, and customer satisfaction.

Walmart's success is also deeply rooted in its efficient supply chain management. The company's logistics strategy focuses on optimising the flow of goods from suppliers to stores, ensuring that products are available to customers at the right time and place. Walmart leverages advanced technology, such as radio-frequency identification (RFID) and data analytics, to track inventory, forecast demand, and manage replenishment processes. The company's investment in an extensive distribution network, including strategically located distribution centres and a fleet of transportation vehicles, ensures seamless logistics operations. By maintaining tight control over its supply chain, Walmart can reduce costs, offer competitive prices, and deliver a superior shopping experience to customers.

Moreover, effective resource management and logistics involve continuous monitoring and improvement. Companies must regularly assess their resource allocation and logistics processes to identify areas for enhancement. This involves analysing performance metrics, gathering feedback, and implementing best practices. For example, a company might conduct regular supply chain audits to assess efficiency, identify bottlenecks, and implement corrective actions. By fostering a culture of continuous improvement, companies can ensure that their resource management and logistics processes remain agile and responsive to changing market conditions.

Building Strong Relationships & Morale

Sun Tzu emphasises the importance of treating soldiers with humanity while maintaining discipline. In the modern business context, this principle translates into the critical need for leaders to build strong relationships with employees and foster a positive organisational culture. Effective leaders must demonstrate empathy, provide unwavering support, and recognise contributions, all while upholding high standards of performance. This balanced approach not only enhances morale but also drives higher levels of engagement and productivity, ultimately contributing to the organisation's success.

Creating a Culture of Trust:

Building strong relationships with employees begins with creating a culture of trust. Trust is the foundation of any successful relationship and is crucial in the workplace. Leaders must be transparent in their communication, honest in their actions, and consistent in their decisions to build and maintain trust. For instance, a leader who regularly updates their team on company performance, future plans, and any changes helps to build a sense of security and trust among employees. Trust fosters an environment where employees feel safe to express their ideas, take risks, and make decisions, knowing they have the support of their leaders.

Promoting Collaboration:

Collaboration is another key element of building strong relationships. Leaders should encourage teamwork and provide opportunities for cross-functional collaboration. This can be achieved through team-building activities, collaborative projects, and open communication channels. By promoting a collaborative culture, leaders can harness the diverse skills and perspectives of their employees, leading to more innovative solutions and improved problem-solving capabilities. For example, a company might implement regular brainstorming sessions where employees from different departments can collaborate on new ideas and projects. This not only strengthens relationships but also drives creativity and innovation within the organisation.

Demonstrating Mutual Respect:

Mutual respect is essential for fostering a positive organisational culture. Leaders must demonstrate respect for their employees by valuing their contributions, listening to their concerns, and treating them with dignity. This involves recognising and appreciating employees' efforts, providing constructive feedback, and addressing any issues promptly and fairly. For instance, a leader who acknowledges an employee's hard work and publicly celebrates their achievements fosters a culture of respect and recognition. This not only boosts morale but also encourages other employees to strive for excellence.

Providing Opportunities for Growth and Development:

Providing opportunities for growth and development is crucial for enhancing morale and engagement. Employees who feel that they have opportunities to learn and advance within the organisation are more likely to be motivated and committed. Leaders should invest in professional development programmes, mentorship opportunities, and career advancement pathways. For example, a company might offer training workshops, leadership development programmes, and access to online learning platforms to help employees develop new skills and advance their careers. By supporting employees' growth, leaders demonstrate their commitment to their team's success and well-being.

Recognising & Rewarding Contributions:

Recognition and rewards play a significant role in maintaining high morale. Leaders must implement recognition programmes that celebrate employees' achievements and contributions. This can include monetary rewards, promotions, public recognition, and non-monetary incentives such as extra time off or special projects. For example, a company might establish an "Employee of the Month" programme to highlight outstanding performance and inspire others. Recognising and rewarding employees not only boosts morale but also reinforces desired behaviours and motivates employees to continue striving for excellence.

Showing Empathy:

Empathy is a critical quality for leaders in building strong relationships. Leaders must show genuine care and concern for their employees' well-being, both personally and professionally. This involves being approachable, actively listening to employees' concerns, and providing support when needed. For instance, a leader who takes the time to check in with employees regularly, offer support during challenging times, and celebrate personal milestones fosters a culture of empathy and connection. This not only strengthens relationships but also creates a supportive and inclusive work environment.

Maintaining High Standards of Performance:

Maintaining high standards of performance is essential for achieving organisational success. Leaders must set clear expectations, provide regular feedback, and hold employees accountable for their performance. This involves setting specific, measurable, achievable, relevant, and time-bound (SMART) goals, conducting performance reviews, and providing constructive feedback. For example, a sales team might have clear targets for revenue growth, customer acquisition, and market penetration, with regular reviews to track progress and provide feedback. By maintaining high standards, leaders ensure that employees are aligned with organisational goals and motivated to perform at their best.

Employee Engagement:

Employee engagement is a critical factor in maintaining morale. Engaged employees are more committed, motivated, and productive. Companies must actively seek to engage employees through meaningful work, opportunities for growth, and a supportive work environment. For example, a company might conduct regular employee engagement surveys to gather feedback and identify areas for improvement. By acting on this feedback and implementing changes that address employees' needs and concerns, companies can enhance engagement and create a more positive work environment.

Leadership Role:

Leadership plays a vital role in maintaining discipline and morale. Leaders must set the tone for the organisation, modelling the behaviours and values that they expect from employees. This involves demonstrating integrity, transparency, and empathy in their interactions with employees. Leaders must also provide clear direction, support, and resources to help employees achieve their goals. For example, a leader who actively listens to employees' concerns, provides regular feedback, and offers guidance and support can build trust and foster a positive work culture. By embodying the principles of discipline and morale, leaders can inspire and motivate employees to perform at their best.

Companies like Google and Microsoft exemplify the successful balance of building strong relationships and maintaining high morale. Google emphasises employee well-being and professional development, fostering a culture of innovation and excellence. The company offers a wide range of benefits and programmes to support employees' well-being, including flexible work arrangements, wellness programmes, and professional development opportunities. By prioritising employee satisfaction and fostering a positive work environment, Google has created a highly engaged and productive workforce that drives innovation and success.

Microsoft, under the leadership of Satya Nadella, has also placed a strong emphasis on employee engagement and satisfaction. Nadella's focus on a growth mindset, continuous learning, and collaboration has transformed the company's culture and driven significant advancements in technology and market leadership. Microsoft provides opportunities for professional development, recognises and rewards employees' contributions, and fosters a culture of innovation and excellence. By maintaining discipline and morale, Microsoft has achieved high levels of employee engagement and organisational performance.

Strategic Patience & Timing

Sun Tzu emphasises the profound importance of strategic patience and timing. He advises waiting for the right moment to deliver an attack and avoiding unnecessary confrontations, an insight that holds significant relevance in the business world. Strategic patience and timing are crucial elements of decision-making, enabling companies to optimise their actions and maximise their impact. By exercising patience and waiting for the most opportune moment to execute strategic initiatives, launch new products, or enter new markets, businesses can enhance their chances of success and secure a competitive edge.

Strategic patience involves a disciplined approach to decision-making, where companies carefully evaluate the timing and potential impact of their actions. This requires a deep understanding of market dynamics, customer behaviours, and competitive landscape. Companies must resist the urge to rush into decisions and instead wait for the optimal conditions that will enhance their chances of success. For instance, a technology company planning to launch a new product might conduct extensive market research to identify the best time for release, considering factors such as seasonal demand, competitor activity, and economic conditions. By exercising strategic patience, the company can ensure that its product launch generates maximum interest and achieves strong market penetration.

Timing is a critical element in strategic decision-making. It involves identifying the precise moment when conditions are most favourable for executing a strategic action. This requires continuous monitoring of the external environment and staying attuned to shifts in market trends, customer preferences, and industry developments. For instance, a retail company might decide to introduce a new clothing line at the start of the holiday shopping season, capitalising on increased consumer spending and heightened market activity. By aligning strategic actions with the most opportune timing, companies can maximise their impact and drive significant results.

Successful companies recognise that timing is not just about launching new products or entering new markets; it also involves knowing when to pause, observe, and adjust strategies. This adaptive approach ensures that companies remain agile and responsive to changing conditions. For example, during an economic downturn, a company might delay a planned expansion to conserve resources and focus on strengthening its core operations. By waiting for more stable economic conditions, the company can mitigate risks and position itself for long-term growth.

Anticipating market trends and aligning strategic actions with these trends is essential for maximising the impact of timing. Companies must leverage data analytics, market research, and industry insights to forecast future trends and identify emerging opportunities. For example, a pharmaceutical company might track advancements in biotechnology and regulatory developments to determine the best time to introduce a new drug. By staying ahead of market trends, the company can capture market share and establish itself as a leader in innovation.

Strategic patience and timing also involve recognising and seizing opportunistic moments. Companies must be ready to act swiftly when the right opportunities arise, even if it means deviating from planned strategies. This requires a balance between patience and agility, where companies remain vigilant and prepared to capitalise on unexpected opportunities. For instance, a financial services firm might take advantage of a sudden market dip to acquire undervalued assets, positioning itself for future gains. By maintaining strategic flexibility and readiness, companies can turn challenges into opportunities and drive growth.

Tesla's success in the electric vehicle (EV) market exemplifies the power of strategic patience and timing. Tesla strategically timed its introduction of electric vehicles to coincide with growing consumer interest in sustainable transportation and advancements in battery technology. By patiently waiting for the market conditions to be favourable, Tesla was able to capture significant consumer interest and establish itself as a leader in the EV market. The company's timing was further reinforced by its investment in building a comprehensive charging infrastructure, ensuring that its customers had access to convenient charging options, thereby enhancing the overall ownership experience.

Tesla's strategic timing extended to its expansion plans and product line diversification. The company introduced the Model S, a high-performance electric sedan, at a time when there was increasing demand for luxury electric vehicles. This was followed by the launch of the Model 3, a more affordable option that targeted the mass market. By carefully timing these product launches, Tesla was able to capture a broad customer base and drive substantial sales growth. Additionally, Tesla's entry into energy solutions, such as solar panels and energy storage systems, was timed to align with the growing focus on renewable energy. This strategic diversification not only reinforced Tesla's commitment to sustainability but also created new revenue streams and growth opportunities.

Moreover, Tesla's approach to strategic patience and timing is evident in its handling of market expansions. The company has gradually expanded its presence in international markets, carefully assessing local conditions and regulatory environments before making significant investments. For example, Tesla's entry into the Chinese market was strategically timed to leverage the country's support for electric vehicles and growing consumer demand. By building a Gigafactory in Shanghai, Tesla was able to produce vehicles locally, reduce costs, and enhance its competitiveness in the Chinese market.

Strategic partnerships and collaborations are also part of Tesla's timing strategy. The company has formed alliances with key suppliers and technology partners to ensure a steady supply of components and access to cutting-edge innovations. For instance, Tesla's partnership with Panasonic for battery production has been instrumental in supporting its ambitious production targets and ensuring the quality and performance of its vehicles. By timing these partnerships to coincide with product launches and market expansions, Tesla has strengthened its market position and operational capabilities.

Summary

Sun Tzu's *The Nine Situations* offers timeless insights that are highly relevant to modern strategic management. The principles of understanding different market conditions, adaptive decision-making, leveraging strategic alliances, managing resources, building strong relationships, and strategic patience provide a robust framework for navigating the complexities of the business world.

CHAPTER 12 – THE ATTACK BY FIRE

*Move not unless you see an advantage;
use not your troops unless there is something to be gained;
fight not unless the position is critical.*

Sun Tzu

Sun Tzu's *The Attack by Fire* illuminates the strategic nuances of leveraging resources and timing for maximum impact. Though initially crafted in the context of ancient warfare, the principles encapsulated in this chapter resonate profoundly with contemporary strategic management practices.

The Strategic Use of Resources

Sun Tzu begins by outlining five distinct methods of attacking with fire: burning soldiers in their camp, burning stores, burning baggage-trains, burning arsenals and magazines, and hurling fire among the enemy. These tactics emphasise the strategic use of available resources to disrupt and weaken the enemy. In today's business environment, resources such as data, capital, technology, and human talent are equivalent to Sun Tzu's "fire." Companies must strategically deploy these resources to create market disruptions, outmanoeuvre competitors, and capture value.

Leveraging Big Data & Analytics:

One of the most powerful resources at a company's disposal is data. By leveraging big data and analytics, companies can gain deep insights into consumer behaviour, market trends, and operational efficiency. This data-driven approach enables companies to tailor their offerings and create personalised experiences that disrupt traditional market players. For example, an e-commerce company might use data analytics to analyse customer browsing and purchasing patterns, allowing it to recommend products that are highly relevant to each individual shopper. This personalised approach not only enhances the customer experience but also drives higher conversion rates and sales. Additionally, data analytics can help companies identify emerging trends and predict future demand, enabling them to stay ahead of the competition and capitalise on new opportunities.

Investing in Cutting-Edge Technology:

Investing in cutting-edge technology is another strategic use of resources that can set a company apart from its competitors. Advanced technologies such as artificial intelligence (AI), machine learning, the Internet of Things (IoT), and blockchain can streamline operations, reduce costs, and enhance product innovation. For example, a manufacturing company might implement IoT sensors on its production line to monitor equipment performance in real time. This allows the company to perform predictive maintenance, reducing downtime and increasing overall efficiency. Similarly, AI-driven automation can optimise supply chain management, improving inventory accuracy and reducing lead times. By embracing technological innovation, companies can enhance their operational capabilities, deliver superior products, and create a sustainable competitive advantage.

Maximising Human Talent:

Human talent is a critical resource that companies must strategically manage to achieve their strategic objectives. This involves attracting, developing, and retaining top talent. Companies must create a supportive work environment that fosters creativity, collaboration, and continuous learning. For example, a technology company might implement professional development programmes, mentorship opportunities, and career advancement pathways to help employees grow and succeed. By investing in employee development, companies can build a skilled and motivated workforce that drives innovation and productivity. Additionally, fostering a culture of inclusion and diversity can bring diverse perspectives and ideas, leading to more creative problem-solving and better business outcomes.

Optimising Financial Resources:

Effective management of financial resources is essential for achieving strategic goals. Companies must allocate their capital efficiently, ensuring that investments align with strategic priorities and deliver maximum returns. This involves rigorous financial planning, budgeting, and performance monitoring. For instance, a company planning to expand its market presence might allocate capital towards marketing campaigns, sales expansion, and new product development. By strategically investing financial resources, the company can drive growth and enhance its competitive position. Additionally, maintaining financial discipline and implementing robust financial controls can help companies manage risks and ensure long-term financial stability.

Strategic Use of Capital:

Capital is a powerful resource that, when strategically deployed, can create significant value and drive competitive advantage. Companies must carefully plan their capital investments to ensure they align with their long-term goals and deliver the highest returns. For example, a company might decide to invest in acquiring a smaller competitor to gain access to new markets, technologies, or customer bases. Such strategic acquisitions can enhance the company's capabilities, expand its market reach, and create synergies that drive growth. Additionally, capital investments in infrastructure, technology, and innovation can enable companies to scale their operations, improve efficiency, and deliver superior products and services.

Creating Market Disruptions:

Strategic use of resources can also involve creating market disruptions that challenge the status quo and position the company as an industry leader. This might involve launching innovative products that redefine customer expectations, entering new markets with unique value propositions, or adopting unconventional business models that differentiate the company from competitors. For example, a ride-sharing company might disrupt the traditional taxi industry by offering a convenient, affordable, and technology-driven alternative. By strategically deploying resources to create market disruptions, companies can capture significant market share, attract new customers, and drive long-term growth.

Collaborating with Strategic Partners:

Leveraging strategic partnerships is another effective way to optimise resources and achieve business objectives. By collaborating with other organisations, companies can pool their resources, share risks, and leverage complementary strengths. For example, a pharmaceutical company might form a partnership with a biotechnology firm to co-develop a new treatment. This collaboration allows both companies to share research and development costs, accelerate the innovation process, and bring the product to market faster. Strategic partnerships can also provide access to new markets, technologies, and expertise, enhancing the company's competitive position.

Enhancing Supply Chain Efficiency:

Optimising supply chain management is a critical aspect of resource management that can drive significant cost savings and operational efficiencies. Companies must streamline their supply chain processes, from sourcing and procurement to production and distribution, to ensure timely delivery and meet customer expectations. For example, a retail company might use advanced logistics software to track inventory levels, forecast demand, and optimise delivery routes. By enhancing supply chain efficiency, companies can reduce lead times, lower transportation costs, and improve service levels. Efficient supply chain management also enables companies to respond quickly to market changes and minimise the impact of disruptions.

Leveraging Intellectual Property:

Intellectual property (IP) is a valuable resource that companies can strategically deploy to protect their innovations and gain a competitive edge. Companies must invest in protecting their patents, trademarks, copyrights, and trade secrets to safeguard their unique technologies and products. For example, a technology company might file patents for its new inventions to prevent competitors from copying its innovations. Additionally, companies can leverage their IP assets to generate revenue through licensing agreements and partnerships. By strategically managing their intellectual property, companies can protect their market position, enhance their brand value, and create additional revenue streams.

Driving Sustainable Practices:

Sustainability is becoming an increasingly important consideration for companies looking to create long-term value. By strategically deploying resources to drive sustainable practices, companies can enhance their reputation, meet regulatory requirements, and attract environmentally conscious customers. For example, a manufacturing company might invest in renewable energy sources, implement energy-efficient technologies, and adopt circular economy principles to reduce waste and minimise its environmental impact. Sustainable practices can also lead to cost savings through reduced energy consumption and waste management. By prioritising sustainability, companies can differentiate themselves from competitors and build a strong, responsible brand.

Preparation & Readiness

Sun Tzu emphasises the critical importance of having the means available and being prepared to use them. This concept highlights the necessity for organisations to maintain a state of readiness and agility. In modern strategic management, this translates to having a robust infrastructure, an adaptable workforce, and contingency plans in place. By ensuring that these elements are effectively managed, companies can navigate uncertainties and respond swiftly to changing market conditions, thereby securing a competitive edge and achieving long-term success.

Robust Infrastructure:

A robust infrastructure forms the backbone of an organisation's operational capabilities. This involves investing in physical facilities, technology systems, and logistical networks that support efficient and resilient operations. Companies must ensure that their infrastructure is designed to withstand disruptions and maintain continuity. For example, a global manufacturing company might invest in state-of-the-art production facilities equipped with advanced automation technologies. These facilities can operate with minimal human intervention, reducing the risk of disruptions caused by labour shortages or safety concerns. Additionally, the company might establish redundant supply chain networks with multiple suppliers and distribution centres to ensure a steady flow of materials and products, even during crises.

Furthermore, a robust infrastructure includes a strong IT framework that supports digital transformation and data-driven decision-making. Companies must invest in scalable and secure IT systems that enable seamless communication, collaboration, and data management. For instance, a financial services firm might implement cloud computing solutions to enhance its data storage and processing capabilities, ensuring that critical information is accessible and protected. By leveraging advanced IT infrastructure, companies can streamline their operations, enhance cybersecurity, and drive innovation.

Adaptable Workforce:

An adaptable workforce is essential for an organisation's ability to respond to evolving market conditions and seize new opportunities. Companies must invest in continuous training and development to ensure that their employees are equipped with the necessary skills and knowledge. This involves offering a range of learning opportunities, such as workshops, online courses, mentorship programmes, and professional certifications. For example, a technology company might provide its employees with access to coding bootcamps and data science training programmes to keep them updated with the latest industry trends and technological advancements. By fostering a culture of continuous learning, companies can build a workforce that is agile, innovative, and prepared to tackle new challenges.

Leadership development is also a critical aspect of workforce adaptability. Companies must identify high-potential employees and provide them with leadership training and development opportunities. This ensures that the organisation has a pipeline of capable leaders who can guide teams through periods of change and uncertainty. For instance, a healthcare organisation might implement a leadership development programme that includes executive coaching, cross-functional projects, and exposure to strategic decision-making processes. By nurturing leadership talent, the organisation can enhance its ability to navigate complex environments and drive strategic initiatives.

Contingency Planning:

Contingency planning is a vital component of preparation and readiness. Companies must develop comprehensive contingency plans that outline how they will respond to various scenarios, such as natural disasters, economic downturns, supply chain disruptions, and cybersecurity threats. These plans should include detailed procedures, communication protocols, and roles and responsibilities to ensure a coordinated and effective response. For example, a retail company might create a business continuity plan that includes backup suppliers, alternative distribution routes, and emergency response teams. By having contingency plans in place, companies can minimise the impact of disruptions and maintain operational stability.

Regular testing and updating of contingency plans are essential to ensure their effectiveness. Companies must conduct drills, simulations, and scenario analyses to evaluate their preparedness and identify areas for improvement. For instance, a financial institution might conduct regular cybersecurity drills to assess its response to potential data breaches and refine its incident response protocols. By continuously refining their contingency plans, companies can enhance their resilience and ensure that they are well-prepared to handle unexpected events.

Flexible Supply Chain:

A flexible supply chain is critical for maintaining operational efficiency and meeting customer demands, especially during periods of disruption. Companies must design their supply chains to be agile and responsive, with the ability to adapt to changing conditions. This involves diversifying suppliers, optimising inventory management, and leveraging technology to enhance visibility and control. For example, a consumer goods company might use advanced supply chain analytics to forecast demand, monitor inventory levels, and optimise transportation routes. By implementing just-in-time inventory practices, the company can reduce carrying costs and improve responsiveness to market changes.

Collaboration with supply chain partners is also essential for building flexibility. Companies must work closely with their suppliers, distributors, and logistics providers to ensure alignment and coordination. This involves sharing information, aligning goals, and developing joint strategies to address potential challenges. For instance, an automotive manufacturer might collaborate with its suppliers to develop contingency plans for potential disruptions, such as supply shortages or transportation delays. By fostering strong partnerships, the company can enhance its supply chain resilience and ensure continuous operations.

Agile Business Processes:

Agile business processes are crucial for enabling organisations to respond quickly to market dynamics and customer needs. Companies must adopt agile methodologies that emphasise flexibility, collaboration, and iterative development. This involves breaking down projects into smaller, manageable tasks, using cross-functional teams, and incorporating feedback loops. For example, a software development company might implement agile practices to deliver incremental updates and enhancements to its products. This iterative approach allows the company to respond to customer feedback and market changes in real time, ensuring that its offerings remain relevant and competitive.

Agile processes also extend to decision-making and strategic planning. Companies must implement flexible planning processes that allow for regular review and adjustment of strategies. This involves setting clear objectives, monitoring performance, and making data-driven decisions. For example, a retail company might conduct quarterly planning sessions to reassess market conditions, evaluate performance, and adjust its strategies accordingly. This adaptive approach ensures that the company remains agile and can quickly pivot in response to new opportunities or threats.

Resilience During Disruptions:

The COVID-19 pandemic has underscored the importance of preparation and readiness in ensuring business continuity during disruptions. Companies that maintained flexible supply chains, robust IT infrastructure, and adaptable workforces were better positioned to navigate the challenges of the pandemic. For instance, many companies swiftly implemented remote work policies to ensure employee safety and maintain productivity. This involved providing employees with the necessary tools, technologies, and support to work effectively from home. Additionally, businesses adapted their operations to meet changing consumer needs, such as shifting to e-commerce, developing new product offerings, and enhancing customer service.

Companies that invested in digital transformation before the pandemic were able to leverage their technological capabilities to maintain operations and drive growth. For example, retailers with robust e-commerce platforms were able to continue serving customers despite physical store closures. Similarly, companies with advanced data analytics capabilities were able to gain insights into changing consumer behaviour and adjust their strategies accordingly. By embracing digital transformation, companies can enhance their resilience and agility, positioning themselves for long-term success.

Timing & Environmental Conditions

Sun Tzu emphasises the importance of understanding the proper season and special days for starting a conflagration, highlighting the critical role of timing and environmental conditions. In the business world, this principle translates into the concept of market timing and a deep understanding of the broader economic, social, and technological environment. Companies must meticulously assess market conditions and identify the optimal timing for launching new products, entering new markets, or executing mergers and acquisitions. By doing so, they can maximise the impact of their strategic actions and enhance their likelihood of success.

Assessing Market Conditions:

Effective market timing begins with a thorough analysis of current market conditions. Companies must gather and analyse data on consumer behaviour, economic indicators, industry trends, and competitive dynamics. This involves utilising various research methods, such as surveys, focus groups, and data analytics, to gain insights into the market environment. For instance, a consumer electronics company planning to launch a new product might conduct market research to understand the latest technological advancements, consumer preferences, and competitor offerings. By assessing market conditions, the company can identify the best time to introduce its product to maximise consumer interest and sales.

Economic Conditions:

Understanding the broader economic environment is crucial for strategic decision-making. Companies must monitor key economic indicators, such as GDP growth, inflation rates, unemployment levels, and consumer spending patterns, to assess the overall health of the economy. For example, a retail company considering expanding its operations might analyse economic data to determine if consumer confidence and spending are on the rise, indicating a favourable time for expansion. Conversely, if economic conditions are uncertain or declining, the company might delay its expansion plans to minimise risks and conserve resources.

Social Trends:

Social trends play a significant role in influencing market conditions and consumer behaviour. Companies must stay attuned to shifts in cultural, demographic, and lifestyle trends to ensure that their products and services remain relevant and appealing. For instance, a fashion brand might monitor social media platforms and influencer trends to identify emerging fashion styles and consumer preferences. By aligning their product offerings with current social trends, companies can capture consumer interest and drive sales. Additionally, understanding social trends can help companies identify new market opportunities and develop targeted marketing campaigns that resonate with specific customer segments.

Technological Advancements:

Technological advancements can create new opportunities and disrupt existing markets. Companies must keep a close eye on technological developments and assess their potential impact on their industry and business model. For example, a healthcare provider might monitor advancements in telemedicine technology and consider integrating virtual consultation services into its offerings. By staying ahead of technological trends, companies can leverage new technologies to enhance their operations, improve customer experiences, and gain a competitive edge. Additionally, early adoption of innovative technologies can position companies as industry leaders and attract tech-savvy customers.

Strategic Timing:

Timing is a critical element in executing strategic initiatives. Companies must identify the precise moment when conditions are most favourable for their actions. This requires continuous monitoring of the external environment and staying attuned to shifts in market trends, customer preferences, and industry developments. For instance, a technology company might decide to launch a new product during a period of high consumer demand for innovative gadgets, such as the holiday shopping season. By aligning strategic actions with the most opportune timing, companies can maximise their impact and drive significant results. Additionally, strategic timing involves knowing when to pause, observe, and adjust strategies to remain agile and responsive to changing conditions.

Market Entry & Expansion:

Entering new markets or expanding existing operations requires careful consideration of timing and environmental conditions. Companies must conduct thorough market research to understand local market dynamics, regulatory requirements, and competitive landscape. For example, a food and beverage company planning to enter an international market might analyse local consumer preferences, cultural nuances, and food regulations to ensure a successful market entry. By timing their entry to align with favourable economic and social conditions, companies can enhance their chances of success and minimise risks. Additionally, strategic partnerships with local firms can provide valuable insights and resources to navigate new markets effectively.

Mergers & Acquisitions:

Executing mergers and acquisitions (M&A) requires precise timing and a deep understanding of market conditions. Companies must assess the financial health and strategic fit of potential acquisition targets, as well as the overall market environment. For instance, a company considering an acquisition might analyse market trends, competitive dynamics, and economic conditions to determine the optimal time for the transaction. By executing M&A during favourable conditions, companies can achieve synergies, expand their market presence, and create value for shareholders. Additionally, well-timed acquisitions can provide access to new technologies, customer bases, and distribution channels.

Navigating Economic Downturns:

During economic downturns, companies must exercise strategic patience and agility to navigate challenging conditions. This might involve delaying major strategic moves, conserving resources, and focusing on core operations to maintain stability. For example, a manufacturing company facing a recession might postpone capital-intensive projects and prioritise cost-cutting measures to preserve cash flow. By waiting for more stable economic conditions, the company can mitigate risks and position itself for long-term growth. Additionally, companies can explore new revenue streams, such as digital transformation and e-commerce, to adapt to changing consumer behaviours and market conditions.

Real-World Example:

Tesla's strategic timing in introducing electric vehicles (EVs) and expanding its product line exemplifies the importance of market timing and environmental conditions. Tesla strategically timed its introduction of EVs to coincide with growing consumer interest in sustainable transportation and advancements in battery technology. By patiently waiting for the market conditions to be favourable, Tesla was able to capture significant consumer interest and establish itself as a leader in the EV market. The company's timing was further reinforced by its investment in building a comprehensive charging infrastructure, ensuring that its customers had access to convenient charging options, thereby enhancing the overall ownership experience.

Tesla's strategic timing extended to its expansion plans and product line diversification. The company introduced the Model S, a high-performance electric sedan, at a time when there was increasing demand for luxury electric vehicles. This was followed by the launch of the Model 3, a more affordable option that targeted the mass market. By carefully timing these product launches, Tesla was able to capture a broad customer base and drive substantial sales growth. Additionally, Tesla's entry into energy solutions, such as solar panels and energy storage systems, was timed to align with the growing focus on renewable energy. This strategic diversification not only reinforced Tesla's commitment to sustainability but also created new revenue streams and growth opportunities.

Tactical Response to Developments

Sun Tzu delineates five possible developments in the use of fire and the corresponding tactical responses. This insightful emphasis on adaptability and responsiveness is crucial for modern businesses navigating the complexities of today's dynamic environment. Companies must be able to pivot their strategies adeptly in response to rapid market changes, competitor actions, and internal developments. This flexibility is paramount to maintaining and enhancing their competitive edge.

Strategic Agility & Real-Time Decision Making:

The ability to make swift and informed decisions is essential in a rapidly changing marketplace. Companies must develop mechanisms to gather real-time data, analyse it promptly, and implement strategic decisions based on these insights. For instance, if a competitor launches a disruptive product, a company must quickly assess the situation by evaluating the potential impact on its market position, customer base, and long-term goals. This assessment requires a thorough analysis of the competitor's strengths and weaknesses, as well as an understanding of market trends and consumer preferences. By leveraging this information, companies can determine whether to respond immediately with a counter-innovation, make strategic adjustments to their existing offerings, or adopt a wait-and-see approach while preparing for a more calculated response.

Proactive Monitoring & Competitive Intelligence:

To stay ahead of the competition, companies must proactively monitor competitor activities and market developments. This involves setting up competitive intelligence systems to track competitors' product launches, marketing strategies, pricing changes, and technological advancements. For example, a consumer electronics company might use advanced data analytics and machine learning algorithms to monitor social media, industry publications, and patent filings for early signals of competitor innovations. By maintaining a vigilant watch on the competitive landscape, companies can anticipate potential threats and identify opportunities to differentiate themselves. This proactive approach allows companies to respond swiftly and strategically to competitor actions, thereby safeguarding their market position and enhancing their competitive advantage.

Adapting to Market Changes:

Market conditions can change rapidly due to various factors such as economic fluctuations, technological disruptions, regulatory shifts, and evolving consumer behaviours. Companies must be agile and adaptable, ready to pivot their strategies in response to these changes. This adaptability involves continuously analysing market data, staying attuned to industry trends, and engaging with customers to understand their evolving needs. For example, during the COVID-19 pandemic, many businesses rapidly adapted their strategies to address new market realities. Brick-and-mortar retailers pivoted to e-commerce platforms to continue serving customers during lockdowns, while companies in the hospitality industry implemented contactless services and enhanced sanitation protocols to ensure customer safety. By staying flexible and responsive, companies can navigate market changes effectively and seize new opportunities for growth.

Internal Alignment & Cross-Functional Collaboration:

Adapting to developments requires seamless internal coordination and cross-functional collaboration. Companies must ensure that all departments, from marketing and sales to research and development and operations, are aligned with the strategic objectives and ready to respond to market changes. This alignment involves fostering a culture of communication, collaboration, and shared goals. For example, a technology company might establish cross-functional teams to work on innovative projects, bringing together expertise from different departments to develop and launch new products swiftly. Regular meetings, clear communication channels, and collaborative tools can enhance coordination and ensure that all team members are aligned and working towards common objectives. By promoting internal alignment and collaboration, companies can respond more effectively to developments and drive innovation.

Scenario Planning & Risk Management:

Effective tactical response involves scenario planning and risk management. Companies must develop contingency plans for various scenarios, such as competitor disruptions, market downturns, and supply chain disruptions. Scenario planning involves creating and analysing multiple scenarios based on different assumptions about the future, allowing companies to prepare for potential outcomes and develop strategies to mitigate risks. For example, a financial services firm might create scenarios based on different interest rate environments to assess their impact on investment portfolios and develop strategies to mitigate risks. By preparing for multiple scenarios, companies can enhance their ability to adapt to changing conditions and maintain resilience.

Leveraging Technology for Agility:

Technology plays a crucial role in enabling companies to respond swiftly and effectively to developments. Advanced technologies such as artificial intelligence, machine learning, and data analytics can provide real-time insights and predictive analytics, empowering companies to make informed decisions. For example, a retail company might use AI-powered analytics to track consumer behaviour and predict demand trends, allowing it to adjust inventory levels and marketing strategies accordingly. Additionally, digital transformation initiatives, such as cloud computing and automation, can enhance operational efficiency and enable companies to scale their operations quickly in response to market changes. By leveraging technology, companies can enhance their agility and responsiveness, positioning themselves for long-term success.

Customer-Centric Approach:

Adapting to developments also involves maintaining a customer-centric approach. Companies must stay connected with their customers, gathering feedback and understanding their changing needs and preferences. This customer-centric approach allows companies to tailor their offerings and strategies to meet customer demands effectively. For example, a software company might gather feedback from users to identify pain points and develop new features that enhance the user experience. By prioritising customer needs and staying attuned to their evolving expectations, companies can build stronger relationships and drive customer loyalty.

Case Study: Amazon's Adaptability:

Amazon's adaptability and responsiveness to market changes and competitor actions serve as a prime example of strategic agility. The company's ability to pivot its strategies and innovate continuously has enabled it to maintain its market leadership and drive sustained growth. Amazon's proactive monitoring and competitive intelligence systems allow it to stay ahead of competitors and identify emerging trends. For instance, Amazon's early recognition of the growing demand for cloud computing services led to the launch of Amazon Web Services (AWS), which has become a significant revenue driver for the company.

During the COVID-19 pandemic, Amazon swiftly adapted its operations to address new market realities. The company implemented safety protocols in its fulfilment centres, expanded its delivery capacity, and introduced new services such as Amazon Pharmacy to meet the increased demand for essential goods and services. Additionally, Amazon's investment in technology, such as AI-powered logistics and automation, enabled it to enhance operational efficiency and respond to market changes effectively. By maintaining a customer-centric approach and prioritising customer needs, Amazon continued to deliver exceptional service and build customer loyalty.

Intelligence & Strategic Planning

Sun Tzu's notion of using fire as an aid to the attack reflects the indispensable importance of intelligence and strategic planning. In the business world, companies must gather and analyse information to make informed strategic decisions, enabling them to navigate complex environments and maintain a competitive edge. This process involves conducting comprehensive market research, competitive analysis, and scenario planning to understand the landscape and devise effective strategies.

Conducting Market Research:

Comprehensive market research is the foundation of effective strategic planning. Companies must gather data on market trends, customer preferences, and industry developments to gain valuable insights into the external environment. This involves employing various research methods, such as surveys, focus groups, and data analytics, to collect and analyse information. For example, a consumer goods company might conduct surveys and focus groups to understand shifting consumer preferences and identify emerging trends. By analysing this data, the company can make informed decisions about product development, marketing strategies, and market entry. Market research helps companies identify opportunities, anticipate changes, and develop strategies that align with market demands.

Competitive Analysis:

Understanding the competitive landscape is crucial for crafting effective strategies. Companies must conduct thorough competitive analysis to identify the strengths and weaknesses of their competitors, assess their market positions, and evaluate their strategic initiatives. This involves analysing competitors' products, pricing, marketing campaigns, and technological capabilities. For instance, a technology company might analyse competitors' product features, customer reviews, and market performance to identify areas where it can differentiate itself. By gaining insights into competitors' strengths and weaknesses, companies can develop strategies that leverage their unique capabilities and resources, positioning themselves more effectively in the market.

Scenario Planning:

Scenario planning is a strategic tool that helps companies prepare for various future scenarios and develop contingency plans. This involves creating and analysing multiple scenarios based on different assumptions about the future, such as economic conditions, regulatory changes, and technological advancements. For example, a financial services firm might create scenarios based on different interest rate environments to assess their impact on investment portfolios and develop strategies to mitigate risks. By exploring potential outcomes and preparing for different scenarios, companies can enhance their resilience and adaptability, ensuring they are well-prepared to navigate uncertainties and capitalise on opportunities.

Leveraging Intelligence for Strategic Decisions:

The insights gained from market research, competitive analysis, and scenario planning provide the foundation for informed strategic decision-making. Companies must leverage this intelligence to develop strategies that align with their goals and objectives. For example, a healthcare provider might use insights from market research to identify growing demand for telemedicine services and develop a strategy to expand its virtual care offerings. Similarly, a manufacturing company might use competitive analysis to identify opportunities for product differentiation and invest in developing innovative features that set it apart from competitors. By leveraging intelligence, companies can make strategic decisions that enhance their competitive advantage and drive long-term growth.

Understanding Competitor Strengths & Weaknesses:

To outmanoeuvre competitors, companies must have a deep understanding of their strengths and weaknesses. This involves conducting a SWOT analysis (Strengths, Weaknesses, Opportunities, Threats) to evaluate competitors' capabilities and identify areas of opportunity. For example, a retail company might analyse a competitor's supply chain efficiency, customer service quality, and product assortment to identify areas where it can improve and differentiate itself. By understanding competitors' weaknesses, companies can develop strategies to exploit these vulnerabilities and gain a competitive edge. Additionally, recognising competitors' strengths allows companies to benchmark their performance and identify areas for improvement.

Identifying Customer Needs:

Understanding customer needs and preferences is critical for developing effective strategies. Companies must gather and analyse customer data to gain insights into their behaviours, pain points, and expectations. This involves leveraging customer feedback, social media analytics, and purchasing data to create a comprehensive understanding of the target audience. For instance, an e-commerce company might analyse customer reviews and purchasing patterns to identify popular products and areas for improvement. By understanding customer needs, companies can tailor their offerings, enhance the customer experience, and build stronger relationships. This customer-centric approach ensures that companies remain relevant and competitive in the market.

Anticipating & Mitigating Risks:

Effective strategic planning involves anticipating potential risks and developing strategies to mitigate them. Companies must identify risks associated with market changes, competitive pressures, regulatory developments, and operational challenges. This involves conducting risk assessments, scenario planning, and developing contingency plans. For example, a pharmaceutical company might identify risks related to regulatory approvals, supply chain disruptions, and market competition. By developing mitigation strategies, such as diversifying suppliers, investing in regulatory compliance, and enhancing product differentiation, the company can minimise the impact of these risks and maintain operational continuity.

Seizing Opportunities:

Strategic planning also involves identifying and capitalising on opportunities. Companies must be proactive in recognising emerging trends, market gaps, and new technologies that can drive growth. This involves continuously monitoring the external environment, gathering intelligence, and being agile in responding to opportunities. For example, a renewable energy company might identify growing demand for solar energy and invest in developing advanced solar panel technology to capture market share. By seizing opportunities, companies can drive innovation, expand their market presence, and create value for stakeholders.

Crafting Strategies to Outmanoeuvre Competitors:

The ultimate goal of intelligence and strategic planning is to develop strategies that outmanoeuvre competitors and achieve sustainable success. This involves leveraging the insights gained from market research, competitive analysis, and scenario planning to create a strategic roadmap that guides the company's actions. For instance, a technology company might develop a strategy to invest in cutting-edge research and development, form strategic partnerships, and enhance customer engagement to differentiate itself from competitors. By aligning their strategies with their unique capabilities and resources, companies can create a competitive advantage and drive long-term growth.

Case Study: Netflix's Strategic Planning:

Netflix's success is a prime example of the power of intelligence and strategic planning. The company continuously gathers and analyses data on consumer preferences, market trends, and competitor actions to inform its strategic decisions. By leveraging big data and analytics, Netflix understands its audience's viewing habits and preferences, enabling it to create personalised content recommendations and enhance the user experience. Additionally, Netflix conducts competitive analysis to identify gaps in the market and develop original content that sets it apart from competitors. By anticipating and mitigating risks, such as content piracy and changing consumer behaviours, Netflix has maintained its market leadership and driven sustained growth.

The Spirit of Enterprise

Sun Tzu warns against the stagnation that results from a lack of enterprise, emphasising the need for continuous innovation and proactive engagement. This principle is highly relevant to modern businesses, where innovation and entrepreneurship serve as critical drivers of growth and success. Companies that cultivate a culture of innovation and encourage employees to think creatively, take risks, and explore new opportunities are better positioned to thrive in dynamic and competitive markets.

Cultivating a Culture of Innovation:

A culture of innovation starts with leadership that prioritises and models innovative thinking. Leaders must set a vision that embraces change and encourages employees to experiment with new ideas. This involves creating an environment where curiosity is valued, and failure is seen as a learning opportunity rather than a setback. For example, a technology company might establish innovation labs where teams can work on cutting-edge projects without the constraints of daily operations. By providing dedicated time and resources for innovation, companies signal their commitment to creativity and experimentation.

Communication plays a crucial role in fostering innovation. Companies must promote open and transparent communication channels that allow ideas to flow freely across all levels of the organisation. This involves regular brainstorming sessions, cross-departmental meetings, and digital platforms for idea sharing. For instance, a global manufacturing firm might implement an online innovation portal where employees can submit ideas, collaborate on projects, and receive feedback from peers and leaders. By facilitating open dialogue, companies can tap into the collective intelligence of their workforce and drive innovative solutions.

Encouraging Risk-Taking & Exploration:

Encouraging employees to take risks and explore new opportunities is essential for nurturing the spirit of enterprise. This requires a shift in mindset where employees feel empowered to venture beyond their comfort zones without fear of retribution. Companies can achieve this by recognising and rewarding innovative efforts, even if they do not always result in immediate success. For example, a financial services firm might introduce an innovation award that celebrates employees who demonstrate bold thinking and creative problem-solving. By acknowledging and celebrating risk-taking, companies create a safe space for innovation to flourish.

Professional development is another key aspect of encouraging exploration. Companies must invest in training and development programmes that equip employees with the skills and knowledge needed to innovate. This includes offering courses on emerging technologies, creative thinking, and innovation management. For example, an automotive company might partner with leading universities to provide employees with access to advanced engineering and design programmes. By continuously enhancing employees' capabilities, companies empower them to explore new ideas and drive innovation.

Intrapreneurship Programmes:

Intrapreneurship programmes are effective tools for fostering innovation within organisations. These programmes provide employees with the resources, autonomy, and support needed to develop new ideas and ventures internally. By nurturing intrapreneurship, companies can harness the entrepreneurial spirit of their workforce and drive significant innovation from within. For instance, a pharmaceutical company might launch an intrapreneurship programme that allows employees to pitch new drug development projects. Successful pitches receive funding, mentorship, and dedicated time to bring their ideas to fruition. This approach not only accelerates innovation but also fosters a sense of ownership and engagement among employees.

Intrapreneurship programmes can take various forms, such as innovation incubators, hackathons, and internal venture funds. For example, a retail company might host an annual innovation challenge where teams compete to develop new products, services, or business models. Winning teams receive financial support and resources to implement their ideas. By providing a structured framework for innovation, companies can channel employees' creativity into impactful initiatives that drive growth and differentiation.

Continuous Evolution & Staying Ahead:

To stay ahead of the competition, companies must continuously evolve and adapt to changing market conditions. This involves a commitment to lifelong learning and a proactive approach to identifying and capitalising on emerging trends. Companies must regularly review their strategies, processes, and offerings to ensure they remain relevant and competitive. For example, a software company might conduct quarterly innovation reviews to assess the progress of ongoing projects, identify new opportunities, and allocate resources accordingly. By maintaining a dynamic and forward-thinking mindset, companies can anticipate market shifts and respond swiftly to changes.

Partnerships and collaborations also play a vital role in continuous evolution. Companies can enhance their innovation capabilities by partnering with external organisations, such as startups, research institutions, and industry consortia. For example, an energy company might collaborate with a cutting-edge technology startup to develop new renewable energy solutions. By leveraging external expertise and resources, companies can accelerate innovation and gain access to new markets and technologies.

Implementing Agile Methodologies:

Adopting agile methodologies can further enhance a company's ability to innovate and respond to market changes. Agile methodologies emphasise flexibility, iterative development, and continuous improvement. By breaking down large projects into smaller, manageable tasks, companies can quickly adapt to changing conditions and make adjustments based on real-time feedback. For example, a telecommunications company might implement agile practices to develop and launch new services rapidly. This iterative approach allows the company to test new ideas, gather customer feedback, and refine its offerings, ensuring they meet market demands and drive customer satisfaction.

Case Study: Google & Microsoft's Culture of Innovation:

Companies like Google and Microsoft exemplify the successful cultivation of a culture of innovation and the spirit of enterprise. Google, known for its innovative approach, fosters a culture that encourages creativity and exploration. The company offers employees the freedom to spend a portion of their time on personal projects through its "20% time" policy, resulting in the development of groundbreaking products such as Gmail and Google News. Google's commitment to continuous learning, open communication, and cross-functional collaboration drives its innovation success.

Microsoft, under the leadership of Satya Nadella, has also transformed its organisational culture to prioritise innovation and entrepreneurship. Nadella's focus on a growth mindset, continuous learning, and collaboration has driven significant advancements in technology and market leadership. Microsoft encourages intrapreneurship through initiatives such as its Garage programme, which provides employees with the resources and autonomy to work on innovative projects. By fostering a culture of innovation, Microsoft has maintained its competitive edge and driven sustained growth.

Ethical Considerations & Long-term Strategy

Sun Tzu's advice against fighting battles out of anger or pique and his emphasis on the enlightened ruler's cautious approach resonate deeply with the importance of ethical considerations and long-term strategy in modern business practices. In today's complex and interconnected world, companies must strike a delicate balance between achieving short-term gains and ensuring long-term sustainability. This requires a commitment to ethical conduct, a clear alignment with core values and mission, and a strategic focus on building lasting competitive advantages, fostering strong relationships with stakeholders, and maintaining a positive reputation.

Balancing Short-term Gains with Long-term Sustainability:

In the pursuit of short-term profits, companies may face pressures to make hasty decisions or take actions that deliver immediate results. However, such decisions can often lead to negative consequences that undermine long-term success. Companies must adopt a holistic perspective that considers both short-term and long-term impacts. This involves implementing strategic planning processes that prioritise sustainable growth and resilience. For example, a manufacturing company might choose to invest in sustainable practices, such as energy-efficient production methods and waste reduction initiatives, even if these investments require significant upfront costs. By prioritising long-term sustainability over short-term gains, the company can build a strong foundation for future growth and enhance its reputation as a responsible corporate citizen.

Aligning Actions with Core Values & Mission:

Ethical considerations are deeply intertwined with a company's core values and mission. Companies must ensure that their actions consistently reflect their ethical principles and commitment to social responsibility. This involves integrating ethical considerations into every aspect of decision-making, from strategic planning to daily operations. For example, a technology company that values privacy and data security must rigorously safeguard customer information and comply with data protection regulations. By aligning actions with core values, companies can build trust with customers, employees, and other stakeholders, fostering loyalty and long-term relationships. Additionally, a strong commitment to ethical conduct can differentiate a company from competitors and enhance its brand reputation.

Avoiding Hasty Decisions Driven by Short-term Pressures:

Hasty decisions driven by short-term pressures or emotional reactions can lead to strategic missteps and damage to a company's reputation. Companies must adopt a measured and deliberate approach to decision-making, especially in times of crisis or uncertainty. This involves conducting thorough analyses, considering multiple perspectives, and seeking input from key stakeholders. For example, a financial services firm facing market volatility might avoid making impulsive investment decisions by conducting comprehensive risk assessments and consulting with financial experts. By taking a thoughtful and calculated approach, the company can navigate challenges effectively and make decisions that support long-term objectives.

Building Sustainable Competitive Advantages:

Long-term success requires companies to build sustainable competitive advantages that are difficult for competitors to replicate. This involves investing in innovation, developing unique value propositions, and continuously improving products and services. For instance, a pharmaceutical company might invest in cutting-edge research and development to create groundbreaking treatments for unmet medical needs. By focusing on innovation and differentiation, the company can establish a strong market position and drive sustained growth. Additionally, companies can build competitive advantages through strategic partnerships, intellectual property protection, and operational excellence. These efforts contribute to long-term resilience and market leadership.

Fostering Strong Relationships with Stakeholders:

Building and maintaining strong relationships with stakeholders is essential for long-term success. Companies must engage with stakeholders, including customers, employees, suppliers, investors, and communities, to understand their needs and expectations. This involves transparent communication, active listening, and collaborative problem-solving. For example, a retail company might engage with customers through surveys and focus groups to gather feedback on product offerings and customer service. By addressing stakeholder concerns and demonstrating a commitment to their well-being, companies can build trust and loyalty. Strong stakeholder relationships also provide valuable insights that inform strategic decision-making and enhance overall performance.

Maintaining a Positive Reputation:

A positive reputation is a valuable asset that contributes to long-term success. Companies must actively manage their reputation by consistently delivering on their promises, demonstrating ethical behaviour, and contributing to the greater good. This involves proactive reputation management strategies, such as effective public relations, corporate social responsibility initiatives, and crisis communication plans. For example, a company facing a product recall might respond transparently and swiftly, taking responsibility and implementing corrective actions. By demonstrating accountability and integrity, the company can mitigate reputational damage and maintain stakeholder trust. Additionally, companies can enhance their reputation by supporting social and environmental causes, such as sustainability, diversity, and community development. These efforts reinforce the company's commitment to making a positive impact and contribute to long-term brand equity.

Case Study: Unilever's Sustainable Living Plan:

Unilever's Sustainable Living Plan exemplifies the integration of ethical considerations and long-term strategy. The company has committed to making sustainable living commonplace by integrating sustainability into its business model and addressing social and environmental challenges. Unilever's plan includes ambitious goals such as reducing the environmental footprint of its products, improving health and well-being, and enhancing livelihoods. By prioritising sustainability, Unilever has not only built a positive reputation but also achieved significant business benefits, including cost savings, innovation, and increased consumer trust. The company's long-term focus on sustainability and ethical conduct has positioned it as a leader in corporate responsibility and contributed to its sustained growth.

Ethical Leadership & Governance:

Ethical leadership and governance are critical for ensuring that a company's actions align with its values and long-term strategy. Leaders must set the tone at the top by modelling ethical behaviour, promoting transparency, and holding themselves and others accountable. This involves establishing robust governance structures, such as ethics committees, compliance programmes, and whistleblower protection policies, to ensure ethical conduct throughout the organisation. For example, a technology company might implement a comprehensive ethics and compliance programme that includes training, monitoring, and reporting mechanisms. By fostering a culture of ethics and integrity, companies can build a strong foundation for long-term success and resilience.

Adapting to Changing Expectations:

As societal expectations evolve, companies must continuously adapt their strategies to meet emerging ethical standards and stakeholder demands. This involves staying informed about regulatory developments, industry best practices, and social trends. For example, increasing awareness of climate change and environmental sustainability has led many companies to adopt more rigorous sustainability practices. A food and beverage company might set ambitious goals for reducing plastic waste, sourcing sustainable ingredients, and minimising carbon emissions. By proactively adapting to changing expectations, companies can demonstrate their commitment to ethical conduct and long-term sustainability, thereby enhancing their competitiveness and relevance.

Summary

Sun Tzu's *The Attack by Fire* offers timeless insights that are remarkably applicable to modern strategic management. The principles of resource utilisation, preparation, timing, adaptability, intelligence, innovation, and ethical considerations provide a comprehensive framework for navigating the complexities of the business world.

CHAPTER 13 — THE USE OF SPIES

*Be subtle! be subtle!
and use your spies for every kind of business.*

Sun Tzu

Sun Tzu's *The Use of Spies* stands out as a testament to the timeless relevance of information gathering and intelligence in achieving strategic advantage. While the context has shifted from the battlegrounds of ancient China to the boardrooms and market landscapes of contemporary corporate strategy, the principles articulated by Sun Tzu remain profoundly applicable.

The Cost of Ignorance & Value of Intelligence

Sun Tzu begins *The Use of Spies* by underscoring the immense cost of prolonged military campaigns and the strategic folly of remaining ignorant about the enemy's condition. This wisdom seamlessly translates to the corporate world, where ignorance of market conditions, competitor moves, and customer preferences can lead to strategic missteps and resource wastage. Just as a general must invest in intelligence to minimise the duration and cost of war, business leaders must prioritise market research and competitive intelligence. By understanding the competitive landscape, companies can make informed decisions, anticipate market shifts, and deploy resources effectively, thereby avoiding costly mistakes.

Importance of Market Research:

Market research is an essential tool for businesses to gain a comprehensive understanding of their environment. This involves collecting data on customer preferences, market trends, and economic conditions. Companies can utilise various methods such as surveys, focus groups, and data analytics to gather this information. For example, a fashion retailer might conduct surveys to understand consumer preferences for the upcoming season. By analysing the gathered data, the company can make informed decisions about product design, pricing, and marketing strategies. Effective market research helps companies identify opportunities, mitigate risks, and stay ahead of the competition.

Competitive Intelligence:

Competitive intelligence involves systematically gathering and analysing information about competitors' activities, strategies, and capabilities. This process enables companies to anticipate competitors' moves and develop strategies to counteract them. For instance, a technology firm might monitor competitors' product launches, patent filings, and market positioning to gain insights into their strategic priorities. By understanding competitors' strengths and weaknesses, the company can identify gaps in the market and develop differentiated products and services. Competitive intelligence also helps companies benchmark their performance against industry standards and identify areas for improvement.

Anticipating Market Shifts:

The business environment is constantly evolving, with market conditions and consumer behaviours changing rapidly. Companies must be proactive in monitoring these shifts to stay competitive. This involves staying attuned to emerging trends, technological advancements, and regulatory changes. For example, a healthcare provider might track developments in telemedicine and digital health technologies to anticipate changes in patient preferences and regulatory requirements. By staying informed, the company can adapt its offerings and strategies to meet evolving market demands. Anticipating market shifts allows companies to be agile and responsive, positioning them for long-term success.

Informed Decision-Making:

Informed decision-making is a cornerstone of effective business strategy. By leveraging intelligence from market research and competitive analysis, companies can make strategic decisions that align with their goals and objectives. For example, a financial services firm might use market research to identify a growing demand for sustainable investment products. Based on this insight, the firm can develop and launch new investment offerings that cater to environmentally conscious investors. Informed decision-making reduces the risk of costly mistakes and enhances the likelihood of achieving desired outcomes.

Resource Allocation:

Effective resource allocation is crucial for maximising business performance. Companies must deploy their financial, human, and technological resources strategically to achieve their objectives. This involves prioritising initiatives that offer the greatest potential for return on investment and align with the company's strategic goals. For instance, a manufacturing company might allocate resources to upgrade its production facilities and adopt advanced manufacturing technologies. By doing so, the company can improve operational efficiency, reduce costs, and enhance product quality. Strategic resource allocation ensures that companies utilise their assets effectively and maintain a competitive edge.

Avoiding Costly Mistakes:

Ignorance in the business world can lead to significant financial losses and strategic setbacks. Companies that fail to invest in intelligence risk making decisions based on incomplete or outdated information. For example, a retail company that neglects to monitor changing consumer preferences may continue to stock products that are no longer in demand. This can result in excess inventory, reduced sales, and financial losses. By prioritising intelligence, companies can avoid such costly mistakes and make data-driven decisions that support long-term success.

Enhancing Strategic Planning:

Strategic planning is an ongoing process that requires continuous monitoring and adaptation. Companies must regularly review and update their strategic plans based on new intelligence and changing market conditions. This involves setting clear goals, developing actionable strategies, and tracking progress. For instance, an automotive company might set a strategic goal to become a leader in electric vehicle (EV) technology. To achieve this, the company can invest in R&D, form partnerships with battery manufacturers, and launch new EV models. By continuously refining its strategic plan based on market intelligence, the company can achieve its objectives and drive innovation.

Leveraging Technology for Intelligence:

Advancements in technology have transformed the way companies gather and analyse intelligence. Big data analytics, artificial intelligence (AI), and machine learning enable companies to process vast amounts of data quickly and derive valuable insights. For example, an e-commerce company might use AI-powered analytics to track customer behaviour and preferences in real time. This allows the company to personalise its marketing campaigns and improve the customer experience. By leveraging technology, companies can enhance their intelligence capabilities and make more informed decisions.

Building a Culture of Intelligence:

Creating a culture that values intelligence and informed decision-making is essential for sustained success. This involves fostering a mindset that prioritises data-driven insights and encourages continuous learning. Companies can achieve this by providing employees with access to training programmes, analytical tools, and data resources. For example, a consumer goods company might offer workshops on data analytics and market research techniques. By empowering employees with the skills and knowledge to gather and analyse intelligence, the company can build a culture of informed decision-making and innovation.

Case Study: Apple's Strategic Use of Intelligence:

Apple's success is a testament to the value of intelligence and informed decision-making. The company's rigorous market research and competitive analysis have enabled it to anticipate consumer trends and develop innovative products that resonate with customers. For example, Apple's introduction of the iPhone was based on extensive research into consumer preferences for mobile devices. By understanding the competitive landscape and identifying gaps in the market, Apple was able to create a product that revolutionised the industry. The company's continuous investment in R&D and market intelligence has allowed it to maintain its leadership position and drive sustained growth.

Foreknowledge & Strategic Decision-Making

Foreknowledge, according to Sun Tzu, is the hallmark of wise leadership and a prerequisite for achieving strategic objectives. This timeless wisdom is highly relevant to modern strategic management, where the use of data analytics, market intelligence, and scenario planning is crucial for informed decision-making. By leveraging big data and advanced analytics, companies can gain predictive insights into market trends, customer behaviour, and competitor actions. This foreknowledge enables strategic foresight, allowing businesses to craft proactive strategies, seize emerging opportunities, and mitigate potential risks. The ability to anticipate and respond to market dynamics is a key differentiator in achieving sustainable competitive advantage.

Leveraging Data Analytics:

Data analytics is a powerful tool that allows companies to extract valuable insights from vast amounts of data. By analysing data from various sources, such as customer transactions, social media interactions, and website traffic, companies can uncover patterns and trends that inform strategic decisions. For example, an online retailer might use data analytics to identify purchasing trends and predict future demand for specific products. This information can guide inventory management, marketing campaigns, and product development. Additionally, data analytics can help companies segment their customer base and tailor their offerings to meet the unique needs of different customer groups. By leveraging data analytics, companies can make data-driven decisions that enhance their competitive advantage and drive growth.

Market Intelligence:

Market intelligence involves gathering and analysing information about market conditions, industry trends, and competitive activities. This process enables companies to stay informed about the external environment and make strategic decisions based on comprehensive insights. For example, a financial services firm might use market intelligence to track regulatory changes, economic indicators, and competitor strategies. By staying attuned to these factors, the firm can anticipate market shifts and adjust its strategies accordingly. Market intelligence also involves monitoring customer feedback and preferences, which can provide valuable insights into market demand and emerging opportunities. By prioritising market intelligence, companies can develop a deep understanding of their competitive landscape and make informed decisions that drive success.

Scenario Planning:

Scenario planning is a strategic tool that helps companies prepare for various future scenarios and develop contingency plans. This involves creating and analysing multiple scenarios based on different assumptions about the future, such as economic conditions, technological advancements, and regulatory changes. For example, a technology company might create scenarios to assess the impact of potential disruptions, such as new market entrants or changes in consumer behaviour. By exploring these scenarios, the company can identify potential risks and opportunities and develop strategies to navigate them. Scenario planning enhances a company's ability to anticipate and respond to market dynamics, ensuring resilience and adaptability in a rapidly changing environment.

Predictive Insights:

Advanced analytics and machine learning algorithms enable companies to gain predictive insights into future market trends and customer behaviour. By analysing historical data and identifying patterns, companies can make accurate forecasts and informed predictions. For example, a healthcare provider might use predictive analytics to forecast patient demand for specific services and allocate resources accordingly. This foresight allows the provider to optimise operations, reduce wait times, and improve patient satisfaction. Predictive insights also enable companies to identify emerging market trends and capitalise on new opportunities before competitors. By leveraging predictive analytics, companies can stay ahead of the curve and drive innovation.

Crafting Proactive Strategies:

Foreknowledge allows companies to craft proactive strategies that position them for success. Rather than reacting to market changes and competitor actions, companies can anticipate these developments and develop strategies to address them proactively. For example, a consumer goods company might use market intelligence to identify a growing demand for eco-friendly products. By developing a line of sustainable products and launching them ahead of competitors, the company can capture market share and build a reputation as a leader in sustainability. Proactive strategies also involve continuous monitoring and adjustment to ensure alignment with market conditions and strategic goals. By adopting a proactive approach, companies can drive growth and maintain a competitive edge.

Seizing Emerging Opportunities:

Foreknowledge enables companies to identify and seize emerging opportunities that drive growth and innovation. This involves staying attuned to industry trends, technological advancements, and regulatory changes that create new market opportunities. For example, an energy company might identify a growing demand for renewable energy solutions and invest in developing advanced solar and wind technologies. By entering the market early and positioning itself as a leader in renewable energy, the company can capture market share and drive significant growth. Seizing emerging opportunities also involves strategic partnerships and collaborations that enhance a company's capabilities and expand its reach. By leveraging foreknowledge, companies can capitalise on new opportunities and drive long-term success.

Mitigating Potential Risks:

Foreknowledge allows companies to anticipate potential risks and develop strategies to mitigate them. This involves conducting risk assessments, scenario planning, and developing contingency plans. For example, a manufacturing company might identify risks related to supply chain disruptions, regulatory changes, and market competition. By developing mitigation strategies, such as diversifying suppliers, investing in regulatory compliance, and enhancing product differentiation, the company can minimise the impact of these risks and maintain operational continuity. Mitigating risks also involves regular monitoring and adjustment to ensure alignment with changing conditions. By prioritising risk management, companies can enhance their resilience and protect their long-term success.

Enhancing Strategic Foresight:

Strategic foresight is the ability to anticipate and respond to future developments in the business environment. This involves staying informed about market trends, technological advancements, and regulatory changes that impact the industry. For example, a telecommunications company might use strategic foresight to anticipate the impact of 5G technology on its operations and develop strategies to leverage this technology for competitive advantage. Enhancing strategic foresight involves continuous learning, scenario planning, and proactive decision-making. By prioritising strategic foresight, companies can stay ahead of the curve and drive innovation.

Building a Data-Driven Culture:

Creating a data-driven culture is essential for leveraging foreknowledge and making informed strategic decisions. This involves fostering a mindset that prioritises data and analytics in decision-making processes. Companies can achieve this by providing employees with access to data analytics tools, training programmes, and resources. For example, a retail company might offer workshops on data analytics and business intelligence techniques. By empowering employees with the skills and knowledge to gather and analyse data, the company can build a culture of informed decision-making and innovation.

Case Study: Amazon's Use of Data Analytics:

Amazon's success is a testament to the value of foreknowledge and data-driven decision-making. The company continuously gathers and analyses data on customer behaviour, market trends, and competitive activities to inform its strategic decisions. By leveraging big data and advanced analytics, Amazon can predict customer preferences, optimise inventory management, and personalise marketing campaigns. For example, Amazon's recommendation engine uses predictive analytics to suggest products based on customers' browsing and purchasing history. This personalised approach drives customer engagement and sales. Additionally, Amazon's investment in data analytics has enabled it to anticipate market shifts and launch new services, such as Amazon Web Services (AWS), that drive significant growth. The company's commitment to data-driven decision-making has been a key differentiator in achieving sustainable competitive advantage.

The Role of Different Types of Spies

Sun Tzu's classification of spies into five categories—local spies, inward spies, converted spies, doomed spies, and surviving spies—provides a nuanced understanding of intelligence gathering that is remarkably applicable to the corporate world. Each type of spy offers a unique source of information, essential for crafting effective strategies and maintaining a competitive edge. In modern business, these categories can be interpreted as different sources and methods of acquiring strategic information.

Local Spies:

Local spies, or employees within a market, provide invaluable on-the-ground insights into local market conditions. These individuals are embedded within the target market and possess firsthand knowledge of local consumer behaviours, market trends, and competitive dynamics. For example, a multinational corporation expanding into a new geographical region might rely on local employees to gather insights about consumer preferences, regulatory environments, and local competitors. This localised intelligence helps the company tailor its products, marketing strategies, and operations to meet the unique needs of the market. By leveraging the knowledge of local spies, companies can make informed decisions that enhance their market entry and growth strategies.

Inward Spies:

Inward spies, or industry insiders, offer valuable intelligence on competitor strategies, industry trends, and technological advancements. These individuals have access to internal information within competitor organisations or industry networks. For instance, a technology company might employ industry insiders to monitor competitors' product development efforts, patent filings, and strategic partnerships. By gaining insights into competitors' strengths and weaknesses, the company can identify gaps in the market and develop innovative solutions that differentiate it from competitors. Inward spies also provide early warnings about potential threats, such as new market entrants or disruptive technologies. This intelligence enables companies to adapt their strategies proactively and maintain a competitive edge.

Converted Spies:

Converted spies are analogous to strategic partnerships or alliances that provide access to new information channels and resources. These partnerships allow companies to share intelligence, pool resources, and collaborate on strategic initiatives. For example, a pharmaceutical company might form an alliance with a biotechnology firm to co-develop new treatments. This partnership provides both companies with access to each other's research, technologies, and market insights. By leveraging the strengths and intelligence of converted spies, companies can accelerate innovation, reduce risks, and enhance their competitive positioning. Strategic partnerships also enable companies to enter new markets and expand their reach through shared networks and resources.

Doomed Spies:

Doomed spies, or deliberate misinformation campaigns, can be used strategically to mislead competitors and create confusion. While the ethical implications of such tactics must be carefully considered, the concept highlights the importance of controlling the narrative and managing competitive intelligence. For example, a company might release misleading information about its product launch dates or strategic priorities to divert competitors' attention and resources. This tactic can buy the company time to develop its initiatives without the pressure of direct competition. However, it is essential for companies to balance the use of misinformation with ethical considerations and ensure that such strategies do not compromise their integrity or reputation.

Surviving Spies:

Surviving spies, or key informants, are individuals who bring back critical information from the competitive landscape. These informants operate within or closely monitor competitors and the broader industry environment. For example, a market research firm might employ surviving spies to conduct in-depth competitor analysis, monitor market trends, and gather insights from industry conferences and events. This intelligence provides companies with a comprehensive understanding of the competitive landscape, enabling them to anticipate market shifts, identify emerging opportunities, and develop robust strategies. Surviving spies also offer valuable feedback on the effectiveness of existing strategies, allowing companies to refine their approaches continuously.

Comprehensive Intelligence Gathering:

By utilising a multifaceted approach to intelligence gathering, companies can build a comprehensive understanding of their competitive environment. This "divine manipulation of the threads," as Sun Tzu calls it, is essential for developing robust strategies and maintaining a competitive edge. Combining insights from local spies, inward spies, converted spies, doomed spies, and surviving spies allows companies to gain a holistic view of the market and make informed decisions. For instance, a consumer electronics company might integrate data from local market research, industry reports, strategic partnerships, and competitor analysis to develop a new product that meets consumer needs and outperforms competitors.

Case Study: Procter & Gamble's Intelligence Gathering:

Procter & Gamble (P&G) exemplifies the strategic use of intelligence gathering in the corporate world. The company employs various methods to gather market intelligence, including local market research, industry analysis, and strategic partnerships. P&G's local market researchers provide on-the-ground insights into consumer preferences, cultural nuances, and market dynamics. This intelligence helps P&G tailor its products and marketing strategies to meet the unique needs of different regions. Additionally, P&G collaborates with research institutions and industry partners to gain access to cutting-edge technologies and innovations. By leveraging a multifaceted approach to intelligence gathering, P&G has maintained its leadership position in the consumer goods industry and driven sustained growth.

Building a Culture of Intelligence:

Creating a culture that values intelligence and informed decision-making is essential for sustained success. Companies must foster a mindset that prioritises data-driven insights and encourages continuous learning. This involves providing employees with access to training programmes, analytical tools, and data resources. For example, a technology company might offer workshops on data analytics and market research techniques. By empowering employees with the skills and knowledge to gather and analyse intelligence, the company can build a culture of informed decision-making and innovation.

Ethical Considerations:

While intelligence gathering is crucial for strategic decision-making, companies must consider the ethical implications of their actions. It is important to balance the pursuit of competitive intelligence with ethical standards and respect for privacy. Companies must ensure that their intelligence-gathering practices comply with legal and regulatory requirements and do not compromise their integrity or reputation. By maintaining high ethical standards, companies can build trust with stakeholders and sustain their competitive advantage in the long term.

The Importance of Secrecy & Trust

Sun Tzu emphasises the paramount importance of secrecy and the careful management of spies, a principle that translates seamlessly to the corporate world where maintaining the confidentiality of strategic plans and proprietary information is crucial. In today's business environment, leaks and breaches can significantly undermine a company's competitive advantage and expose vulnerabilities that competitors can exploit. Therefore, it is essential for companies to implement robust cybersecurity measures and foster a culture of discretion among employees.

Maintaining Confidentiality:

Confidentiality is the cornerstone of protecting sensitive information. Companies must ensure that their strategic plans, proprietary technologies, and internal communications are safeguarded against unauthorised access. This involves implementing comprehensive cybersecurity protocols, such as encryption, secure access controls, and regular security audits. For example, a financial institution might use advanced encryption technologies to protect client data and transaction information. Additionally, companies must establish clear policies and training programmes to educate employees about the importance of confidentiality and the risks associated with data breaches. By maintaining strict confidentiality, companies can protect their intellectual property, strategic initiatives, and competitive positioning.

Implementing Robust Cybersecurity Measures:

Cybersecurity is a critical component of maintaining secrecy in the digital age. Companies must invest in cutting-edge technologies and best practices to secure their information systems against cyber threats. This includes deploying firewalls, intrusion detection systems, and antivirus software to prevent unauthorised access and malicious attacks. For instance, a healthcare provider might use multi-factor authentication and advanced threat detection to protect patient records and medical data. Regular security assessments and penetration testing can help identify vulnerabilities and strengthen defences. By prioritising cybersecurity, companies can mitigate the risk of data breaches and ensure the integrity and confidentiality of their information.

Fostering a Culture of Discretion:

Creating a culture of discretion involves promoting awareness and accountability among employees regarding the handling of sensitive information. Companies must emphasise the importance of discretion through regular training sessions, internal communications, and leadership example. For example, a tech company might conduct workshops on data privacy and secure communication practices. Employees should be encouraged to report any suspicious activities or potential breaches to designated security teams. By fostering a culture of discretion, companies can reduce the risk of inadvertent leaks and ensure that all employees are aligned with the organisation's commitment to confidentiality.

Management of Intelligence Resources:

The management of intelligence resources requires a leadership approach that values integrity, transparency, and creativity. Just as Sun Tzu emphasises the need for benevolence, straightforwardness, and subtle ingenuity in managing spies, modern business leaders must ensure the reliability and truthfulness of intelligence reports. This involves building trust with intelligence resources, such as data analysts, market researchers, and strategic consultants, and fostering an environment where they can operate effectively.

Integrity and Transparency:

Integrity and transparency are essential for building trust within an organisation. Leaders must demonstrate ethical behaviour, open communication, and a commitment to honesty in all interactions. For example, a multinational corporation might implement a code of conduct that outlines ethical standards and expectations for all employees. By promoting a culture of integrity and transparency, companies can build a strong foundation of trust that supports effective intelligence gathering and decision-making. Employees are more likely to share accurate and reliable information when they trust their leaders and believe in the organisation's values.

Creativity and Ingenuity:

Creativity and ingenuity are critical for developing innovative solutions and strategies. Leaders must encourage intelligence resources to think outside the box and explore new approaches to gathering and analysing information. For example, a marketing team might use social media analytics and sentiment analysis to gain insights into consumer behaviour and preferences. By fostering a culture of creativity, companies can enhance their ability to generate valuable intelligence and stay ahead of competitors. Additionally, leaders should provide the necessary tools, training, and support to enable intelligence resources to excel in their roles.

Ensuring the Reliability of Intelligence Reports:

The reliability of intelligence reports is crucial for making sound strategic decisions. Companies must implement rigorous processes for validating and verifying the accuracy of information. This involves cross-referencing data from multiple sources, conducting thorough analyses, and seeking input from subject matter experts. For example, a manufacturing company might use data triangulation to confirm market research findings and ensure the accuracy of competitive intelligence. By ensuring the reliability of intelligence reports, companies can make informed decisions that drive growth and success.

Developing Robust Strategies:

Secrecy and trust are essential for developing robust strategies that give companies a competitive edge. By protecting sensitive information and fostering a culture of integrity, companies can confidently pursue strategic initiatives without the risk of leaks or breaches. For example, an automotive company might develop a groundbreaking electric vehicle in secrecy, ensuring that competitors are unaware of its innovations until the official launch. This strategic advantage allows the company to capture market share and establish itself as a leader in the industry.

Case Study: Apple's Commitment to Secrecy:

Apple is renowned for its commitment to secrecy and the careful management of its strategic plans and proprietary information. The company employs stringent security measures and fosters a culture of discretion to protect its innovations. For example, Apple uses secure access controls, non-disclosure agreements, and compartmentalised workflows to ensure that sensitive information is only accessible to authorised personnel. This commitment to secrecy has allowed Apple to maintain a competitive edge and generate excitement around its product launches. Additionally, Apple's leadership values integrity, transparency, and creativity, fostering a culture where employees are motivated to contribute to the company's success while maintaining confidentiality.

Implementing Best Practices for Confidentiality:

Companies can implement best practices to enhance confidentiality and trust. This includes regular security training, clear policies and procedures, and ongoing monitoring and auditing. For example, a financial services firm might conduct quarterly security assessments and provide employees with training on data protection and secure communication. By continuously improving their security practices, companies can protect sensitive information and build a reputation for reliability and trustworthiness.

Building Trust with Stakeholders:

Building trust with stakeholders is essential for long-term success. Companies must demonstrate their commitment to ethical conduct, transparency, and confidentiality in all interactions. For example, a pharmaceutical company might engage with regulatory authorities, healthcare providers, and patients to ensure compliance with data privacy regulations and build trust in its products. By fostering strong relationships based on trust, companies can enhance their reputation, attract loyal customers, and achieve sustained growth.

Application of Intelligence in Strategic Models

The principles outlined in *The Use of Spies* by Sun Tzu can be seamlessly integrated into various strategic models and frameworks used by modern businesses to enhance decision-making and strategic planning. Intelligence gathering is a critical component of these models, providing the necessary insights to identify opportunities, mitigate threats, and develop robust strategies. Let's explore how intelligence can be applied to some of the most widely used strategic models and frameworks in greater detail.

SWOT Analysis (Strengths, Weaknesses, Opportunities, Threats):

SWOT analysis is a foundational tool in strategic planning that helps organisations identify internal strengths and weaknesses, as well as external opportunities and threats. Intelligence gathered from competitive analysis plays a crucial role in identifying these external factors. By collecting data on competitors' strengths, market trends, and potential threats, companies can gain a comprehensive understanding of the external environment. For instance, a tech company might use competitive intelligence to identify emerging technologies and market gaps that present new opportunities for innovation. Conversely, intelligence on competitors' strategic initiatives and market positioning can highlight potential threats that the company needs to address. By integrating intelligence into SWOT analysis, organisations can develop informed strategies that leverage their strengths, address weaknesses, capitalise on opportunities, and mitigate risks.

Porter's Five Forces Model:

Porter's Five Forces model is a powerful framework for analysing the competitive forces and market dynamics that influence an industry's attractiveness and profitability. Understanding these forces requires continuous intelligence gathering. The five forces include the threat of new entrants, the bargaining power of suppliers, the bargaining power of buyers, the threat of substitute products or services, and the intensity of competitive rivalry. By gathering intelligence on each of these forces, companies can make strategic decisions to enhance their market position. For example, a pharmaceutical company might use intelligence on regulatory changes and competitor strategies to assess the threat of new entrants. Additionally, understanding the bargaining power of suppliers and buyers can inform procurement and pricing strategies. By leveraging intelligence, companies can navigate the competitive landscape more effectively and develop strategies that enhance their competitive advantage.

Scenario Planning:

Scenario planning is a crucial tool for strategic foresight that relies heavily on accurate and timely information to construct plausible future scenarios and develop contingency plans. This process involves identifying key drivers of change, such as technological advancements, economic shifts, and regulatory developments, and exploring their potential impact on the organisation. Intelligence plays a pivotal role in identifying these drivers and providing the data needed to build realistic scenarios. For example, an automotive company might use intelligence on advancements in electric vehicle technology and changes in environmental regulations to create scenarios for the future of the automotive industry. By exploring these scenarios, the company can develop contingency plans to address potential risks and capitalise on emerging opportunities. Scenario planning enables organisations to be proactive, adaptable, and resilient in the face of uncertainty.

PEST Analysis (Political, Economic, Social, Technological):

PEST analysis is another strategic tool that helps organisations assess the external macro-environmental factors that can impact their operations. Intelligence gathering is essential for understanding these factors and their implications. For instance, political intelligence can provide insights into regulatory changes, trade policies, and geopolitical risks. Economic intelligence can inform companies about market trends, inflation rates, and consumer spending patterns. Social intelligence can shed light on demographic shifts, cultural trends, and changes in consumer behaviour. Technological intelligence can identify emerging technologies and innovations that could disrupt the industry. By integrating intelligence into PEST analysis, organisations can develop strategies that are aligned with the external environment and anticipate changes that could impact their business.

Blue Ocean Strategy:

Blue Ocean Strategy is a strategic framework that encourages companies to create new market spaces, or "blue oceans," rather than competing in existing, saturated markets, or "red oceans." Intelligence gathering is critical for identifying opportunities to create blue oceans. By analysing market trends, customer needs, and competitor activities, companies can identify unmet demands and emerging opportunities. For example, a consumer electronics company might use market intelligence to identify a gap in the market for a new, innovative product that addresses unmet customer needs. By developing a blue ocean strategy, the company can create a new market space with reduced competition and significant growth potential. Intelligence enables companies to think creatively and identify opportunities for differentiation and value innovation.

Balanced Scorecard:

The Balanced Scorecard is a strategic management tool that provides a holistic view of organisational performance by measuring key performance indicators (KPIs) across four perspectives: financial, customer, internal processes, and learning and growth. Intelligence gathering is essential for identifying the right KPIs and setting targets that align with strategic objectives. For example, financial intelligence can inform revenue targets and cost management strategies. Customer intelligence can provide insights into customer satisfaction and retention rates. Intelligence on internal processes can help identify areas for operational improvement and efficiency gains. Learning and growth intelligence can inform talent development and innovation initiatives. By integrating intelligence into the Balanced Scorecard, organisations can track their progress, make data-driven decisions, and achieve their strategic goals.

Competitive Benchmarking:

Competitive benchmarking is a strategic practice that involves comparing an organisation's performance, products, and processes with those of its competitors. Intelligence gathering is crucial for obtaining accurate and relevant data for benchmarking. This includes analysing competitors' financial performance, market share, product offerings, and customer satisfaction levels. For example, a retail company might use competitive intelligence to benchmark its pricing strategies, inventory management, and customer service against leading competitors. By identifying gaps and areas for improvement, the company can develop strategies to enhance its competitive position. Competitive benchmarking provides organisations with valuable insights and best practices that drive continuous improvement and competitive advantage.

Value Chain Analysis:

Value chain analysis is a strategic tool that examines the internal activities within an organisation to identify areas where value can be added and competitive advantage can be achieved. Intelligence gathering is essential for understanding each stage of the value chain, from inbound logistics and operations to marketing and after-sales service. For example, a manufacturing company might use intelligence to analyse its supply chain, production processes, and distribution networks. By identifying inefficiencies and areas for improvement, the company can optimise its value chain to reduce costs, enhance product quality, and improve customer satisfaction. Intelligence enables organisations to make informed decisions that enhance value creation and competitive advantage.

Case Study: Tesla's Application of Intelligence in Strategic Models:

Tesla's success is a testament to the effective application of intelligence in strategic models. The company continuously gathers and analyses intelligence on market trends, technological advancements, and competitor activities to inform its strategic decisions. For instance, Tesla uses SWOT analysis to identify its strengths in innovation and brand loyalty, and to address weaknesses such as production bottlenecks. By leveraging market intelligence, Tesla identifies opportunities for growth in the electric vehicle market and anticipates potential threats from regulatory changes and new entrants.

Tesla also uses Porter's Five Forces model to understand the competitive forces in the automotive industry. By analysing the threat of new entrants, the bargaining power of suppliers and buyers, the threat of substitutes, and the intensity of competitive rivalry, Tesla develops strategies to maintain its market leadership.

Scenario planning plays a crucial role in Tesla's strategic foresight. The company explores various scenarios related to advancements in battery technology, changes in consumer preferences, and shifts in environmental regulations. By developing contingency plans, Tesla ensures that it remains agile and resilient in a rapidly changing industry.

Competitive Intelligence as a Strategic Imperative

In today's fast-paced and highly competitive business environment, the ability to gather, analyse, and act on competitive intelligence has become a strategic imperative for companies seeking to maintain and enhance their market positions. Competitive intelligence involves the systematic collection and analysis of information about competitors, market conditions, and industry trends. This information is crucial for making informed strategic decisions, anticipating market shifts, and identifying opportunities for innovation and growth.

Importance of Competitive Intelligence:

Competitive intelligence provides companies with a deep understanding of the external environment, enabling them to stay ahead of competitors and respond proactively to market changes. By monitoring competitors' activities, companies can gain insights into their strategies, strengths, and weaknesses. This information allows companies to benchmark their performance, identify gaps in their offerings, and develop strategies to differentiate themselves in the market. Additionally, competitive intelligence helps companies anticipate potential threats, such as new market entrants or disruptive technologies, and develop contingency plans to mitigate risks.

Investment in Data Analytics & Market Intelligence:

Leading companies like Amazon, Google, and Apple invest heavily in data analytics and market intelligence to maintain their competitive positions. These companies recognise that the ability to process vast amounts of data and extract valuable insights is a key differentiator in the digital age. By employing sophisticated algorithms and advanced analytics, these companies can track competitor movements, analyse customer data, and predict market trends with a high degree of accuracy. For example, Amazon uses data analytics to monitor pricing strategies, inventory levels, and customer preferences, allowing it to optimise its operations and deliver personalised experiences to customers.

Tracking Competitor Movements:

Tracking competitor movements is a critical component of competitive intelligence. Companies must continuously monitor competitors' product launches, marketing campaigns, partnerships, and technological advancements. This information provides valuable insights into competitors' strategic priorities and areas of focus. For example, Google monitors competitors' developments in search engine technology, advertising platforms, and cloud computing services. By understanding competitors' strategies, Google can identify areas where it can improve its offerings and develop innovative solutions to stay ahead of the competition.

Analysing Customer Data:

Customer data is a valuable resource that provides insights into consumer behaviour, preferences, and trends. Companies like Apple use advanced analytics to analyse customer data from various sources, such as sales transactions, online interactions, and social media. This analysis allows Apple to understand customer needs, identify emerging trends, and tailor its products and marketing strategies accordingly. For instance, by analysing customer feedback and purchasing patterns, Apple can develop new features for its products, improve customer satisfaction, and drive loyalty. Additionally, customer data helps companies identify potential markets and customer segments, enabling them to expand their reach and increase revenue.

Predicting Market Trends:

The ability to predict market trends is a significant advantage in the competitive landscape. Companies use predictive analytics to forecast future market conditions, consumer demand, and industry developments. This foresight allows companies to make proactive strategic decisions and capitalise on emerging opportunities. For example, Amazon uses predictive analytics to forecast demand for its products, optimise inventory levels, and streamline its supply chain operations. By anticipating market trends, Amazon can ensure that it has the right products available at the right time, enhancing customer satisfaction and driving sales.

Reflecting Sun Tzu's Teachings:

The practices of leading companies reflect Sun Tzu's teachings on the critical role of foreknowledge and the strategic advantage conferred by superior intelligence. Sun Tzu emphasises the importance of understanding the competitive landscape, gathering accurate information, and making informed decisions. Similarly, companies that prioritise competitive intelligence are better equipped to navigate the complexities of the business environment and achieve sustained success. By leveraging data analytics, market intelligence, and predictive insights, companies can develop robust strategies, mitigate risks, and maintain a competitive edge.

Case Study: Amazon's Competitive Intelligence:

Amazon's success is a prime example of the strategic importance of competitive intelligence. The company continuously gathers and analyses data on competitors, market conditions, and customer behaviour to inform its strategic decisions. For instance, Amazon monitors competitors' pricing strategies, product offerings, and customer reviews to identify opportunities for differentiation and improvement. This intelligence allows Amazon to develop competitive pricing models, optimise its product assortment, and enhance the customer experience. Additionally, Amazon's investment in data analytics and predictive analytics enables it to forecast demand, streamline operations, and maintain its leadership position in the e-commerce industry.

Implementing Competitive Intelligence Programmes:

To effectively leverage competitive intelligence, companies must implement structured programmes that integrate data collection, analysis, and strategic decision-making. This involves establishing dedicated teams or departments responsible for competitive intelligence, investing in advanced analytics tools, and fostering a culture of data-driven decision-making. For example, a financial services firm might create a competitive intelligence unit that monitors market trends, analyses competitor strategies, and provides insights to senior leadership. By formalising competitive intelligence programmes, companies can ensure that they have the necessary resources and processes in place to gather and utilise valuable information.

Fostering a Culture of Continuous Improvement:

Competitive intelligence is not a one-time effort but an ongoing process that requires continuous monitoring and adaptation. Companies must foster a culture of continuous improvement, where employees are encouraged to seek out new information, challenge assumptions, and explore innovative solutions. This involves providing training and development opportunities to enhance employees' analytical skills, promoting collaboration across departments, and recognising contributions to competitive intelligence efforts. For instance, a technology company might hold regular workshops on data analytics and market research techniques to empower employees to gather and analyse intelligence effectively.

Ethical Considerations:

While competitive intelligence is essential for strategic decision-making, companies must adhere to ethical standards and legal requirements in their intelligence-gathering practices. This involves respecting competitors' intellectual property, avoiding deceptive practices, and ensuring compliance with data privacy regulations. By maintaining high ethical standards, companies can build trust with stakeholders and sustain their competitive advantage in the long term. For example, a pharmaceutical company might implement a code of conduct that outlines ethical guidelines for competitive intelligence activities, ensuring that all employees understand and adhere to the company's values.

Leveraging Technology for Competitive Intelligence:

Advancements in technology have transformed the way companies gather and analyse competitive intelligence. Big data analytics, artificial intelligence (AI), and machine learning enable companies to process vast amounts of data quickly and derive actionable insights. For instance, Google uses AI-powered analytics to monitor search trends, analyse user behaviour, and identify emerging opportunities in digital advertising. By leveraging technology, companies can enhance their intelligence capabilities, make more informed decisions, and stay ahead of the competition.

Summary

Sun Tzu's *The Use of Spies* offers enduring wisdom that is remarkably relevant to modern strategic management. The principles of intelligence gathering, foreknowledge, secrecy, and strategic foresight articulated by Sun Tzu are as applicable today as they were in ancient times. By integrating these principles into their strategic management practices, contemporary business leaders can navigate the complexities of the modern market, outmanoeuvre competitors, and achieve sustainable success. The timeless insights of Sun Tzu continue to illuminate the path to strategic excellence, underscoring the fundamental truth that knowledge is power and foreknowledge is the key to victory.

CONCLUSION

As we conclude our exploration of Sun Tzu's *The Art of War* through the lens of modern business management, it becomes evident that the ancient wisdom of this military treatise holds profound relevance for today's corporate leaders. Each of the 13 chapters provides timeless strategies that, when adapted to the business context, offer valuable insights into leadership, strategic planning, and competitive advantage.

Laying the Foundation for Success

The journey begins with *Laying Plans*, emphasising the importance of careful preparation and strategic foresight. Just as a general must consider every detail before engaging in battle, CEOs must meticulously plan their initiatives, aligning their vision with actionable goals. By investing time in thorough planning, companies can navigate uncertainties and position themselves for success.

Resource Management & Strategic Investments

In *Waging War*, we explored the parallels between managing resources in warfare and in business. Effective resource allocation, cost control, and strategic investments are crucial for sustaining growth and competitiveness. Companies that master these principles can maximise their returns and build a resilient foundation for long-term success.

Crafting & Executing Effective Strategies

Attack by Stratagem highlights the significance of strategic thinking and the element of surprise. In the corporate world, crafting innovative strategies and anticipating market dynamics are key to staying ahead of competitors. By leveraging intelligence and psychological tactics, businesses can create differentiation and capture market share.

Flexibility & Adaptability in Operations

Tactical Dispositions and *Manoeuvring* emphasise the importance of positioning and agility. In an ever-changing business landscape, flexibility in operations and the ability to pivot quickly are vital. Companies must continuously evaluate their market position and be ready to adjust their strategies to seize opportunities and mitigate risks.

Harnessing Momentum & Motivating Teams

In *Energy*, we delved into the principles of maintaining momentum and motivating teams. High performance and sustained focus are essential for driving innovation and achieving strategic goals. By fostering a culture of energy and enthusiasm, leaders can inspire their teams to excel and deliver outstanding results.

Identifying Strengths & Exploiting Weaknesses

Weak Points & Strong teaches us to recognise and leverage our strengths while identifying and exploiting competitors' weaknesses. A keen understanding of competitive dynamics allows businesses to position themselves effectively and capitalise on their unique capabilities.

Adaptability & Strategic Variation

Variation of Tactics underscores the necessity of adaptability and the use of diverse strategies. In business, one-size-fits-all approaches rarely lead to success. Instead, companies must develop a repertoire of tactics tailored to different scenarios, ensuring they can respond effectively to varying market conditions.

Operational Excellence & Efficient Logistics

The Army on the March and *Terrain* provide valuable lessons in managing operations and understanding the business environment. Efficient logistics, supply chain management, and a deep awareness of regulatory landscapes are critical for operational excellence and market success.

Navigating Complex Situations & Driving Innovation

The Nine Situations and *The Attack by Fire* highlight strategies for navigating complex business situations and driving innovation. Companies that embrace change, leverage technological advancements, and turn challenges into opportunities are better positioned to lead in their industries.

The Power of Intelligence & Information Gathering

Finally, *The Use of Spies* emphasises the critical importance of intelligence and information gathering. Informed decision-making, competitive intelligence, and data-driven strategies are essential for maintaining a competitive edge and achieving sustained success.

Embracing Timeless Wisdom for Modern Success

The enduring relevance of Sun Tzu's teachings lies in their adaptability and applicability across different eras and contexts. By integrating these timeless strategies into modern business practices, CEOs and leaders can navigate the complexities of today's corporate landscape with greater confidence and agility.

Commitment to Ethical Leadership

As we apply these principles, it is crucial to uphold ethical standards and lead with integrity. The wisdom of Sun Tzu, while tactical and strategic, also underscores the importance of benevolence, transparency, and ethical conduct. In the pursuit of success, maintaining trust and fostering positive relationships with stakeholders are paramount.

Continuous Learning & Strategic Innovation

In closing, the journey of mastering the art of war in business is ongoing. Continuous learning, strategic innovation, and an unwavering commitment to excellence are the hallmarks of successful leadership. By embracing the lessons of Sun Tzu, modern CEOs can cultivate a strategic mindset that drives sustainable growth and competitive advantage.

May the insights gleaned from this book inspire you to think strategically, lead with vision, and achieve extraordinary success in your business endeavours. The path to mastery is not a destination but a journey, and the timeless wisdom of Sun Tzu will continue to guide and illuminate the way.

By melding the ancient strategies of Sun Tzu with contemporary business insights, *The Art of War for CEOs* aims to equip you with the knowledge and tools needed to thrive in an ever-changing landscape. As you embark on this journey of strategic enlightenment, remember that the true art of war lies not only in the battlefield but also in the wisdom to lead with foresight, adaptability, and integrity.

APPENDIX – SUN TZU ON THE ART OF WAR

SUN TZU ON THE ART OF WAR
THE OLDEST MILITARY TREATISE IN THE WORLD

Translated from the Chinese by LIONEL GILES, M.A. (1910)

I. LAYING PLANS

1. Sun Tzŭ said: The art of war is of vital importance to the State.
2. It is a matter of life and death, a road either to safety or to ruin. Hence it is a subject of inquiry which can on no account be neglected.
3. The art of war, then, is governed by five constant factors, to be taken into account in one's deliberations, when seeking to determine the conditions obtaining in the field.
4. These are: (1) The Moral Law; (2) Heaven; (3) Earth; (4) The Commander; (5) Method and discipline.
5. The Moral Law causes the people to be in complete accord with their ruler, so that they will follow him regardless of their lives, undismayed by any danger.
6. Heaven signifies night and day, cold and heat, times and seasons.
7. Earth comprises distances, great and small; danger and security; open ground and narrow passes; the chances of life and death.
8. The Commander stands for the virtues of wisdom, sincerity, benevolence, courage and strictness.
9. By Method and discipline are to be understood the marshalling of the army in its proper subdivisions, the gradations of rank among the officers, the maintenance of roads by which supplies may reach the army, and the control of military expenditure.
10. These five heads should be familiar to every general: he who knows them will be victorious; he who knows them not will fail.
11. Therefore, in your deliberations, when seeking to determine the military conditions, let them be made the basis of a comparison, in this wise:—
12. (1) Which of the two sovereigns is imbued with the Moral law?
    (2) Which of the two generals has most ability?
    (3) With whom lie the advantages derived from Heaven and Earth?
    (4) On which side is discipline most rigorously enforced?
    (5) Which army is the stronger?
    (6) On which side are officers and men more highly trained?
    (7) In which army is there the greater constancy both in reward and punishment?
13. By means of these seven considerations I can forecast victory or defeat.
14. The general that hearkens to my counsel and acts upon it, will conquer: let such a one be retained in command! The general that hearkens not to my counsel nor acts upon it, will suffer defeat:—let such a one be dismissed!
15. While heeding the profit of my counsel, avail yourself also of any helpful circumstances over and beyond the ordinary rules.
16. According as circumstances are favourable, one should modify one's plans.
17. All warfare is based on deception.

18. Hence, when able to attack, we must seem unable; when using our forces, we must seem inactive; when we are near, we must make the enemy believe we are far away; when far away, we must make him believe we are near.
19. Hold out baits to entice the enemy. Feign disorder, and crush him.
20. If he is secure at all points, be prepared for him. If he is in superior strength, evade him.
21. If your opponent is of choleric temper, seek to irritate him. Pretend to be weak, that he may grow arrogant.
22. If he is taking his ease, give him no rest. If his forces are united, separate them.
23. Attack him where he is unprepared, appear where you are not expected.
24. These military devices, leading to victory, must not be divulged beforehand.
25. Now the general who wins a battle makes many calculations in his temple ere the battle is fought. The general who loses a battle makes but few calculations beforehand. Thus do many calculations lead to victory, and few calculations to defeat: how much more no calculation at all! It is by attention to this point that I can foresee who is likely to win or lose.

II. WAGING WAR

1. Sun Tzǔ said: In the operations of war, where there are in the field a thousand swift chariots, as many heavy chariots, and a hundred thousand mail-clad soldiers, with provisions enough to carry them a thousand li, the expenditure at home and at the front, including entertainment of guests, small items such as glue and paint, and sums spent on chariots and armour, will reach the total of a thousand ounces of silver per day. Such is the cost of raising an army of 100,000 men.
2. When you engage in actual fighting, if victory is long in coming, the men's weapons will grow dull and their ardour will be damped. If you lay siege to a town, you will exhaust your strength.
3. Again, if the campaign is protracted, the resources of the State will not be equal to the strain.
4. Now, when your weapons are dulled, your ardour damped, your strength exhausted and your treasure spent, other chieftains will spring up to take advantage of your extremity. Then no man, however wise, will be able to avert the consequences that must ensue.
5. Thus, though we have heard of stupid haste in war, cleverness has never been seen associated with long delays.
6. There is no instance of a country having benefited from prolonged warfare.
7. It is only one who is thoroughly acquainted with the evils of war that can thoroughly understand the profitable way of carrying it on.
8. The skilful soldier does not raise a second levy, neither are his supply-wagons loaded more than twice.
9. Bring war material with you from home, but forage on the enemy. Thus the army will have food enough for its needs.
10. Poverty of the State exchequer causes an army to be maintained by contributions from a distance. Contributing to maintain an army at a distance causes the people to be impoverished.
11. On the other hand, the proximity of an army causes prices to go up; and high prices cause the people's substance to be drained away.
12. When their substance is drained away, the peasantry will be afflicted by heavy exactions.
13. With this loss of substance and exhaustion of strength, the homes of the people will be stripped bare, and three-tenths of their incomes will be dissipated; while Government expenses for broken chariots, worn-out horses, breast-plates and helmets, bows and arrows, spears and shields, protective mantlets, draught-oxen and heavy wagons, will amount to four-tenths of its total revenue.

14. Hence a wise general makes a point of foraging on the enemy. One cartload of the enemy's provisions is equivalent to twenty of one's own, and likewise a single picul of his provender is equivalent to twenty from one's own store.
15. Now in order to kill the enemy, our men must be roused to anger; that there may be advantage from defeating the enemy, they must have their rewards.
16. Therefore in chariot fighting, when ten or more chariots have been taken, those should be rewarded who took the first. Our own flags should be substituted for those of the enemy, and the chariots mingled and used in conjunction with ours. The captured soldiers should be kindly treated and kept.
17. This is called, using the conquered foe to augment one's own strength.
18. In war, then, let your great object be victory, not lengthy campaigns.
19. Thus it may be known that the leader of armies is the arbiter of the people's fate, the man on whom it depends whether the nation shall be in peace or in peril.

III. ATTACK BY STRATAGEM

1. Sun Tzǔ said: In the practical art of war, the best thing of all is to take the enemy's country whole and intact; to shatter and destroy it is not so good. So, too, it is better to capture an army entire than to destroy it, to capture a regiment, a detachment or a company entire than to destroy them.
2. Hence to fight and conquer in all your battles is not supreme excellence; supreme excellence consists in breaking the enemy's resistance without fighting.
3. Thus the highest form of generalship is to baulk the enemy's plans; the next best is to prevent the junction of the enemy's forces; the next in order is to attack the enemy's army in the field; and the worst policy of all is to besiege walled cities.
4. The rule is, not to besiege walled cities if it can possibly be avoided. The preparation of mantlets, movable shelters, and various implements of war, will take up three whole months; and the piling up of mounds over against the walls will take three months more.
5. The general, unable to control his irritation, will launch his men to the assault like swarming ants, with the result that one-third of his men are slain, while the town still remains untaken. Such are the disastrous effects of a siege.
6. Therefore the skilful leader subdues the enemy's troops without any fighting; he captures their cities without laying siege to them; he overthrows their kingdom without lengthy operations in the field.
7. With his forces intact he will dispute the mastery of the Empire, and thus, without losing a man, his triumph will be complete. This is the method of attacking by stratagem.
8. It is the rule in war, if our forces are ten to the enemy's one, to surround him; if five to one, to attack him; if twice as numerous, to divide our army into two.
9. If equally matched, we can offer battle; if slightly inferior in numbers, we can avoid the enemy; if quite unequal in every way, we can flee from him.
10. Hence, though an obstinate fight may be made by a small force, in the end it must be captured by the larger force.
11. Now the general is the bulwark of the State: if the bulwark is complete at all points; the State will be strong; if the bulwark is defective, the State will be weak.
12. There are three ways in which a ruler can bring misfortune upon his army:—
13. (1) By commanding the army to advance or to retreat, being ignorant of the fact that it cannot obey. This is called hobbling the army.
14. (2) By attempting to govern an army in the same way as he administers a kingdom, being ignorant of the conditions which obtain in an army. This causes restlessness in the soldier's minds.

15. (3) By employing the officers of his army without discrimination, through ignorance of the military principle of adaptation to circumstances. This shakes the confidence of the soldiers.
16. But when the army is restless and distrustful, trouble is sure to come from the other feudal princes. This is simply bringing anarchy into the army, and flinging victory away.
17. Thus we may know that there are five essentials for victory:
    (1) He will win who knows when to fight and when not to fight.
    (2) He will win who knows how to handle both superior and inferior forces.
    (3) He will win whose army is animated by the same spirit throughout all its ranks.
    (4) He will win who, prepared himself, waits to take the enemy unprepared.
    (5) He will win who has military capacity and is not interfered with by the sovereign.
    Victory lies in the knowledge of these five points.
18. Hence the saying: If you know the enemy and know yourself, you need not fear the result of a hundred battles. If you know yourself but not the enemy, for every victory gained you will also suffer a defeat. If you know neither the enemy nor yourself, you will succumb in every battle.

IV. TACTICAL DISPOSITIONS

1. Sun Tzŭ said: The good fighters of old first put themselves beyond the possibility of defeat, and then waited for an opportunity of defeating the enemy.
2. To secure ourselves against defeat lies in our own hands, but the opportunity of defeating the enemy is provided by the enemy himself.
3. Thus the good fighter is able to secure himself against defeat, but cannot make certain of defeating the enemy.
4. Hence the saying: One may know how to conquer without being able to do it.
5. Security against defeat implies defensive tactics; ability to defeat the enemy means taking the offensive.
6. Standing on the defensive indicates insufficient strength; attacking, a superabundance of strength.
7. The general who is skilled in defence hides in the most secret recesses of the earth; he who is skilled in attack flashes forth from the topmost heights of heaven. Thus on the one hand we have ability to protect ourselves; on the other, a victory that is complete.
8. To see victory only when it is within the ken of the common herd is not the acme of excellence.
9. Neither is it the acme of excellence if you fight and conquer and the whole Empire says, "Well done!"
10. To lift an autumn hair is no sign of great strength; to see sun and moon is no sign of sharp sight; to hear the noise of thunder is no sign of a quick ear.
11. What the ancients called a clever fighter is one who not only wins, but excels in winning with ease.
12. Hence his victories bring him neither reputation for wisdom nor credit for courage.
13. He wins his battles by making no mistakes. Making no mistakes is what establishes the certainty of victory, for it means conquering an enemy that is already defeated.
14. Hence the skilful fighter puts himself into a position which makes defeat impossible, and does not miss the moment for defeating the enemy.
15. Thus it is that in war the victorious strategist only seeks battle after the victory has been won, whereas he who is destined to defeat first fights and afterwards looks for victory.
16. The consummate leader cultivates the moral law, and strictly adheres to method and discipline; thus it is in his power to control success.
17. In respect of military method, we have, firstly, Measurement; secondly, Estimation of quantity; thirdly, Calculation; fourthly, Balancing of chances; fifthly, Victory.

18. Measurement owes its existence to Earth; Estimation of quantity to Measurement; Calculation to Estimation of quantity; Balancing of chances to Calculation; and Victory to Balancing of chances.
19. A victorious army opposed to a routed one, is as a pound's weight placed in the scale against a single grain.
20. The onrush of a conquering force is like the bursting of pent-up waters into a chasm a thousand fathoms deep. So much for tactical dispositions.

V. ENERGY

1. Sun Tzǔ said: The control of a large force is the same principle as the control of a few men: it is merely a question of dividing up their numbers.
2. Fighting with a large army under your command is nowise different from fighting with a small one: it is merely a question of instituting signs and signals.
3. To ensure that your whole host may withstand the brunt of the enemy's attack and remain unshaken—this is effected by manoeuvres direct and indirect.
4. That the impact of your army may be like a grindstone dashed against an egg—this is effected by the science of weak points and strong.
5. In all fighting, the direct method may be used for joining battle, but indirect methods will be needed in order to secure victory.
6. Indirect tactics, efficiently applied, are inexhaustible as Heaven and Earth, unending as the flow of rivers and streams; like the sun and moon, they end but to begin anew; like the four seasons, they pass away but to return once more.
7. There are not more than five musical notes, yet the combinations of these five give rise to more melodies than can ever be heard.
8. There are not more than five primary colours (blue, yellow, red, white, and black), yet in combination they produce more hues than can ever be seen.
9. There are not more than five cardinal tastes (sour, acrid, salt, sweet, bitter), yet combinations of them yield more flavours than can ever be tasted.
10. In battle, there are not more than two methods of attack—the direct and the indirect; yet these two in combination give rise to an endless series of manoeuvres.
11. The direct and the indirect lead on to each other in turn. It is like moving in a circle—you never come to an end. Who can exhaust the possibilities of their combination?
12. The onset of troops is like the rush of a torrent which will even roll stones along in its course.
13. The quality of decision is like the well-timed swoop of a falcon which enables it to strike and destroy its victim.
14. Therefore the good fighter will be terrible in his onset, and prompt in his decision.
15. Energy may be likened to the bending of a crossbow; decision, to the releasing of the trigger.
16. Amid the turmoil and tumult of battle, there may be seeming disorder and yet no real disorder at all; amid confusion and chaos, your array may be without head or tail, yet it will be proof against defeat.
17. Simulated disorder postulates perfect discipline; simulated fear postulates courage; simulated weakness postulates strength.
18. Hiding order beneath the cloak of disorder is simply a question of subdivision; concealing courage under a show of timidity presupposes a fund of latent energy; masking strength with weakness is to be effected by tactical dispositions.
19. Thus one who is skilful at keeping the enemy on the move maintains deceitful appearances, according to which the enemy will act. He sacrifices something, that the enemy may snatch at it.
20. By holding out baits, he keeps him on the march; then with a body of picked men he lies in wait for him.

21. The clever combatant looks to the effect of combined energy, and does not require too much from individuals. Hence his ability to pick out the right men and utilise combined energy.
22. When he utilises combined energy, his fighting men become as it were like unto rolling logs or stones. For it is the nature of a log or stone to remain motionless on level ground, and to move when on a slope; if four-cornered, to come to a standstill, but if round-shaped, to go rolling down.
23. Thus the energy developed by good fighting men is as the momentum of a round stone rolled down a mountain thousands of feet in height. So much on the subject of energy.

VI. WEAK POINTS AND STRONG

1. Sun Tzŭ said: Whoever is first in the field and awaits the coming of the enemy, will be fresh for the fight; whoever is second in the field and has to hasten to battle, will arrive exhausted.
2. Therefore the clever combatant imposes his will on the enemy, but does not allow the enemy's will to be imposed on him.
3. By holding out advantages to him, he can cause the enemy to approach of his own accord; or, by inflicting damage, he can make it impossible for the enemy to draw near.
4. If the enemy is taking his ease, he can harass him; if well supplied with food, he can starve him out; if quietly encamped, he can force him to move.
5. Appear at points which the enemy must hasten to defend; march swiftly to places where you are not expected.
6. An army may march great distances without distress, if it marches through country where the enemy is not.
7. You can be sure of succeeding in your attacks if you only attack places which are undefended. You can ensure the safety of your defence if you only hold positions that cannot be attacked.
8. Hence that general is skilful in attack whose opponent does not know what to defend; and he is skilful in defence whose opponent does not know what to attack.
9. O divine art of subtlety and secrecy! Through you we learn to be invisible, through you inaudible; and hence we can hold the enemy's fate in our hands.
10. You may advance and be absolutely irresistible, if you make for the enemy's weak points; you may retire and be safe from pursuit if your movements are more rapid than those of the enemy.
11. If we wish to fight, the enemy can be forced to an engagement even though he be sheltered behind a high rampart and a deep ditch. All we need do is attack some other place that he will be obliged to relieve.
12. If we do not wish to fight, we can prevent the enemy from engaging us even though the lines of our encampment be merely traced out on the ground. All we need do is to throw something odd and unaccountable in his way.
13. By discovering the enemy's dispositions and remaining invisible ourselves, we can keep our forces concentrated, while the enemy's must be divided.
14. We can form a single united body, while the enemy must split up into fractions. Hence there will be a whole pitted against separate parts of a whole, which means that we shall be many to the enemy's few.
15. And if we are able thus to attack an inferior force with a superior one, our opponents will be in dire straits.
16. The spot where we intend to fight must not be made known; for then the enemy will have to prepare against a possible attack at several different points; and his forces being thus distributed in many directions, the numbers we shall have to face at any given point will be proportionately few.
17. For should the enemy strengthen his van, he will weaken his rear; should he strengthen his rear, he will weaken his van; should he strengthen his left, he will weaken his right; should he

strengthen his right, he will weaken his left. If he sends reinforcements everywhere, he will everywhere be weak.
18. Numerical weakness comes from having to prepare against possible attacks; numerical strength, from compelling our adversary to make these preparations against us.
19. Knowing the place and the time of the coming battle, we may concentrate from the greatest distances in order to fight.
20. But if neither time nor place be known, then the left wing will be impotent to succour the right, the right equally impotent to succour the left, the van unable to relieve the rear, or the rear to support the van. How much more so if the furthest portions of the army are anything under a hundred li apart, and even the nearest are separated by several li!
21. Though according to my estimate the soldiers of Yüeh exceed our own in number, that shall advantage them nothing in the matter of victory. I say then that victory can be achieved.
22. Though the enemy be stronger in numbers, we may prevent him from fighting. Scheme so as to discover his plans and the likelihood of their success.
23. Rouse him, and learn the principle of his activity or inactivity. Force him to reveal himself, so as to find out his vulnerable spots.
24. Carefully compare the opposing army with your own, so that you may know where strength is superabundant and where it is deficient.
25. In making tactical dispositions, the highest pitch you can attain is to conceal them; conceal your dispositions, and you will be safe from the prying of the subtlest spies, from the machinations of the wisest brains.
26. How victory may be produced for them out of the enemy's own tactics—that is what the multitude cannot comprehend.
27. All men can see the tactics whereby I conquer, but what none can see is the strategy out of which victory is evolved.
28. Do not repeat the tactics which have gained you one victory, but let your methods be regulated by the infinite variety of circumstances.
29. Military tactics are like unto water; for water in its natural course runs away from high places and hastens downwards.
30. So in war, the way is to avoid what is strong and to strike at what is weak.
31. Water shapes its course according to the nature of the ground over which it flows; the soldier works out his victory in relation to the foe whom he is facing.
32. Therefore, just as water retains no constant shape, so in warfare there are no constant conditions.
33. He who can modify his tactics in relation to his opponent and thereby succeed in winning, may be called a heaven-born captain.
34. The five elements (water, fire, wood, metal, earth) are not always equally predominant; the four seasons make way for each other in turn. There are short days and long; the moon has its periods of waning and waxing.

VII. MANOEUVRING

1. Sun Tzŭ said: In war, the general receives his commands from the sovereign.
2. Having collected an army and concentrated his forces, he must blend and harmonise the different elements thereof before pitching his camp.
3. After that, comes tactical manoeuvring, than which there is nothing more difficult. The difficulty of tactical manoeuvring consists in turning the devious into the direct, and misfortune into gain.
4. Thus, to take a long and circuitous route, after enticing the enemy out of the way, and though starting after him, to contrive to reach the goal before him, shows knowledge of the artifice of deviation.

5. Manoeuvring with an army is advantageous; with an undisciplined multitude, most dangerous.
6. If you set a fully equipped army in march in order to snatch an advantage, the chances are that you will be too late. On the other hand, to detach a flying column for the purpose involves the sacrifice of its baggage and stores.
7. Thus, if you order your men to roll up their buff-coats, and make forced marches without halting day or night, covering double the usual distance at a stretch, doing a hundred li in order to wrest an advantage, the leaders of all your three divisions will fall into the hands of the enemy.
8. The stronger men will be in front, the jaded ones will fall behind, and on this plan only one-tenth of your army will reach its destination.
9. If you march fifty li in order to outmanoeuvre the enemy, you will lose the leader of your first division, and only half your force will reach the goal.
10. If you march thirty li with the same object, two-thirds of your army will arrive.
11. We may take it then that an army without its baggage-train is lost; without provisions it is lost; without bases of supply it is lost.
12. We cannot enter into alliances until we are acquainted with the designs of our neighbours.
13. We are not fit to lead an army on the march unless we are familiar with the face of the country —its mountains and forests, its pitfalls and precipices, its marshes and swamps.
14. We shall be unable to turn natural advantages to account unless we make use of local guides.
15. In war, practise dissimulation, and you will succeed. Move only if there is a real advantage to be gained.
16. Whether to concentrate or to divide your troops, must be decided by circumstances.
17. Let your rapidity be that of the wind, your compactness that of the forest.
18. In raiding and plundering be like fire, in immovability like a mountain.
19. Let your plans be dark and impenetrable as night, and when you move, fall like a thunderbolt.
20. When you plunder a countryside, let the spoil be divided amongst your men; when you capture new territory, cut it up into allotments for the benefit of the soldiery.
21. Ponder and deliberate before you make a move.
22. He will conquer who has learnt the artifice of deviation. Such is the art of manoeuvring.
23. The Book of Army Management says: On the field of battle, the spoken word does not carry far enough: hence the institution of gongs and drums. Nor can ordinary objects be seen clearly enough: hence the institution of banners and flags.
24. Gongs and drums, banners and flags, are means whereby the ears and eyes of the host may be focussed on one particular point.
25. The host thus forming a single united body, is it impossible either for the brave to advance alone, or for the cowardly to retreat alone. This is the art of handling large masses of men.
26. In night-fighting, then, make much use of signal-fires and drums, and in fighting by day, of flags and banners, as a means of influencing the ears and eyes of your army.
27. A whole army may be robbed of its spirit; a commander-in-chief may be robbed of his presence of mind.
28. Now a soldier's spirit is keenest in the morning; by noonday it has begun to flag; and in the evening, his mind is bent only on returning to camp.
29. A clever general, therefore, avoids an army when its spirit is keen, but attacks it when it is sluggish and inclined to return. This is the art of studying moods.
30. Disciplined and calm, to await the appearance of disorder and hubbub amongst the enemy:—this is the art of retaining self-possession.
31. To be near the goal while the enemy is still far from it, to wait at ease while the enemy is toiling and struggling, to be well-fed while the enemy is famished:—this is the art of husbanding one's strength.
32. To refrain from intercepting an enemy whose banners are in perfect order, to refrain from attacking an army drawn up in calm and confident array:—this is the art of studying circumstances.

33. It is a military axiom not to advance uphill against the enemy, nor to oppose him when he comes downhill.
34. Do not pursue an enemy who simulates flight; do not attack soldiers whose temper is keen.
35. Do not swallow a bait offered by the enemy. Do not interfere with an army that is returning home.
36. When you surround an army, leave an outlet free. Do not press a desperate foe too hard.
37. Such is the art of warfare.

VIII. VARIATION OF TACTICS

1. Sun Tzǔ said: In war, the general receives his commands from the sovereign, collects his army and concentrates his forces.
2. When in difficult country, do not encamp. In country where high roads intersect, join hands with your allies. Do not linger in dangerously isolated positions. In hemmed-in situations, you must resort to stratagem. In a desperate position, you must fight.
3. There are roads which must not be followed, armies which must be not attacked, towns which must not be besieged, positions which must not be contested, commands of the sovereign which must not be obeyed.
4. The general who thoroughly understands the advantages that accompany variation of tactics knows how to handle his troops.
5. The general who does not understand these, may be well acquainted with the configuration of the country, yet he will not be able to turn his knowledge to practical account.
6. So, the student of war who is unversed in the art of war of varying his plans, even though he be acquainted with the Five Advantages, will fail to make the best use of his men.
7. Hence in the wise leader's plans, considerations of advantage and of disadvantage will be blended together.
8. If our expectation of advantage be tempered in this way, we may succeed in accomplishing the essential part of our schemes.
9. If, on the other hand, in the midst of difficulties we are always ready to seize an advantage, we may extricate ourselves from misfortune.
10. Reduce the hostile chiefs by inflicting damage on them; and make trouble for them, and keep them constantly engaged; hold out specious allurements, and make them rush to any given point.
11. The art of war teaches us to rely not on the likelihood of the enemy's not coming, but on our own readiness to receive him; not on the chance of his not attacking, but rather on the fact that we have made our position unassailable.
12. There are five dangerous faults which may affect a general:
    (1) Recklessness, which leads to destruction;
    (2) cowardice, which leads to capture;
    (3) a hasty temper, which can be provoked by insults;
    (4) a delicacy of honour which is sensitive to shame;
    (5) over-solicitude for his men, which exposes him to worry and trouble.
13. These are the five besetting sins of a general, ruinous to the conduct of war.
14. When an army is overthrown and its leader slain, the cause will surely be found among these five dangerous faults. Let them be a subject of meditation.

IX. THE ARMY ON THE MARCH

1. Sun Tzŭ said: We come now to the question of encamping the army, and observing signs of the enemy. Pass quickly over mountains, and keep in the neighbourhood of valleys.
2. Camp in high places, facing the sun. Do not climb heights in order to fight. So much for mountain warfare.
3. After crossing a river, you should get far away from it.
4. When an invading force crosses a river in its onward march, do not advance to meet it in mid-stream. It will be best to let half the army get across, and then deliver your attack.
5. If you are anxious to fight, you should not go to meet the invader near a river which he has to cross.
6. Moor your craft higher up than the enemy, and facing the sun. Do not move up-stream to meet the enemy. So much for river warfare.
7. In crossing salt-marshes, your sole concern should be to get over them quickly, without any delay.
8. If forced to fight in a salt-marsh, you should have water and grass near you, and get your back to a clump of trees. So much for operations in salt-marshes.
9. In dry, level country, take up an easily accessible position with rising ground to your right and on your rear, so that the danger may be in front, and safety lie behind. So much for campaigning in flat country.
10. These are the four useful branches of military knowledge which enabled the Yellow Emperor to vanquish four several sovereigns.
11. All armies prefer high ground to low, and sunny places to dark.
12. If you are careful of your men, and camp on hard ground, the army will be free from disease of every kind, and this will spell victory.
13. When you come to a hill or a bank, occupy the sunny side, with the slope on your right rear. Thus you will at once act for the benefit of your soldiers and utilise the natural advantages of the ground.
14. When, in consequence of heavy rains up-country, a river which you wish to ford is swollen and flecked with foam, you must wait until it subsides.
15. Country in which there are precipitous cliffs with torrents running between, deep natural hollows, confined places, tangled thickets, quagmires and crevasses, should be left with all possible speed and not approached.
16. While we keep away from such places, we should get the enemy to approach them; while we face them, we should let the enemy have them on his rear.
17. If in the neighbourhood of your camp there should be any hilly country, ponds surrounded by aquatic grass, hollow basins filled with reeds, or woods with thick undergrowth, they must be carefully routed out and searched; for these are places where men in ambush or insidious spies are likely to be lurking.
18. When the enemy is close at hand and remains quiet, he is relying on the natural strength of his position.
19. When he keeps aloof and tries to provoke a battle, he is anxious for the other side to advance.
20. If his place of encampment is easy of access, he is tendering a bait.
21. Movement amongst the trees of a forest shows that the enemy is advancing. The appearance of a number of screens in the midst of thick grass means that the enemy wants to make us suspicious.
22. The rising of birds in their flight is the sign of an ambuscade. Startled beasts indicate that a sudden attack is coming.
23. When there is dust rising in a high column, it is the sign of chariots advancing; when the dust is low, but spread over a wide area, it betokens the approach of infantry. When it branches out in different directions, it shows that parties have been sent to collect firewood. A few clouds of dust moving to and fro signify that the army is encamping.
24. Humble words and increased preparations are signs that the enemy is about to advance. Violent language and driving forward as if to the attack are signs that he will retreat.

25. When the light chariots come out first and take up a position on the wings, it is a sign that the enemy is forming for battle.
26. Peace proposals unaccompanied by a sworn covenant indicate a plot.
27. When there is much running about and the soldiers fall into rank, it means that the critical moment has come.
28. When some are seen advancing and some retreating, it is a lure.
29. When the soldiers stand leaning on their spears, they are faint from want of food.
30. If those who are sent to draw water begin by drinking themselves, the army is suffering from thirst.
31. If the enemy sees an advantage to be gained and makes no effort to secure it, the soldiers are exhausted.
32. If birds gather on any spot, it is unoccupied. Clamour by night betokens nervousness.
33. If there is disturbance in the camp, the general's authority is weak. If the banners and flags are shifted about, sedition is afoot. If the officers are angry, it means that the men are weary.
34. When an army feeds its horses with grain and kills its cattle for food, and when the men do not hang their cooking-pots over the camp-fires, showing that they will not return to their tents, you may know that they are determined to fight to the death.
35. The sight of men whispering together in small knots or speaking in subdued tones points to disaffection amongst the rank and file.
36. Too frequent rewards signify that the enemy is at the end of his resources; too many punishments betray a condition of dire distress.
37. To begin by bluster, but afterwards to take fright at the enemy's numbers, shows a supreme lack of intelligence.
38. When envoys are sent with compliments in their mouths, it is a sign that the enemy wishes for a truce.
39. If the enemy's troops march up angrily and remain facing ours for a long time without either joining battle or taking themselves off again, the situation is one that demands great vigilance and circumspection.
40. If our troops are no more in number than the enemy, that is amply sufficient; it only means that no direct attack can be made. What we can do is simply to concentrate all our available strength, keep a close watch on the enemy, and obtain reinforcements.
41. He who exercises no forethought but makes light of his opponents is sure to be captured by them.
42. If soldiers are punished before they have grown attached to you, they will not prove submissive; and, unless submissive, then will be practically useless. If, when the soldiers have become attached to you, punishments are not enforced, they will still be useless.
43. Therefore soldiers must be treated in the first instance with humanity, but kept under control by means of iron discipline. This is a certain road to victory.
44. If in training soldiers commands are habitually enforced, the army will be well-disciplined; if not, its discipline will be bad.
45. If a general shows confidence in his men but always insists on his orders being obeyed, the gain will be mutual.

X. TERRAIN

1. Sun Tzŭ said: We may distinguish six kinds of terrain, to wit: (1) Accessible ground; (2) entangling ground; (3) temporising ground; (4) narrow passes; (5) precipitous heights; (6) positions at a great distance from the enemy.
2. Ground which can be freely traversed by both sides is called accessible.
3. With regard to ground of this nature, be before the enemy in occupying the raised and sunny spots, and carefully guard your line of supplies. Then you will be able to fight with advantage.

4. Ground which can be abandoned but is hard to re-occupy is called entangling.
5. From a position of this sort, if the enemy is unprepared, you may sally forth and defeat him. But if the enemy is prepared for your coming, and you fail to defeat him, then, return being impossible, disaster will ensue.
6. When the position is such that neither side will gain by making the first move, it is called temporising ground.
7. In a position of this sort, even though the enemy should offer us an attractive bait, it will be advisable not to stir forth, but rather to retreat, thus enticing the enemy in his turn; then, when part of his army has come out, we may deliver our attack with advantage.
8. With regard to narrow passes, if you can occupy them first, let them be strongly garrisoned and await the advent of the enemy.
9. Should the enemy forestall you in occupying a pass, do not go after him if the pass is fully garrisoned, but only if it is weakly garrisoned.
10. With regard to precipitous heights, if you are beforehand with your adversary, you should occupy the raised and sunny spots, and there wait for him to come up.
11. If the enemy has occupied them before you, do not follow him, but retreat and try to entice him away.
12. If you are situated at a great distance from the enemy, and the strength of the two armies is equal, it is not easy to provoke a battle, and fighting will be to your disadvantage.
13. These six are the principles connected with Earth. The general who has attained a responsible post must be careful to study them.
14. Now an army is exposed to six several calamities, not arising from natural causes, but from faults for which the general is responsible. These are: (1) Flight; (2) insubordination; (3) collapse; (4) ruin; (5) disorganisation; (6) rout.
15. Other conditions being equal, if one force is hurled against another ten times its size, the result will be the flight of the former.
16. When the common soldiers are too strong and their officers too weak, the result is insubordination. When the officers are too strong and the common soldiers too weak, the result is collapse.
17. When the higher officers are angry and insubordinate, and on meeting the enemy give battle on their own account from a feeling of resentment, before the commander-in-chief can tell whether or no he is in a position to fight, the result is ruin.
18. When the general is weak and without authority; when his orders are not clear and distinct; when there are no fixed duties assigned to officers and men, and the ranks are formed in a slovenly haphazard manner, the result is utter disorganisation.
19. When a general, unable to estimate the enemy's strength, allows an inferior force to engage a larger one, or hurls a weak detachment against a powerful one, and neglects to place picked soldiers in the front rank, the result must be a rout.
20. These are six ways of courting defeat, which must be carefully noted by the general who has attained a responsible post.
21. The natural formation of the country is the soldier's best ally; but a power of estimating the adversary, of controlling the forces of victory, and of shrewdly calculating difficulties, dangers and distances, constitutes the test of a great general.
22. He who knows these things, and in fighting puts his knowledge into practice, will win his battles. He who knows them not, nor practises them, will surely be defeated.
23. If fighting is sure to result in victory, then you must fight, even though the ruler forbid it; if fighting will not result in victory, then you must not fight even at the ruler's bidding.
24. The general who advances without coveting fame and retreats without fearing disgrace, whose only thought is to protect his country and do good service for his sovereign, is the jewel of the kingdom.
25. Regard your soldiers as your children, and they will follow you into the deepest valleys; look on them as your own beloved sons, and they will stand by you even unto death.

26. If, however, you are indulgent, but unable to make your authority felt; kind-hearted, but unable to enforce your commands; and incapable, moreover, of quelling disorder: then your soldiers must be likened to spoilt children; they are useless for any practical purpose.
27. If we know that our own men are in a condition to attack, but are unaware that the enemy is not open to attack, we have gone only halfway towards victory.
28. If we know that the enemy is open to attack, but are unaware that our own men are not in a condition to attack, we have gone only halfway towards victory.
29. If we know that the enemy is open to attack, and also know that our men are in a condition to attack, but are unaware that the nature of the ground makes fighting impracticable, we have still gone only halfway towards victory.
30. Hence the experienced soldier, once in motion, is never bewildered; once he has broken camp, he is never at a loss.
31. Hence the saying: If you know the enemy and know yourself, your victory will not stand in doubt; if you know Heaven and know Earth, you may make your victory complete.

XI. THE NINE SITUATIONS

1. Sun Tzŭ said: The art of war recognises nine varieties of ground: (1) Dispersive ground; (2) facile ground; (3) contentious ground; (4) open ground; (5) ground of intersecting highways; (6) serious ground; (7) difficult ground; (8) hemmed-in ground; (9) desperate ground.
2. When a chieftain is fighting in his own territory, it is dispersive ground.
3. When he has penetrated into hostile territory, but to no great distance, it is facile ground.
4. Ground the possession of which imports great advantage to either side, is contentious ground.
5. Ground on which each side has liberty of movement is open ground.
6. Ground which forms the key to three contiguous states, so that he who occupies it first has most of the Empire at his command, is ground of intersecting highways.
7. When an army has penetrated into the heart of a hostile country, leaving a number of fortified cities in its rear, it is serious ground.
8. Mountain forests, rugged steeps, marshes and fens—all country that is hard to traverse: this is difficult ground.
9. Ground which is reached through narrow gorges, and from which we can only retire by tortuous paths, so that a small number of the enemy would suffice to crush a large body of our men: this is hemmed in ground.
10. Ground on which we can only be saved from destruction by fighting without delay, is desperate ground.
11. On dispersive ground, therefore, fight not. On facile ground, halt not. On contentious ground, attack not.
12. On open ground, do not try to block the enemy's way. On ground of intersecting highways, join hands with your allies.
13. On serious ground, gather in plunder. In difficult ground, keep steadily on the march.
14. On hemmed-in ground, resort to stratagem. On desperate ground, fight.
15. Those who were called skilful leaders of old knew how to drive a wedge between the enemy's front and rear; to prevent co-operation between his large and small divisions; to hinder the good troops from rescuing the bad, the officers from rallying their men.
16. When the enemy's men were scattered, they prevented them from concentrating; even when their forces were united, they managed to keep them in disorder.
17. When it was to their advantage, they made a forward move; when otherwise, they stopped still.
18. If asked how to cope with a great host of the enemy in orderly array and on the point of marching to the attack, I should say: "Begin by seizing something which your opponent holds dear; then he will be amenable to your will."

19. Rapidity is the essence of war: take advantage of the enemy's unreadiness, make your way by unexpected routes, and attack unguarded spots.
20. The following are the principles to be observed by an invading force: The further you penetrate into a country, the greater will be the solidarity of your troops, and thus the defenders will not prevail against you.
21. Make forays in fertile country in order to supply your army with food.
22. Carefully study the well-being of your men, and do not overtax them. Concentrate your energy and hoard your strength. Keep your army continually on the move, and devise unfathomable plans.
23. Throw your soldiers into positions whence there is no escape, and they will prefer death to flight. If they will face death, there is nothing they may not achieve. Officers and men alike will put forth their uttermost strength.
24. Soldiers when in desperate straits lose the sense of fear. If there is no place of refuge, they will stand firm. If they are in the heart of a hostile country, they will show a stubborn front. If there is no help for it, they will fight hard.
25. Thus, without waiting to be marshalled, the soldiers will be constantly on the qui vive; without waiting to be asked, they will do your will; without restrictions, they will be faithful; without giving orders, they can be trusted.
26. Prohibit the taking of omens, and do away with superstitious doubts. Then, until death itself comes, no calamity need be feared.
27. If our soldiers are not overburdened with money, it is not because they have a distaste for riches; if their lives are not unduly long, it is not because they are disinclined to longevity.
28. On the day they are ordered out to battle, your soldiers may weep, those sitting up bedewing their garments, and those lying down letting the tears run down their cheeks. But let them once be brought to bay, and they will display the courage of a Chu or a Kuei.
29. The skilful tactician may be likened to the shuai-jan. Now the shuai-jan is a snake that is found in the Ch'ang mountains. Strike at its head, and you will be attacked by its tail; strike at its tail, and you will be attacked by its head; strike at its middle, and you will be attacked by head and tail both.
30. Asked if an army can be made to imitate the shuai-jan, I should answer, Yes. For the men of Wu and the men of Yüeh are enemies; yet if they are crossing a river in the same boat and are caught by a storm, they will come to each other's assistance just as the left hand helps the right.
31. Hence it is not enough to put one's trust in the tethering of horses, and the burying of chariot wheels in the ground.
32. The principle on which to manage an army is to set up one standard of courage which all must reach.
33. How to make the best of both strong and weak—that is a question involving the proper use of ground.
34. Thus the skilful general conducts his army just as though he were leading a single man, willy-nilly, by the hand.
35. It is the business of a general to be quiet and thus ensure secrecy; upright and just, and thus maintain order.
36. He must be able to mystify his officers and men by false reports and appearances, and thus keep them in total ignorance.
37. By altering his arrangements and changing his plans, he keeps the enemy without definite knowledge. By shifting his camp and taking circuitous routes, he prevents the enemy from anticipating his purpose.
38. At the critical moment, the leader of an army acts like one who has climbed up a height and then kicks away the ladder behind him. He carries his men deep into hostile territory before he shows his hand.
39. He burns his boats and breaks his cooking-pots; like a shepherd driving a flock of sheep, he drives his men this way and that, and none knows whither he is going.

40. To muster his host and bring it into danger:—this may be termed the business of the general.
41. The different measures suited to the nine varieties of ground; the expediency of aggressive or defensive tactics; and the fundamental laws of human nature: these are things that must most certainly be studied.
42. When invading hostile territory, the general principle is, that penetrating deeply brings cohesion; penetrating but a short way means dispersion.
43. When you leave your own country behind, and take your army across neighbourhood territory, you find yourself on critical ground. When there are means of communication on all four sides, the ground is one of intersecting highways.
44. When you penetrate deeply into a country, it is serious ground. When you penetrate but a little way, it is facile ground.
45. When you have the enemy's strongholds on your rear, and narrow passes in front, it is hemmed-in ground. When there is no place of refuge at all, it is desperate ground.
46. Therefore, on dispersive ground, I would inspire my men with unity of purpose. On facile ground, I would see that there is close connection between all parts of my army.
47. On contentious ground, I would hurry up my rear.
48. On open ground, I would keep a vigilant eye on my defences. On ground of intersecting highways, I would consolidate my alliances.
49. On serious ground, I would try to ensure a continuous stream of supplies. On difficult ground, I would keep pushing on along the road.
50. On hemmed-in ground, I would block any way of retreat. On desperate ground, I would proclaim to my soldiers the hopelessness of saving their lives.
51. For it is the soldier's disposition to offer an obstinate resistance when surrounded, to fight hard when he cannot help himself, and to obey promptly when he has fallen into danger.
52. We cannot enter into alliance with neighbouring princes until we are acquainted with their designs. We are not fit to lead an army on the march unless we are familiar with the face of the country—its mountains and forests, its pitfalls and precipices, its marshes and swamps. We shall be unable to turn natural advantages to account unless we make use of local guides.
53. To be ignorant of any one of the following four or five principles does not befit a warlike prince.
54. When a warlike prince attacks a powerful state, his generalship shows itself in preventing the concentration of the enemy's forces. He overawes his opponents, and their allies are prevented from joining against him.
55. Hence he does not strive to ally himself with all and sundry, nor does he foster the power of other states. He carries out his own secret designs, keeping his antagonists in awe. Thus he is able to capture their cities and overthrow their kingdoms.
56. Bestow rewards without regard to rule, issue orders without regard to previous arrangements; and you will be able to handle a whole army as though you had to do with but a single man.
57. Confront your soldiers with the deed itself; never let them know your design. When the outlook is bright, bring it before their eyes; but tell them nothing when the situation is gloomy.
58. Place your army in deadly peril, and it will survive; plunge it into desperate straits, and it will come off in safety.
59. For it is precisely when a force has fallen into harm's way that is capable of striking a blow for victory.
60. Success in warfare is gained by carefully accommodating ourselves to the enemy's purpose.
61. By persistently hanging on the enemy's flank, we shall succeed in the long run in killing the commander-in-chief.
62. This is called ability to accomplish a thing by sheer cunning.
63. On the day that you take up your command, block the frontier passes, destroy the official tallies, and stop the passage of all emissaries.
64. Be stern in the council-chamber, so that you may control the situation.
65. If the enemy leaves a door open, you must rush in.
66. Forestall your opponent by seizing what he holds dear, and subtly contrive to time his arrival on the ground.

67. Walk in the path defined by rule, and accommodate yourself to the enemy until you can fight a decisive battle.
68. At first, then, exhibit the coyness of a maiden, until the enemy gives you an opening; afterwards emulate the rapidity of a running hare, and it will be too late for the enemy to oppose you.

XII. THE ATTACK BY FIRE

1. Sun Tzŭ said: There are five ways of attacking with fire. The first is to burn soldiers in their camp; the second is to burn stores; the third is to burn baggage-trains; the fourth is to burn arsenals and magazines; the fifth is to hurl dropping fire amongst the enemy.
2. In order to carry out an attack, we must have means available. The material for raising fire should always be kept in readiness.
3. There is a proper season for making attacks with fire, and special days for starting a conflagration.
4. The proper season is when the weather is very dry; the special days are those when the moon is in the constellations of the Sieve, the Wall, the Wing or the Cross-bar; for these four are all days of rising wind.
5. In attacking with fire, one should be prepared to meet five possible developments:
6. (1) When fire breaks out inside the enemy's camp, respond at once with an attack from without.
7. (2) If there is an outbreak of fire, but the enemy's soldiers remain quiet, bide your time and do not attack.
8. (3) When the force of the flames has reached its height, follow it up with an attack, if that is practicable; if not, stay where you are.
9. (4) If it is possible to make an assault with fire from without, do not wait for it to break out within, but deliver your attack at a favourable moment.
10. (5) When you start a fire, be to windward of it. Do not attack from the leeward.
11. A wind that rises in the daytime lasts long, but a night breeze soon falls.
12. In every army, the five developments connected with fire must be known, the movements of the stars calculated, and a watch kept for the proper days.
13. Hence those who use fire as an aid to the attack show intelligence; those who use water as an aid to the attack gain an accession of strength.
14. By means of water, an enemy may be intercepted, but not robbed of all his belongings.
15. Unhappy is the fate of one who tries to win his battles and succeed in his attacks without cultivating the spirit of enterprise; for the result is waste of time and general stagnation.
16. Hence the saying: The enlightened ruler lays his plans well ahead; the good general cultivates his resources.
17. Move not unless you see an advantage; use not your troops unless there is something to be gained; fight not unless the position is critical.
18. No ruler should put troops into the field merely to gratify his own spleen; no general should fight a battle simply out of pique.
19. If it is to your advantage, make a forward move; if not, stay where you are.
20. Anger may in time change to gladness; vexation may be succeeded by content.
21. But a kingdom that has once been destroyed can never come again into being; nor can the dead ever be brought back to life.
22. Hence the enlightened ruler is heedful, and the good general full of caution. This is the way to keep a country at peace and an army intact.

XIII. THE USE OF SPIES

1. Sun Tzŭ said: Raising a host of a hundred thousand men and marching them great distances entails heavy loss on the people and a drain on the resources of the State. The daily expenditure will amount to a thousand ounces of silver. There will be commotion at home and abroad, and men will drop down exhausted on the highways. As many as seven hundred thousand families will be impeded in their labour.
2. Hostile armies may face each other for years, striving for the victory which is decided in a single day. This being so, to remain in ignorance of the enemy's condition simply because one grudges the outlay of a hundred ounces of silver in honours and emoluments, is the height of inhumanity.
3. One who acts thus is no leader of men, no present help to his sovereign, no master of victory.
4. Thus, what enables the wise sovereign and the good general to strike and conquer, and achieve things beyond the reach of ordinary men, is foreknowledge.
5. Now this foreknowledge cannot be elicited from spirits; it cannot be obtained inductively from experience, nor by any deductive calculation.
6. Knowledge of the enemy's dispositions can only be obtained from other men.
7. Hence the use of spies, of whom there are five classes: (1) Local spies; (2) inward spies; (3) converted spies; (4) doomed spies; (5) surviving spies.
8. When these five kinds of spy are all at work, none can discover the secret system. This is called "divine manipulation of the threads." It is the sovereign's most precious faculty.
9. Having local spies means employing the services of the inhabitants of a district.
10. Having inward spies, making use of officials of the enemy.
11. Having converted spies, getting hold of the enemy's spies and using them for our own purposes.
12. Having doomed spies, doing certain things openly for purposes of deception, and allowing our own spies to know of them and report them to the enemy.
13. Surviving spies, finally, are those who bring back news from the enemy's camp.
14. Hence it is that with none in the whole army are more intimate relations to be maintained than with spies. None should be more liberally rewarded. In no other business should greater secrecy be preserved.
15. Spies cannot be usefully employed without a certain intuitive sagacity.
16. They cannot be properly managed without benevolence and straightforwardness.
17. Without subtle ingenuity of mind, one cannot make certain of the truth of their reports.
18. Be subtle! be subtle! and use your spies for every kind of business.
19. If a secret piece of news is divulged by a spy before the time is ripe, he must be put to death together with the man to whom the secret was told.
20. Whether the object be to crush an army, to storm a city, or to assassinate an individual, it is always necessary to begin by finding out the names of the attendants, the aides-de-camp, the door-keepers and sentries of the general in command. Our spies must be commissioned to ascertain these.
21. The enemy's spies who have come to spy on us must be sought out, tempted with bribes, led away and comfortably housed. Thus they will become converted spies and available for our service.
22. It is through the information brought by the converted spy that we are able to acquire and employ local and inward spies.
23. It is owing to his information, again, that we can cause the doomed spy to carry false tidings to the enemy.
24. Lastly, it is by his information that the surviving spy can be used on appointed occasions.
25. The end and aim of spying in all its five varieties is knowledge of the enemy; and this knowledge can only be derived, in the first instance, from the converted spy. Hence it is essential that the converted spy be treated with the utmost liberality.
26. Of old, the rise of the Yin dynasty was due to I Chih who had served under the Hsia. Likewise, the rise of the Chou dynasty was due to Lü Ya who had served under the Yin.

27. Hence it is only the enlightened ruler and the wise general who will use the highest intelligence of the army for purposes of spying and thereby they achieve great results. Spies are a most important element in war, because on them depends an army's ability to move.

www.ingramcontent.com/pod-product-compliance
Lightning Source LLC
Chambersburg PA
CBHW052317220526
45472CB00001B/161